JOHN WILLIS'

SCREEN WORLD

1970

Volume 21

CROWN PUBLISHERS, INC.
419 PARK AVENUE SOUTH
NEW YORK

Library of Congress Catalog Card No. 50-3023

The editor expresses his sincere gratitude to the following who assisted in making this volume possible:

Angelis Alexandris
Alan Arce
Porter Bennett
Mike Berman
Marian Billings
Albert Boyars
Arthur Canton
Marc Cutler
John Dartigue
Patty Ecker
Darrell Flugg
Larry Forley
Paula Fraser
Sidney Ganis
Bernard Glaser
Melvin Gold
Jack Goldstein
Alexandra Grant
Larry Kardish
Roger Karnbad
Seymour Krawitz
Martin Levy
Vince Licardi
Jim Lichtenberg
Ernst Lichtenstein
Milton Livingston
Wynn Loewenthal
Arlene Ludwig
Rosa Madell
Eric Naumann
John O'Rourke
Louis Ortiz
Milton Platt
Ruth Pologe
Jay Remer
Alan Rogers
Ovi Rosario
Peggy Rosenthal
Sheldon Roskin
Arthur Rubine
Michael Scrimenti
Eve Siegel
Kenneth Silverman
Diane Solomon
Ted Spiegel
Al Steen
Marilyn Stewart
John Sutherland
Dan Talbot
Don Velde
Paula Vogel
William Wang
Harold Weisenthal
Bill Werneth
Valerie West
Fred Weterick

This volume is gratefully dedicated to the
innumerable personnel, past and present,
in the many companies' publicity and still
departments whose gracious cooperation,
generous assistance, and endless patience
have contributed immeasurably to making
SCREEN WORLD an internationally recognized
historical record of films
in the United States

JON VOIGHT and DUSTIN HOFFMAN
in "Midnight Cowboy"
ACADEMY AWARD BEST PICTURE OF 1969

CONTENTS

EDITOR: JOHN WILLIS

Assistant Editor: Stanley Reeves

Staff: Frances Crampon, Harold Stephens, Lucy Williams

1. Paul Newman

2. John Wayne

3. Steve McQueen

4. Dustin Hoffman

5. Clint Eastwood

6. Sidney Poitier

7. Lee Marvin

8. Jack Lemmon

9. Katharine Hepburn

10. Barbra Streisand

11. Dean Martin

12. Joanne Woodward

13. Walter Matthau

14. Richard Burton

15. Raquel Welch

16. Jane Fonda

17. Elizabeth Taylor

18. Peter Fonda

19. Julie Andrews

20. Faye Dunaway

1969 RELEASES

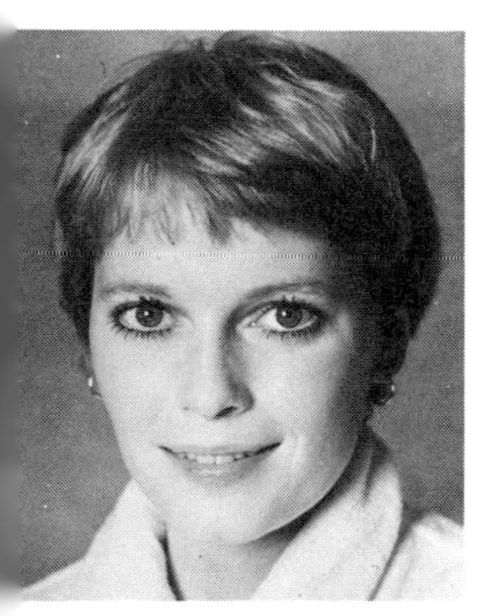
21. Mia Farrow

22. Elvis Presley

23. Sandy Dennis

24. Warren Beatty

25. James Garner

Vanessa Redgrave

Anthony Quinn

Liza Minnelli

PENDULUM

(COLUMBIA) Produced and Written by Stanley Niss; Director, George Schaefer; Photography, Lionel Lindon; Music, Walter Scharf; Assistant Director, David Salven; In Technicolor; January release.

CAST

Capt. Frank Mathews	George Peppard
Adele Mathews	Jean Seberg
Woodrow Wilson King	Richard Kiley
Deputy Chief Hildebrand	Charles McGraw
Mrs. Eileen Sanderson	Madeleine Sherwood
Paul Martin Sanderson	Robert F. Lyons
Lt. Smithson	Frank Marth
Liz Tennant	Marj Dusay
Senator Cole	Paul McGrath
Richard D'Angelo	Stewart Moss
Effie	Isabell Sanford
Det. "Red" Thornton	Dana Elcar
Brooks Elliott	Harry Lewis
Mary Schumacher	Mildred Trares
Myra	Robin Raymond
Mrs. Wilma Elliott	Phyllis Hill
Judge Kinsella	S. John Launer
Attorney Grady Butler	Jock MacKelvie
Deputy Marshall Barnes	Richard Guizon
Detective Jelinek	Logan Ramsey
Detective Hanauer	Douglas Henderson
Garland	Gene Boland

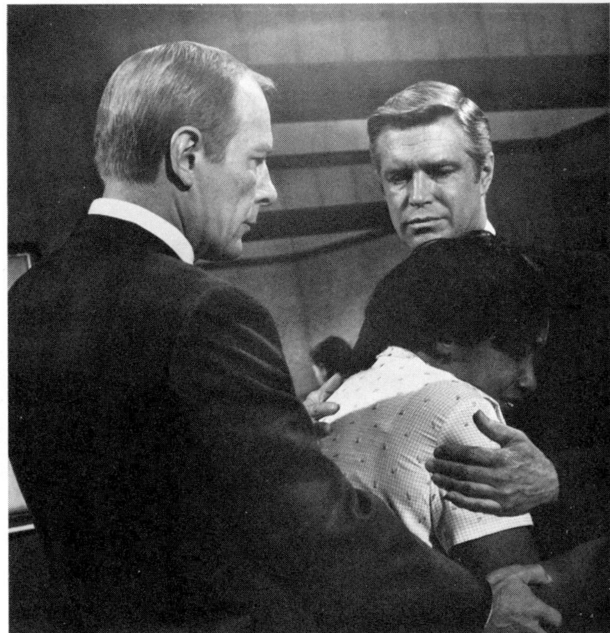

George Peppard, Robert Lyons, Madeleine Sherwood. Above: Jean Seberg, George Peppard

Jean Seberg, George Peppard, Charles McGraw. Above: Frank Marth, Isabell Sanford, George Peppard. Top: George Peppard, Richard Kiley

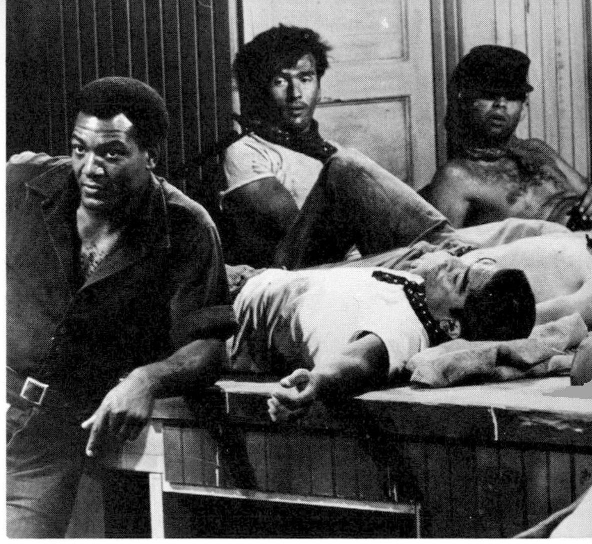

THE RIOT

(PARAMOUNT) Producer, William Castle; Associate Producer, Dona Holloway; Director, Buzz Kulik; Screenplay, James Poe; From novel by Frank Elli; Photography, Robert Hauser; Assistant Director, Danny McCauley; In Technicolor; January release.

CAST

Cully	Jim Brown
Red	Gene Hackman
Surefoot	Ben Carruthers
Bugsy	Mike Kellin
Grossman	Gerald O'Loughlin
"Big Mary"	Clifford David
Jake	Bill Walker
"Gertie"	Ricky Summers

Top: Jim Brown, Gene Hackman

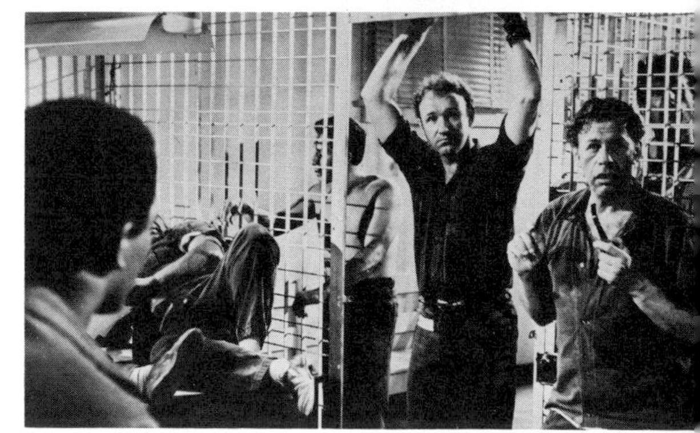

Gene Hackman, Mike Kellin. Above: Ben Carruthers, Jim Brown. Top: Jim Brown

THE STALKING MOON

(NATIONAL GENERAL) Producer, Alan J. Pakula; Director, Robert Mulligan; Photography, Charles Lang; Screenplay, Alvin Sargent; Adaptation, Wendell Mayes; From novel of same name by Theodore V. Olsen; Music, Fred Karlin; Costumes, Seth Banks, Dorothy Jeakins, Grace Harris; Assistant Director, Don Kranze; In Panavision and Technicolor; January release.

CAST

Sam Varner	Gregory Peck
Sarah Carver	Eva Marie Saint
Nick Tana	Robert Forster
Boy	Noland Clay
Ned	Russell Thorson
Major	Frank Silvera
Purdue	Lonny Chapman
Stationmaster	Lou Frizell
Sgt. Rudabaugh	Henry Beckman
Dace	Charles Tyner
Doctor	Richard Bull
Rachel	Sandy Wyeth
Julio	Joaquin Martinez
Stage Driver Shelby	Red Morgan
Salvaje	Nathaniel Narcisco

Noland Clay, Eva Marie Saint. Above: Robert Forster, Gregory Peck

Gregory Peck. Above: Gregory Peck, Nathaniel Narcisco

HELLFIGHTERS

(**UNIVERSAL**) Producer, Robert Arthur; Director, Andrew V. McLaglen; Screenplay, Clair Huffaker; Photography, William H. Clothier; Music, Leonard Rosenman; Costumes, Edith Head; Assistant Director, Terry Morse, Jr.; In Technicolor; January release.

CAST

Chance Buckman	John Wayne
Tish Buckman	Katharine Ross
Greg Parker	Jim Hutton
Madelyn Buckman	Vera Miles
Jack Lomax	Jay C. Flippen
Joe Horn	Bruce Cabot
George Harris	Edward Faulkner
Irene Foster	Barbara Stuart
Colonel Valdez	Edmund Hashim
Amal Bokru	Valentin De Vargas
Madame Loo	Frances Fong
General Lopez	Alberto Morin
Harry York	Alan Caillou
Helen Meadows	Laraine Stephens
Jim Hatch	John Alderson
Dr. Songla	Lal Chand Mehra
Zamora	Rudy Diaz
Gumdrop	Bebe Louie

Vera Miles, Katharine Ross, John Wayne, Jim Hutton. Above: Edmund Hashim, Katharine Ross, Jim Hutton, Bruce Cabot

John Wayne, Vera Miles. Top Left: John Wayne, Jim Hutton

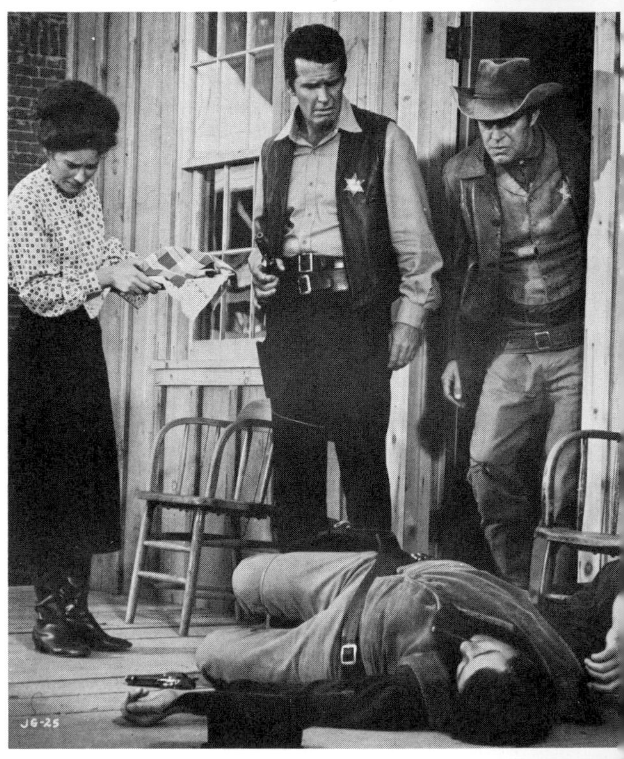

SUPPORT YOUR LOCAL SHERIFF!

(UNITED ARTISTS) Producer, William Bowers; Director, Burt Kennedy; Screenplay, William Bowers; Photography, Harry Strading; Assistant Director, Ray DeCamp; A Cherokee Production in DeLuxe Color; February release.

CAST

Jason McCullough	James Garner
Prudy Perkins	Joan Hackett
Pa Danby	Walter Brennan
Oily Perkins	Harry Morgan
Henry Jackson	Henry Jones
Fred Johnson	Walter Burke
Luke Danby	Dick Peabody
Tom Danby	Gene Evans
Joe Danby	Bruce Dern
Thomas Devery	Willis Bouchey

Top: Gene Evans, Walter Brennan, Dick Peabody. Below: James Garner, Joan Hackett

Center: Henry Jones, Joan Hackett. Above: Joan Hackett, James Garner, Jack Elam. Top: (center) Walter Brennan, Bruce Dern

THE WRECKING CREW

(COLUMBIA) Producer, Irving Allen; Director, Phil Karlson; Screenplay, William McGivern; Based on novel by Donald Hamilton; Photography, Sam Leavitt; Music, Hugo Montenegro; Song, Mack David, DeVol; Costumes, Moss Mabry; Associate Producer, Harold F. Kress; Assistant Director, Jerome Siegel; A Meadway-Claude Picture in Technicolor; February release.

CAST

Matt Helm	Dean Martin
Linka Karensky	Elke Sommer
Freya Carlson	Sharon Tate
Yu-Rang	Nancy Kwan
Count Contini	Nigel Green
Lola Medina	Tina Louise
MacDonald	John Larch
Karl	John Brascia
Kim	Weaver Levy
Gregor	Wilhelm von Homburg
Ching	Bill Saito
Toki	Fuji
Frankie	Pepper Martin

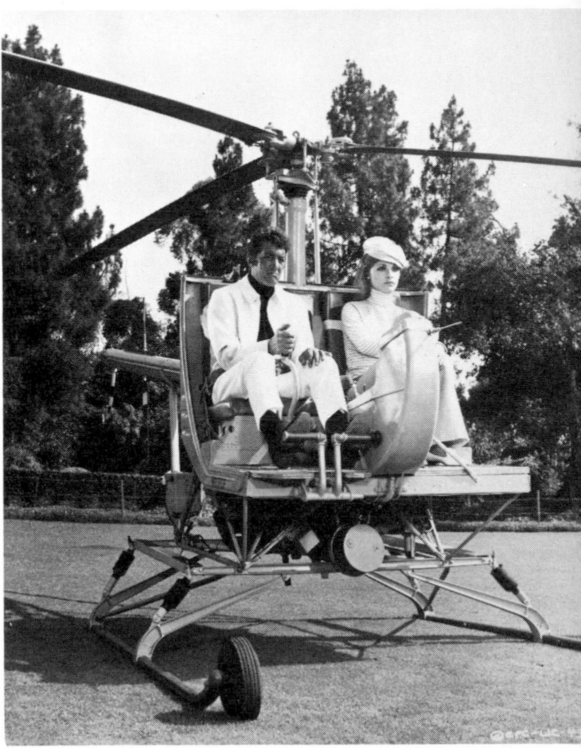

Dean Martin, John Larch. Above: Tina Louise. Top Right: Elke Sommer, Nigel Green

Dean Martin, Nancy Kwan
Above: Dean Martin, Sharon Tate

MY SIDE OF THE MOUNTAIN

(PARAMOUNT) Producer, Robert B. Radnitz; Director, James B. Clark; Photography, Denys Coop; Screenplay, Ted Sherdeman, Jane Klove, Joanna Crawford; Based on Novel by Jean George; In Panavision and Technicolor; March release.

CAST

Sam Gribley .... Ted Eccles
Bando .... Theodore Bikel
Miss Turner .... Tudi Wiggins
Mr. Gribley .... Frank Perry
Mrs. Gribley .... Peggi Loder
Daughter 1 .... Gina Dick
Daughter 2 .... Karen Pearson
Little Boy .... Danny McIlravey
Mrs. Fielder .... Cosette Lee
Hunters .... Larry Reynolds, Tom Harvey, Paul Herbert
Boys .... Ralph Endersby, George Allan
Ranger .... Patrick Pervion

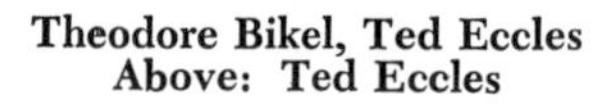

Theodore Bikel, Ted Eccles
Above: Ted Eccles

Tudi Wiggins, Ted Eccles (also above).
Top: Ted Eccles, Theodore Bikel

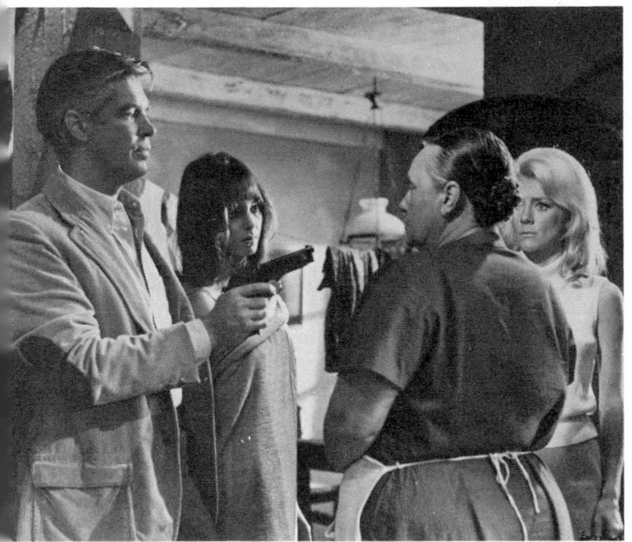

Inger Stevens, George Peppard. Above: Peppard, Rosemary Dexter, Ave Ninchi, Inger Stevens. Top: George Peppard, Barnaby Shaw, Orson Welles.

Top Right: Peppard. Keith Michell, Barnaby Shaw. Below: Inger Stevens, Patience Collier

HELLO DOWN THERE

(PARAMOUNT) Executive Producer, Ivan Tors; Producer, George Sherman; Director, Jack Arnold; Screenplay, Frank Telford, John McGreevey; Music, Jeff Barry; Assistant Directors, William C. Gerrity, Nat Holt, Jr.; Photography, Cliff Poland; In Technicolor; March release.

CAST

Fred Miller	Tony Randall
Vivian Miller	Janet Leigh
T. R. Hollister	Jim Backus
Nate Ashbury	Roddy McDowall
Mel Cheever	Ken Berry
Himself	Merv Griffin
Lorrie Miller	Kay Cole
Tommie Miller	Gary Tigerman
Harold Webster	Richard Dreyfuss
Marvin Webster	Lou Wagner
Nyrtle Ruth	Charlotte Rae
Mrs. Webster	Henny Backus
Mr. Webster	Bud Hoey
Alan Briggs	Frank Schuller
Dr. Cara Wells	Lee Meredith
Admiral	Bruce Gordon
Sonarman	Harvey Lembeck
Jonah	Arnold Stang

SAM WHISKEY

(**UNITED ARTISTS**) Producers, Jules Levy, Arthur Gardner, Arnold Laven; Director, Arnold Laven; Story and Screenplay, William W. Norton; Photography, Robert Moreno; Music, Herschel Burke Gilbert; Assistant Directors, Burt Astor, Russell Vreeland; In DeLuxe Color; March release.

CAST

Sam Whiskey	Burt Reynolds
O. W. Bandy	Clint Walker
Jedidiah Hooker	Ossie Davis
Laura Breckinridge	Angie Dickinson
Fat Henry Hobson	Rick Davis
Fisherman	Del Reeves
Mint Superintendent Perkins	William Schallert

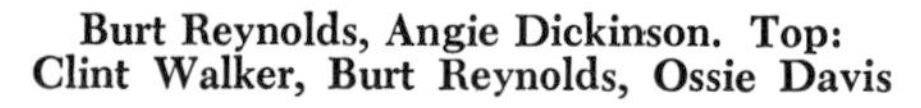

Burt Reynolds, Angie Dickinson. Top: Clint Walker, Burt Reynolds, Ossie Davis

HOUSE OF CARDS

(**UNIVERSAL**) Producer, Dick Berg; Director, John Guillermin; Screenplay, Irving Ravetch, Harriet Frank, Jr.; Based on novel by Stanley Ellin; Photography, Piero Portalupi; Music, Francis Lai; Assistant Director, Tony Brandt; In Technicolor; March release.

CAST

Reno	George Peppard
Anne	Inger Stevens
Leschenhaut	Orson Welles
Morillon	Keith Michell
Claude de Gonde	Ralph Michael
Matilde Vosiers	Maxine Audley
Bourdon	William Job
Edmond Vosier	Peter Bayliss
Gabrielle	Patience Collier
Paul	Barnaby Shaw
Signora Braggi	Ave Ninchi
Monk	Renzo Palmer
Trevi Policeman	Francesco Mule
Daniella	Rosemary Dexter
Louis Le Buc	Raoul Delfosse
Jeanne-Marie	Perrette Pradier
Veronique	Genevieve Cluny
Jesse Hardee	James Mishler
Driot	Jean Louis
Maguy	Jacques Roux
French Conductor	Jean Hebey
Georges	Jacques Stany

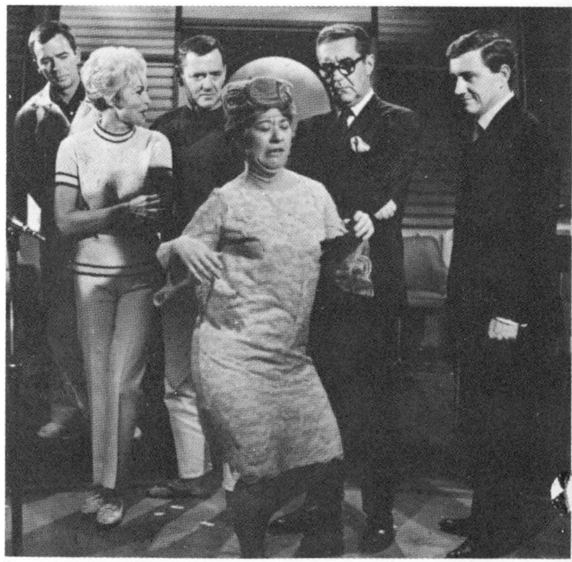

Ken Berry, Janet Leigh, Tony Randall, Charlotte Rae, Jim Backus, Merv Griffin. Above: Kay Cole, Tony Randall, Janet Leigh, Gary Tigerman

THE BIG BOUNCE

(WARNER BROS.-7 ARTS) Producer, William Dozier; Director, Alex March; Screenplay, Robert Dozier; From novel by Elmore Leonard; Photography, Howard R. Schwartz; Music, Michael Curb; Lyrics, Guy Hemric; Assistant Director, Steve Bernhardt; A Greenway Production in Panavision and Technicolor; March release.

CAST

Jack Ryan	Ryan O'Neal
Nancy Barker	Leigh Taylor-Young
Ray Ritchie	James Daly
Bob Rogers	Robert Webber
Girl in #12	Lee Grant
Cheryl	Cindy Eilbacher
Sam Turner	Noam Pitlik
Boy in Dune Buggy	Kevin O'Neal
Sam Mirakian	Van Heflin

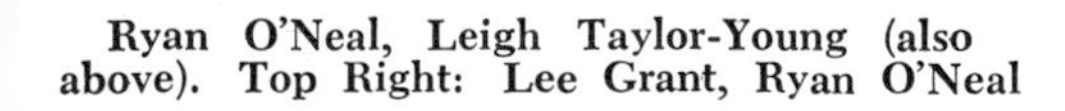

Ryan O'Neal, Leigh Taylor-Young (also above). Top Right: Lee Grant, Ryan O'Neal

Leigh Taylor-Young. Above: Ryan O'Neal, Van Heflin

Rita Moreno, Jess Hahn, Marlon Brando
Above: Brando, Moreno, Pamela Franklin, Richard Boone. Top: Brando, Hughes Wanner

THE NIGHT OF THE FOLLOWING DAY

(UNIVERSAL) Executive Producers, Jerry Gershwin, Elliott Kastner; Produced, Directed, and Written by Hubert Cornfield; Based on novel "The Snatchers" by Lionel White; Photography, Jean Klissak; Costumes, Pierre Marcade; In Technicolor; March release.

CAST

Chauffeur	Marlon Brando
Leer	Richard Boone
The Blonde	Rita Moreno
The Girl	Pamela Franklin
Friendly	Jess Hahn
Fisherman/Cop	Gerard Buhr
Father	Hughes Wanner
Bartender	Jacques Marin

Top Right: Moreno, Brando. Below: Brando, Franklin

SWEET CHARITY

(UNIVERSAL) Producer, Robert Arthur; Director-Choreographer, Bob Fosse; Screenplay, Peter Stone; Based on play by Neil Simon, Cy Coleman, Dorothy Fields; Photography, Robert Surtees; Songs, Cy Coleman, Dorothy Fields; Costumes, Edith Head; Assistant Director, Douglas Green; In Technicolor; April release.

CAST

Charity	Shirley MacLaine
Oscar	John McMartin
Vittorio	Ricardo Montalban
Big Daddy	Sammy Davis, Jr.
Nickie	Chita Rivera
Helene	Paula Kelly
Herman	Stubby Kaye
Ursula	Barbara Bouchet
Charlie	Dante D'Paulo
Nicholsby	Alan Hewitt
Manford	Nolan Leary

Top Left:
Renata Vasalle, Paula Kelly, Kathryn Doby, Chita Rivera, Louise Quick

Shirley MacLaine, John McMartin. Above: Shirley MacLaine, Renata Vasalle.

Shirley MacLaine, Ricardo Montalban
Above: Shirley MacLaine

100 RIFLES

(20th CENTURY-FOX) Producer, Marvin Schwartz; Director, Tom Gries; Screenplay, Clair Huffaker, Tom Gries; Based on novel by Robert MacLeod; Music, Jerry Goldsmith; Photography, Cecilio Paniagua; Assistant Director, Tony Tarruella; In DeLuxe Color; April release.

CAST

Lyedecker	Jim Brown
Sarita	Raquel Welch
Yaqui Joe	Burt Reynolds
Verdugo	Fernando Lamas
Grimes	Dan O'Herlihy
Von Klemme	Hans Gudegast
Humara	Michael Forest
Sgt. Paletes	Aldo Sambrell
Girl in hotel	Soledad Miranda
Padre Francisco	Albert Dalbes
Lopez	Carlos Bravo
Sarita's Father	Jose Manuel Martin

Right: Burt Reynolds, Raquel Welch, Jim Brown. Below: Raquel Welch, Jim Brown

THE MAD ROOM

(COLUMBIA) Producer, Norman Maurer; Director, Bernard Girard; Screenplay, Bernard Girard, A. Z. Martin; Based on screenplay by Garrett Fort, Reginald Denham; From play "Ladies in Retirement" by Reginald Denham, Edward Percy; Photography, Harry Stradling, Jr.; Assistant Director, Rusty Meek; Music, David Grusin; Costumes, Moss Mabry; In Berkey Pathe Color; April release.

CAST

Ellen Hardy	Stella Stevens
Mrs. Armstrong	Shelley Winters
Sam Aller	Skip Ward
Chris	Carol Cole
Nate	Severn Darden
Mrs. Racine	Beverly Garland
George	Michael Burns
Mandy	Barbara Sammeth
Mrs. Ericson	Jenifer Bishop
Edna	Gloria Manon
Dr. Marion Kincaid	Lloyd Haynes
Armand Racine	Lou Kane

Shelley Winters. Left Center: Skip Ward, Stella Stevens

ANGEL IN MY POCKET

(UNIVERSAL) Producer, Ed Montagne; Director, Alan Rafkin; Photography, William Margulies; Assistant Director, Phil Bowles; In Technicolor; April release.

CAST

Sam Whitehead	Andy Griffith
Bubba	Jerry Van Dyke
Racine	Kay Medford
Axel Gresham	Edgar Buchanan
Art Shields	Gary Collins
Mary Elizabeth	Lee Meriwether
Will Sinclair	Henry Jones

Left: Todd Starke, Lee Meriwether, Kay Medford, Andy Griffith, Amber Smale, Jerry Van Dyke. Below: Andy Griffith, Joy Harmon

Jim Brown, Ricky Cordell, Robert Coote. Right Center: Madlyn Rhue, Jim Brown

KENNER

(MGM) Producer, Mary Phillips Murray; Director, Steve Sekely; Screenplay, Harold Clemins, John R. Loring; Based on story by Mary P. Murray; Music, Prem Dhawan, Piero Piccioni; Photography, Dieter Liphardt; Assistant Directors, Bluey Hill, Baba Shaikh; Choreographer, Sudarshan Kumar; Costumes, Janice Bond; An M & N Production in Metrocolor; April release.

CAST

Kenner	Jim Brown
Anasuya	Madlyn Rhue
Henderson	Robert Coote
Saji	Ricky Cordell
Tom Jordan	Charles Horvath
Sandy	Prem Nath
Young Sikh	Kuljit Singh
Mother Superior	Sulochana
Sister Katherine	Ursula Prince
American Friend	Tony North
Ring Referee	Ming Hung
Gym Owner	R. P. Wright
Customs Officer	Nitin Sethi
Young Hindu	Mahendra Jhaveri
Shoe Merchant	G. S. Aasie
Bald Disciple	Ravi Kaant
First Robed Man	Hercules
Second Robed Man	Khalil Amir

SMITH!

(BUENA VISTA) Producer, Bill Anderson; Director, Michael O'Herlihy; Screenplay, Louis Pelletier; Based on book by Paul St. Pierre; Music, Robert F. Brunner; Photography, Robert C. Moreno; A Walt Disney Production in Technicolor; April release.

CAST

Smith	Glenn Ford
Norah	Nancy Olson
Judge	Dean Jagger
Vince Heber	Keenan Wynn
Walter Charlie	Warren Oates
Ol' Antoine	Chief Dan George
Gabriel Jimmyboy	Frank Ramirez
Mr. Edwards	John Randolph
Albie	Christopher Shea
Peterpaul	Ricky Cordell

Dean Jagger, Chief Dan George
Top: Glenn Ford, Warren Oates

Chief Dan George, Glenn Ford, Christopher Shea. Above: Nancy Olson, Glenn Ford

THE ILLUSTRATED MAN

(WARNER BROS.-7 ARTS) Producers, Howard B. Kreitsek, Ted Mann; Director, Jack Smight; Screenplay, Howard B. Kreitsek; Based on novel by Ray Bradbury; Photography, Philip Lathrop; Assistant Director, Terry Nelson; Costumes, Anthea Sylbert; Music, Jerry Goldsmith; An AKM Production in Technicolor; April release.

CAST

Carl	Rod Steiger
Felicia	Claire Bloom
Willie	Robert Drivas
Pickard	Don Dubbins
Simmons	Jason Evers
John	Tim Weldon
Anna	Christie Matchett

Top: Claire Bloom, Rod Steiger (also below)

Robert Drivas, Rod Steiger. Above: Rod Steiger. Top: Christie Matchett, Rod Steiger, Tim Weldon

THE LOVE BUG

(BUENA VISTA) Producer, Bill Walsh; Director, Robert Stevenson; Screenplay, Bill Walsh, Don DaGradi; Based on story by Gordon Buford; Costumes, Bill Thomas; Photography, Edward Colman; Music, George Bruns; Assistant Director, Christopher Hibler; A Walt Disney Production in Technicolor; April release.

CAST

Jim	Dean Jones
Carole	Michele Lee
Thorndyke	David Tomlinson
Tennessee	Buddy Hackett
Havershaw	Joe Flynn
Mr. Wu	Benson Fong
Detective	Joe E. Ross
Police Sergeant	Barry Kelley
Carhop	Iris Adrian

and Andy Granatelli, Ned Glass, Gil Lamb, Nicole Jaffe, Russ Caldwell, P. L. Renoudet, Alan Fordney, Gary Owens, Robert Foulk, Wally Boag, Max Balchowsky, Brian Fong, Stan Duke, Chick Hearn, Pedro Gonzalez-Gonzalez

Top: Dean Jones, Buddy Hackett, and below with Michele Lee

Iris Adrian, Michele Lee, Dean Jones. Top: Buddy Hackett, Michele Lee, Dean Jones

IF IT'S TUESDAY, THIS MUST BE BELGIUM

(UNITED ARTISTS) Producer, Stan Margulies; Director, Mel Stuart; Executive Producer, David L. Wolper; Story and Screenplay, David Shaw; Photography, Vilis Lapenieks; Assistant Director, Patrick O'Brien; In DeLuxe Color; April release.

CAST

Samantha	Suzanne Pleshette
Charlie	Ian McShane
Jenny Grant	Mildred Natwick
Fred Ferguson	Murray Hamilton
John Marino	Sandy Baron
Jack Harmon	Michael Constantine
Harve Blakely	Norman Fell
Edna Ferguson	Peggy Cass
Bert Greenfield	Marty Ingels
Freda	Pamela Britton
Bo	Luke Halpin
Harry Dix	Aubrey Morris
Irma Blakely	Reva Rose
Shelly Ferguson	Hilary Thompson
Giuseppi	Mario Carotenuto
Mrs. Featherstone	Patricia Routledge
Gina	Marina Berti
Fiat Driver's Wife	Linda Di Felice
German Sergeant	Paul Esser
Dot	Jenny White
Marcel	Roger Six
George	Frank Lattimore

and Guest Stars Senta Berger, John Cassavetes, Joan Collins, Vittorio De Sica, Donovan, Anita Ekberg, Ben Gazzara, Virna Lisi, Elsa Martinelli, Catherine Spaak, Robert Vaughn

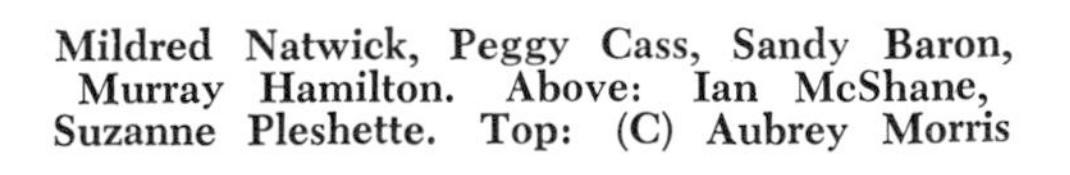

Mildred Natwick, Peggy Cass, Sandy Baron, Murray Hamilton. Above: Ian McShane, Suzanne Pleshette. Top: (C) Aubrey Morris

Norman Fell, Reva Rose. Above: Marty Ingels, Hilary Thompson, Michael Constantine, Patricia Routledge (back), Pamela Britton, Sandy Baron

SALESMAN

(MAYSLES) Produced, Directed, Written by Albert and David Maysles; Photography, Albert Maysles; April release.

CAST

The Badger	Paul Brennan
The Gipper	Charles McDevitt
The Rabbit	James Baker
The Bull	Raymond Martos
Sales Manager	Kennie Turner
Theological Consultant	Melbourne I. Feltman
Motel Maid	Margaret McCarron

Paul Brennan (L). Top: Paul Brennan, Charles McDevitt

Melbourne I. Feltman
Above: Paul Brennan

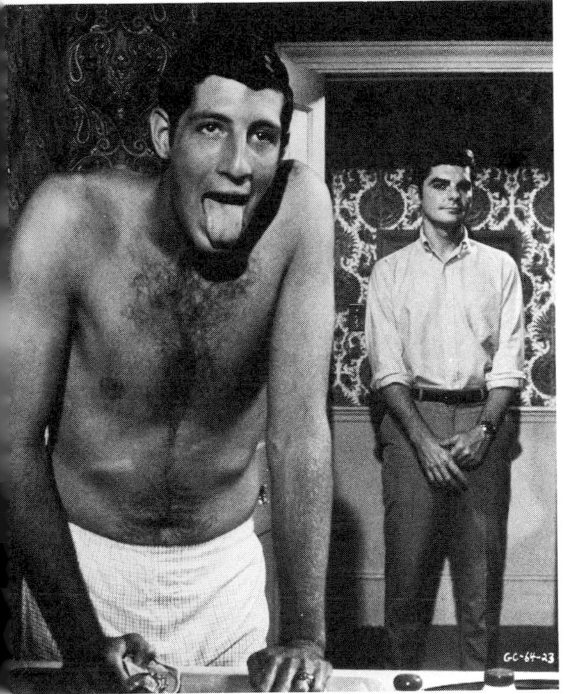

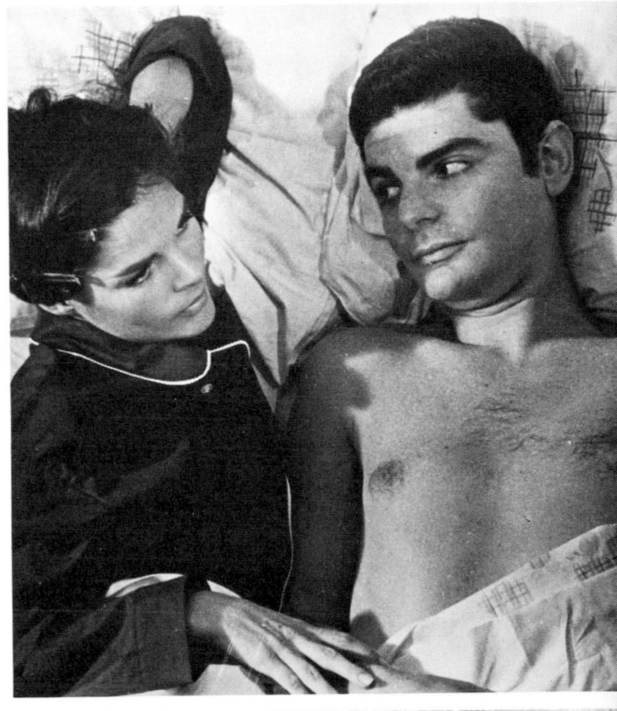

GOODBYE, COLUMBUS

(PARAMOUNT) Producer, Stanley Jaffe; Director, Larry Peerce; Associate Producer, Tony LaMarca; Screenplay, Arnold Schulman; Photography, Gerald Hirschfeld; Assistant Director, Steve Barnett; A Willow Tree Production in WideScreen and Color; April release.

CAST

Neil	Richard Benjamin
Brenda	Ali MacGraw
Mr. Patimkin	Jack Klugman
Mrs. Patimkin	Nan Martin
Ron	Michael Meyers
Julie	Lori Shelle
Carlotta	Royce Wallace
Aunt Gladys	Sylvie Straus
Doris	Kay Cummings
Don Farber	Michael Nurie
Aunt Molly	Betty Greyson
Uncle Leo	Monroe Arnold
Sarah Ehrlich	Elaine Swain
Busboy	Richard Wexler
Uncle Max	Rubin Schafer
Model	Jackie Smith
John McKee	Bill Derringer
Simp	Mari Gorman
Harriet	Gail Ommerle

Top: Rubin Schafer, Richard Benjamin, Sylvie Straus. Below: Michael Meyers, Richard Benjamin

Richard Benjamin, Ali MacGraw (also above) Top: Ali MacGraw, Jack Klugman, Richard Benjamin, Monroe Arnold

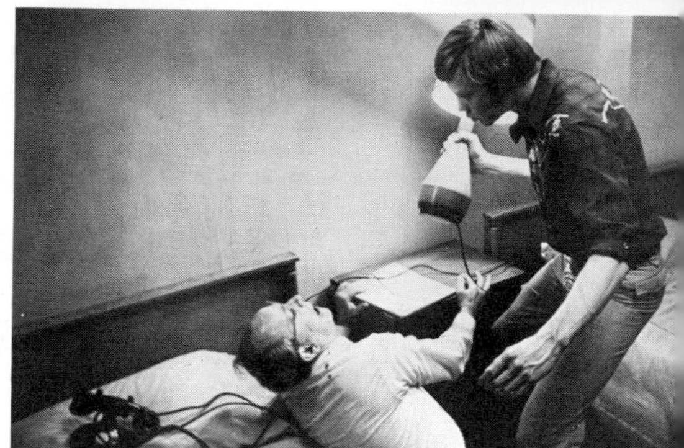

Jon Voight, Sylvia Miles. Above: Voight, Viva, Gastone Rossilli, Dustin Hoffman
Top: Jon Voight

MIDNIGHT COWBOY

(UNITED ARTISTS) Producer, Jerome Hellman; Director, John Schlesinger; Screenplay, Waldo Salt; Based on novel by James Leo Herlihy; Photography, Adam Holender; Costumes, Ann Roth; Associate Producer, Kenneth Utt; A Jerome Hellman-John Schlesinger Production in DeLuxe Color; May release.

CAST

Ratso .... Dustin Hoffman
Joe Buck .... Jon Voight
Cass .... Sylvia Miles
Mr. O'Daniel .... John McGiver
Shirley .... Brenda Vaccaro
Towny .... Barnard Hughes
Sally Buck .... Ruth White
Annie .... Jennifer Salt
Woodsy Niles .... Gil Rankin
Little Joe .... Gary Owens, T. Tom Marlow
Ralph .... George Eppersen
Cafeteria Manager .... Al Scott
Mother on bus .... Linda Davis
Old Cowhand .... J. T. Masters
Old Lady .... Arlene Reeder
Rich Lady .... Georgann Johnson
Jackie .... Jonathan Kramer
Young Student .... Bob Balaban
TV Bishop .... Anthony Holland
Freaked-out Lady .... Jan Tice
Bartender .... Paul Benjamin
Vegetable Grocers .. Peter Scalia, Vito Siracusa
Hat shop owner .... Peter Zamaglias
Hotel Clerk .... Arthur Anderson
Laundromat Ladies ...... Tina Scala, Alma Felix
Escort service man .... Richard Clarke
Frantic Lady .... Ann Thomas
Gretel McAlbertson .... Viva
Hansel McAlbertson .... Gastone Rossilli
Waitress .... Joan Murphy
Bus Driver .... Al Stetson
and Ultra Violet, Paul Jabara, International Velvet, William Dorr, Cecelia Lipson, Taylor Mead, Paul Morrissey

Top: Brenda Vaccaro, Jon Voight
Below: Barnard Hughes, Jon Voight
ACADEMY AWARD BEST PICTURE OF 1969

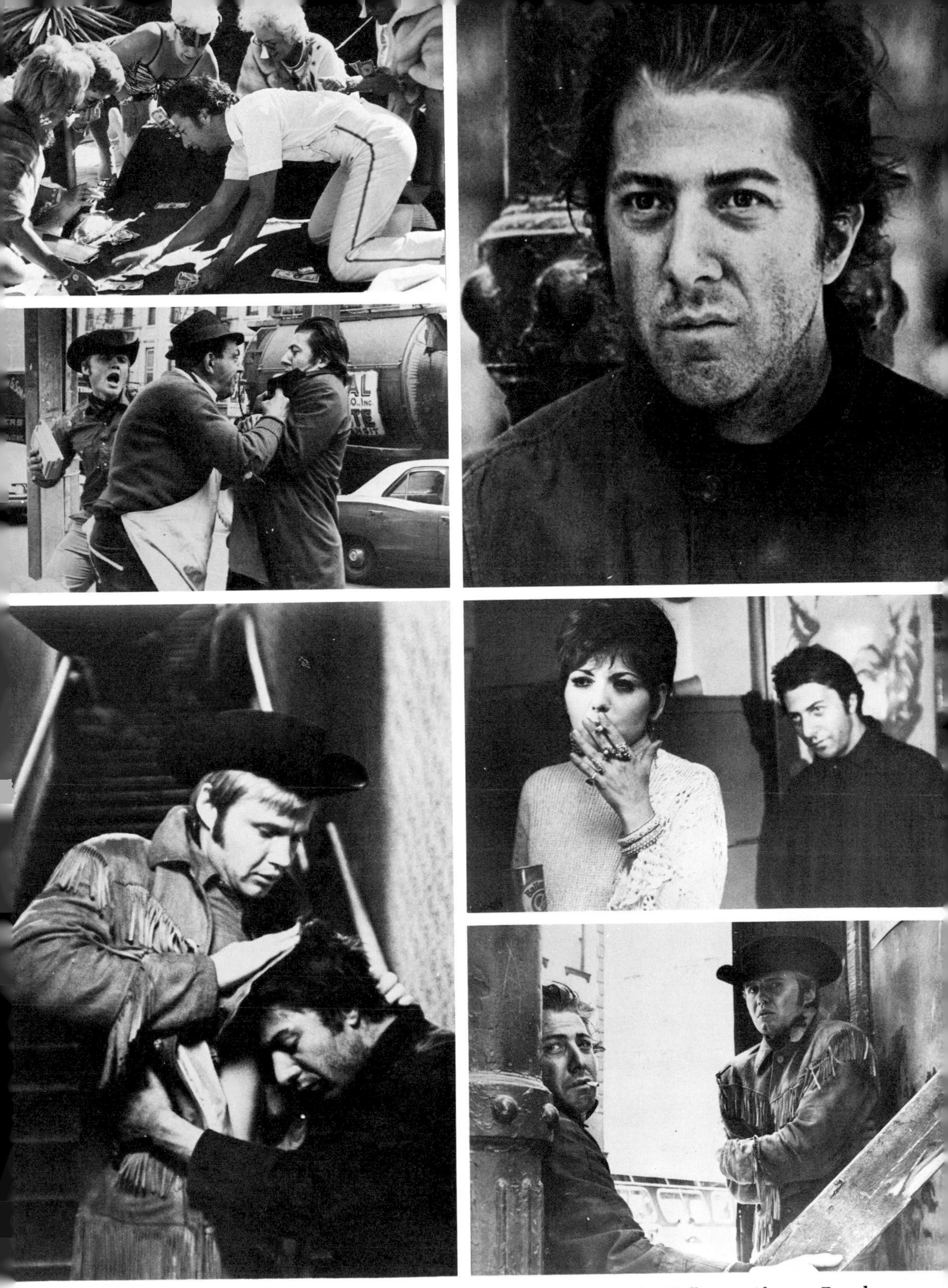

Dustin Hoffman, Jon Voight, and above with Peter Scalia. Top: Dustin Hoffman

Jon Voight, Dustin Hoffman. Above: Brenda Vaccaro, Dustin Hoffman. Top: Dustin Hoffman

IMPASSE

(UNITED ARTISTS) Executive Producer, Aubrey Schenck; Producer, Hal Klein; Director, Richard Benedict; Screenplay, John C. Higgins; Photography, Mars B. Rasca; Music, Philip Springer; Assistant Director, Donald Verk; In DeLuxe Color; May release.

CAST

Pat Morrison	Burt Reynolds
Bobby Jones	Anne Francis
Hansen	Lyle Bettger
Draco	Rodolfo Acosta
Wombat	Jeff Corey
Trev Jones	Clarke Gordon
Mariko	Miko Mayama
Penny	Joanne Dalsass
Jesus	Vic Diaz
Pear Blossom	Dely Atay-Atayan
Nakajima	Bruno Punzalan
Maria Bonita	Lily Campillos
Sherry	Shirley Gorospe
Kiling	Bessie Barredo
Interne	Robert Wang
Kuli	Eddie Nicart

Top Left: Anne Francis, Burt Reynolds

HARD CONTRACT

(20th CENTURY-FOX) Producer, Marvin Schwartz; Director, S. Lee Pogostin; Screenplay and Story, S. Lee Pogostin; Music, Alex North; Photography, Jack Hildyard; Assistant Directors, Julio Sempere, Kip Gowans; In Panavision and DeLuxe Color; May release.

CAST

John Cunningham	James Coburn
Sheila	Lee Remick
Adrianne	Lilli Palmer
Ramsey	Burgess Meredith
Alexi	Patrick Magee
Michael Carlson	Sterling Hayden
Maurice	Claude Dauphin
Evelyn Carlson	Helen Cherry
Ellen	Karen Black
Belgian Prostitute	Sabine Sun

HEAVEN WITH A GUN

(MGM) Producers, Frank King, Maurice King; Director, Lee H. Katzin; Screenplay, Richard Carr; Music, Johnny Mandel; Photography, Fred Koenekamp; Associate Producers, Herman King, Red Hershon; Assistant Director, William P. Owens; A King Brothers Production in Panavision and MetroColor; May release.

CAST

Jim Killian	Glenn Ford
Madge McCloud	Carolyn Jones
Leloopa	Barbara Hershey
Asa Beck	John Anderson
Coke Beck	David Carradine
Mace	J. D. Cannon
Garvey	Noah Beery
Gus Sampson	Harry Townes
Bart Patterson	William Bryant
Mrs. Patterson	Virginia Gregg
Abraham Murdock	James Griffith
Ned Hunter	Roger Perry
Gilcher	Claude Woolman
Scotty Andrews	Ed Bakey
Mrs. Andrews	Barbara Babcock
Doc Foster	James Chandler
Emily	Angelique Pettyjohn
Jan	Jessica James
Bar Girl	Bee Tompkins
Willy	Bill Catching
Indian	Al Wyatt
Charlie	Ed McCready
Townspeople	Eddie Crispell, Barbara Dombre

James Chandler, Carolyn Jones, Glenn Ford, Barbara Hershey

THE APRIL FOOLS

(NATIONAL GENERAL) Producer, Gordon Carroll; Director, Stuart Rosenberg; Screenplay, Hal Dresner; Title Song Music, Burt Bacharach; Lyrics, Hal David; Sung by Dionne Warwick; Music, Marvin Hamlisch; Photography, Michel Hugo; Associate Producer, Carter DeHaven, Jr.; Assistant Director, Hank Moonjean; Costumes, Donfeld; Choreographer, Marc Wilder; A Cinema Center Presentation, A Jalem Production in Technicolor; May release.

CAST

Howard Brubaker	Jack Lemmon
Catherine Gunther	Catherine Deneuve
Ted Gunther	Peter Lawford
Benson	Harvey Korman
Phyllis Bubaker	Sally Kellerman
Leslie Hopkins	Melinda Dillon
Don Hopkins	Kenneth Mars
Mimsy Shrader	Janice Carroll
Potter Shrader	Jack Weston
Grace Greenlaw	Myrna Loy
Andre Greenlaw	Charles Boyer
Walters	David Doyle
Stanley Brubaker	Gary Dubin
Party Singer	Susan Barrett
Secretary	Dee Gardner
Doorman	Tom Ahearne

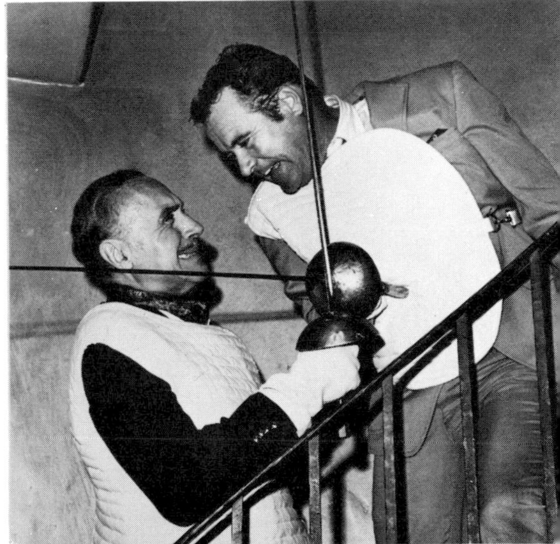

Peter Lawford, Catherine Deneuve. Above: Jack Weston, Jack Lemmon. Top: Catherine Deneuve, Jack Lemmon

Janice Carroll, Harvey Korman
Above: Charles Boyer, Jack Lemmon

WHERE IT'S AT

(UNITED ARTISTS) Producer, Frank Ross; Director, Garson Kanin; Associate Producer, Richard Ross; Assistant Directors, John Chulay, David Hawks, Dick Bennett; Photography, Burnett Guffey; Screenplay, Garson Kanin; A Frank Ross-T.F.T. Production in DeLuxe Color; May release.

CAST

A. C. Smith	David Janssen
Andy	Robert Drivas
Diana Mayhew	Rosemary Forsyth
Molly Hirsch	Brenda Vaccaro
Willie	Don Rickles
Betty Avery	Warrene Ott
Phyllis Horrigan	Edy Williams
Ralph	Vince Howard

Robert Drivas, David Janssen. Above: Rosemary Forsyth, Robert Drivas

Robert Drivas, Edy Williams. Above: Robert Drivas, Brenda Vaccaro. Top: David Janssen, Vince Howard, Robert Drivas

WINNING

(UNIVERSAL) Director, James Goldstone; Screenplay, Howard Rodman; Photography, Richard Moore; Assistant Director, Earl Bellamy; A Newman-Forman Production in Technicolor and Panavision; May release.

CAST

Capua	Paul Newman
Elora	Joanne Woodward
Charley	Richard Thomas, Jr.
Erding	Robert Wagner
Leo Crawford	David Sheiner
Larry Morechek	Clu Gulager
Battineau	Barry Ford
Sam Jagin	Bob Quarry
Miss Redburne 200	Eileen Wesson

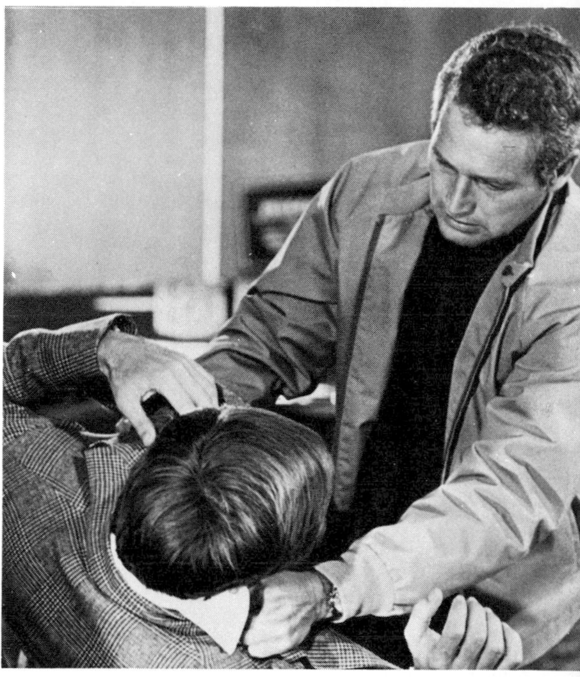

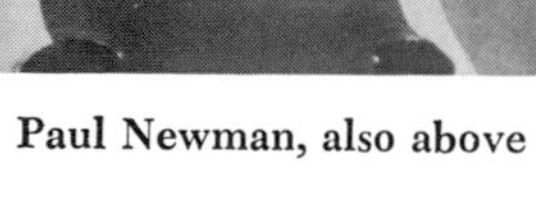

Paul Newman, also above

Paul Newman, and above with Robert Wagner
Top: Paul Newman, Joanne Woodward

McKENNA'S GOLD

(COLUMBIA) Produced and Written by Carl Foreman; Director, J. Lee Thompson; Co-Producer, Dimitri Tiomkin; Photography, Joseph MacDonald; Assistant Director, Dave Salven; In Panavision and Technicolor; May release.

CAST

Mackenna	Gregory Peck
Colorado	Omar Sharif
Tibbs	Telly Savalas
Inga	Camilla Sparv
Sanchez	Keenan Wynn
Hesh-ke	Julie Newmar
Editor	Lee J. Cobb
Preacher	Raymond Massey
Storekeeper	Burgess Meredith
Englishman	Anthony Quayle
Old Adams	Edward G. Robinson
Baker	Eli Wallach
Hachita	Ted Cassidy
Avila	Richard Peabody
Monkey	Robert Phillips
Besh	Rudy Diaz
Young Englishman	J. Robert Porter
Boy	John Garfield, Jr.
Prairie Dog	Eduardo Ciannelli
Judge Bergerman	Trevor Bardette
Old Woman	Madeleine Taylor-Holmes
Pima	Shelley Morrison
Laguna	Pepe Callahan
Lieutenant	Duke Hobbie

Top: Telly Savalas, Omar Sharif, Gregory Peck
Below: Camilla Sparv, Gregory Peck

Omar Sharif, Gregory Peck. Above: Raymond Massey, John Garfield, Jr., Edward G. Robinson. Top: Anthony Quayle, Massey, J. Robert Porter, Eli Wallach, Omar Sharif, Gregory Peck

A SESSION WITH THE COMMITTEE

(COMMONWEALTH UNITED) Executive Producer, Alan Myerson; Producer-Director, Del Jack; Created and staged by Alan Myerson; Musical Conductor, P. William Mathieu; Produced by Commonwealth United in association with SpectraMedia/Alan Myerson; In Technicolor; May release.

CAST

Peter Bonerz
Barbara Bosson
Garry Goodrow
Carl Gottlieb
Jessica Myerson
Christopher Ross
Melvin Stewart
Don Sturdy

Top Right: The Committee

CHASTITY

(AMERICAN INTERNATIONAL) Produced and Written by Sonny Bono; Director, Alessio de Paola; Photography, Ben Coleman; Assistant Director, William Lukather; Music, Sonny Bono; Costumes, Sadie Hayes; In Color; June release.

CAST

Chastity .... Cher
Diana Midnight .... Barbara London
Eddie .... Stephen Whittaker
Tommy .... Tom Nolan
Cab Driver .... Danny Zapien
First Truck Driver .... Elmer Valentine
Salesman .... Burke Rhind
Husband .... Richard Armstrong
Master of Ceremonies .... Joe Light
Church Lady .... Dolly Hunt
Second Truck Driver .... Jason Clarke

Right Center: Barbara London, Cher

THE VALLEY OF GWANGI

(WARNER BROS.-7 ARTS) Producer, Charles H. Schneer; Director, James O'Connolly; Screenplay, William E. Bast; Additional Material, Julian More; Photography, Erwin Hillier; Associate Producer, Visual Effects, Ray Harryhausen; Music, Jerome Moross; Assistant Director, Pedro Vidal; In Dynamation and Technicolor; June release.

CAST

Tuck .... James Franciscus
T. J. .... Gila Golan
Champ .... Richard Carlson
Professor Bromley .... Laurence Naismith
Tia Zorina .... Freda Jackson
Carlos .... Gustavo Rojo
Rowdy .... Dennis Kilbane
Bean .... Mario De Barros
Lope .... Curtis Arden

James Franciscus, Gila Golan

THE WILD BUNCH

(WARNER BROS.-7 ARTS) Producer, Phil Feldman; Director, Sam Peckinpah; Screenplay, Walon Green, Sam Peckinpah; Story, Walon Green, Roy N. Sickner; Photography, Lucien Ballard; Associate Producer, Roy N. Sickner; Music, Jerry Fielding; Assistant Directors, Cliff Coleman, Fred Gamon; June release.

CAST

Pike	William Holden
Dutch	Ernest Borgnine
Thornton	Robert Ryan
Sykes	Edmond O'Brien
Lyle Gorch	Warren Oates
Angel	Jaime Sanchez
Tector Gorch	Ben Johnson
Mapache	Emilio Fernandez
Coffer	Strother Martin
T. C.	L. Q. Jones
Harrigan	Albert Dekker
Crazy Lee	Bo Hopkins
Wainscoat	Bud Taylor
Zamorra	Jorge Russek
Herrera	Alfonso Arau
Don Jose	Chano Urueta
Teresa	Sonia Amelio
Aurora	Aurora Clavel
Elsa	Elsa Cardenas

William Holden, Ernest Borgnine, Ben Johnson, Warren Oates, Jaime Sanchez. Top: Edmond O'Brien, William Holden

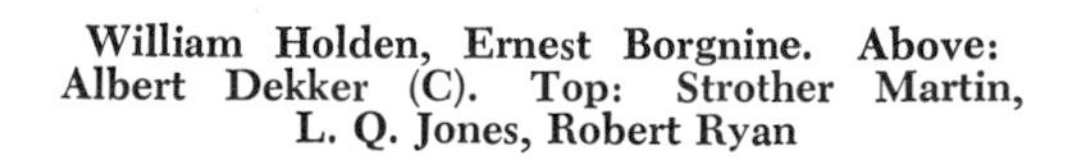

William Holden, Ernest Borgnine. Above: Albert Dekker (C). Top: Strother Martin, L. Q. Jones, Robert Ryan

Ernest Borgnine, William Holden (also above)

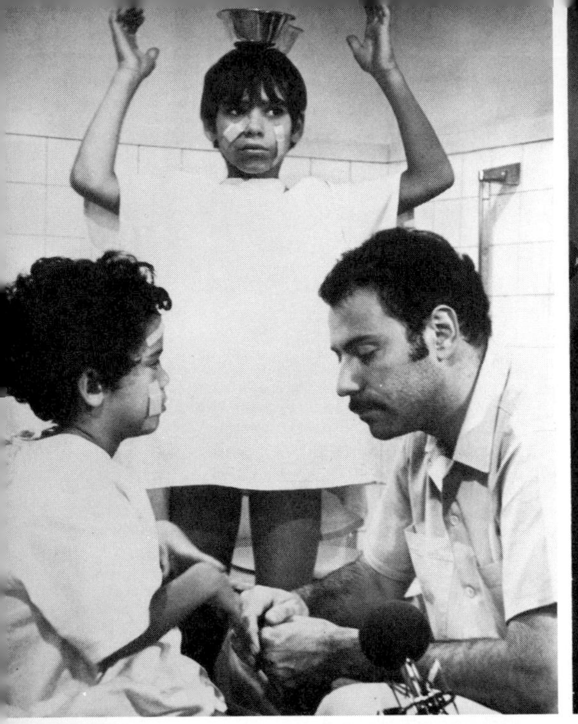

POPI

(UNITED ARTISTS) Producer, Herbert B. Leonard; Director, Arthur Hiller; Screenplay, Tina and Lester Pine; Assistant Directors, Pete Scoppa, Don Moody; Photography, Andrew Laszlo; Music, Dominic Frontiere; Costumes, Albert Wolsky; In DeLuxe Color; June release.

CAST

Abraham .... Alan Arkin
Lupe .... Rita Moreno
Junior .... Miguel Alejandro
Luis .... Ruben Figueroa
Harmon .... John Harkins
Miss Musto .... Joan Tompkins
Pickett .... Anthony Holland
Diaz .... Arny Freeman
Receptionist .... Barbara Dana
Mrs. Cruz .... Antonia Rey
Dr. Perle .... Arnold Soboloff
Novitas Man .... Victor Junquera
Silvia .... Gladys Velez

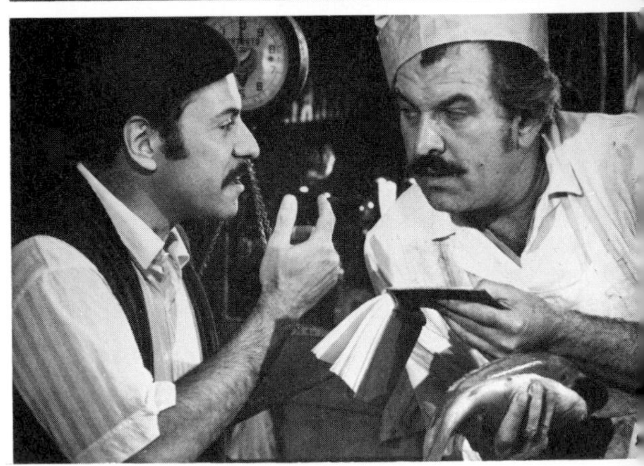

Top: Miguel Alejandro, Ruben Figueroa, Alan Arkin. Below: Alan Arkin, Rita Moreno

Alan Arkin, Arny Freeman. Above: Alan Arkin, Miguel Alejandro, Ruben Figueroa

Top: Miguel Alejandro, Ruben Figueroa

Elsa Lanchester
Top: Bill Mumy

RASCAL

(BUENA VISTA) Producer, James Algar; Director, Norman Tokar; Screenplay, Harold Swanton; Based on book by Sterling North; Photography, William Snyder; Music, Buddy Baker; Song, Bobby Russell; Costumes, Rosemary O'Ell; Assistant Director, Christopher Hibler; A Walt Disney Production in Technicolor; June release.

CAST

Willard North	Steve Forrest
Sterling North	Bill Mumy
Theo North	Pamela Toll
Miss Whalen	Bettye Ackerman
Mrs. Satterfield	Elsa Lanchester
Garth Shadwick	Henry Jones
Cy Jenkins	John Fiedler
Rev. Thurman	Jonathan Daly
Mr. Pringle	Herbert Anderson
Miss Pince-nez	Maudie Prickett
Walter Dabbitt	Richard Erdman
Norman Bradshaw	Steve Carlson
Constable Stacey	Robert Emhardt
Narrator	Walter Pidgeon

LAST SUMMER

(ALLIED ARTISTS) Producers, Alfred W. Crown, Sidney Beckerman; Director, Frank Perry; Associate Producer, Joel Glickman; Screenplay, Eleanor Perry; Assistant Directors, Terry Donnelly, Gene Sultan; Photography, Gerald Hirschfeld; Music, John Simon; Costumes, Theoni Aldredge; Adapted from novel by Evan Hunter; In Eastmancolor; June release.

CAST

Sandy	Barbara Hershey
Peter	Richard Thomas
Dan	Bruce Davison
Rhoda	Cathy Burns
Anibal	Ernesto Gonzalez
Mr. Caudell	Peter Turgeon
Townies	Lou Gary, Andrew Krance, Wayne Mayer

Bruce Davison, Cathy Burns, Richard Thomas, Barbara Hershey. Above: (L) Barbara Hershey, Richard Thomas, (R) Richard Thomas, Barbara Hershey, Bruce Davison. Top: Richard Thomas, Barbara Hershey, Bruce Davison

Bruce Davison, Cathy Burns, Barbara Hershey, Richard Thomas

Jack Palance, Omar Sharif

CHE!

(20th CENTURY-FOX) Producer, Sy Bartlett; Director, Richard Fleischer; Screenplay, Michael Wilson, Sy Bartlett; Story, Sy Bartlett, David Karp; Music, Lalo Schifrin; Photography, Charles Wheeler; Assistant Director, Richard Glassman; In Panavision and DeLuxe Color; June release.

CAST

Che Guevara .... Omar Sharif
Fidel Castro .... Jack Palance
Ramon Valdez .... Cesare Danova
Faustino Morales .... Robert Loggia
Guillermo .... Woody Strode
Anita Marquez .... Barbara Luna
Goatherd .... Frank Silvera
Capt. Vasquez .... Albert Paulsen
Tania .... Linda Marsh
Felipe Munoz .... Tom Troupe
Willy .... Rudy Diaz
Rolando .... Perry Lopez
Pablo Rojas .... Abraham Sofaer
Col Salazar .... Richard Angarola
Celia Sanchez .... Sarita Vara
Raul Castro .... Paul Bertoya
Antonio .... Sid Haig
Juan Almeida .... Adolph Caesar
Hector .... Paul Picerni
Camilo Cienfuegos .... Ray Martell

EYE OF THE CAT

(UNIVERSAL) Producers, Bernard Schwartz, Phillip Hazelton; Director, David Lowell Rich; Screenplay, Joseph Stefano; Photography, Russell Mett, Ellsworth Fredricks; Music, Lalo Schifrin; Costumes, Edith Head; Assistant Director, Joseph Cavalier; In Technicolor; June release.

CAST

Wylie .... Michael Sarrazin
Kassia .... Gayle Hunnicutt
Aunt Danny .... Eleanor Parker
Luke .... Tim Henry
Dr. Mills .... Laurence Naismith
Poor Dear .... Jennifer Leak
Bendetto .... Linden Chiles
Bellemondo .... Mark Herron
Socialite .... Annabelle Garth

Right: Gayle Hunnicut, Michael Sarrazin

THE BRIDGE AT REMAGEN

(UNITED ARTISTS) Producer, David L. Wolper; Director, John Guillermin; Screenplay, Theodore Strauss, William Roberts, Ray Rigby; Associate Producers, Julian Ludwig, Theodore Strauss; Photography, Stanley Cortez; Assistant Director, Reggie Callow; Costumer, Frank Balchus; In Panavision and DeLuxe Color; June release.

CAST

Lt. Phil Hartman .... George Segal
Maj. Paul Kreuger .... Robert Vaughn
Sgt. Angelo (Angel) .... Ben Gazzara
Maj. Barnes .... Bradford Dillman
Brig. Gen. Shinner .... E. G. Marshall
Gen. Von Brock .... Peter Van Eyck
Col. Jellicoe .... Matt Clark
Col. Dent .... Fritz Ford
Lt. Pattison .... Tom Heaton
Cpl. Grebs .... Bo Hopkins
Pvt. Bissell .... Robert Logan
Capt. Colt .... Paul Prokop
Pvt. Slavek .... Steve Sandor
Pvt. Glover .... Frank Webb
Capt. Carl Schmidt .... Hans Christian Blech
Capt. Otto Baumann .... Joachim Hansen
S. S. Gen. Gerlach .... Gunter Meisner
Field Marshal Von Sturmer .... Richard Munch
Emil Holzgang .... Heinz Reincke
Greta Holzgang .... Sonja Ziemann
Lt. Zimring .... Vit Olmer
Pvt. Manfred .... Rudolf Jelinek
The Girl .... Anna Gael

George Segal, Ben Gazzara

THE MALTESE BIPPY

(MGM) Producers, Everett Freeman, Robert Enders; Director, Norman Panama; Screenplay, Everett Freeman, Ray Singer; Story, Everett Freeman; Photography, William H. Daniels; Music, Nelson Riddle; Assistant Director, Arthur Jacobson; Costumes, Moss Mabry; A Freeman-Enders Production in Panavision and Metrocolor; June release.

CAST

Sam Smith	Dan Rowan
Ernest Grey	Dick Martin
Robin Sherwood	Carol Lynley
Carlotta Ravenswood	Julie Newmar
Molly Fletcher	Mildred Natwick
Mr. Ravenswood	Fritz Weaver
Lt. Tim Crane	Robert Reed
Dr. Charles Strauss	David Hurst
Sgt. Kelvaney	Dana Elcar
Axel Kronstadt	Leon Askin
Adolph Springer	Alan Oppenheimer
Helga	Eddra Gale
Tony	Arthur Batanides
Saundra	Pamela Rodgers
Joanna Clay	Jenifer Bishop
Mrs. Potter	Maudie Prickett
Harold Fenster	Garry Walberg
Mona	Carol-Jean Thompson
Wesling	Jerry Mann

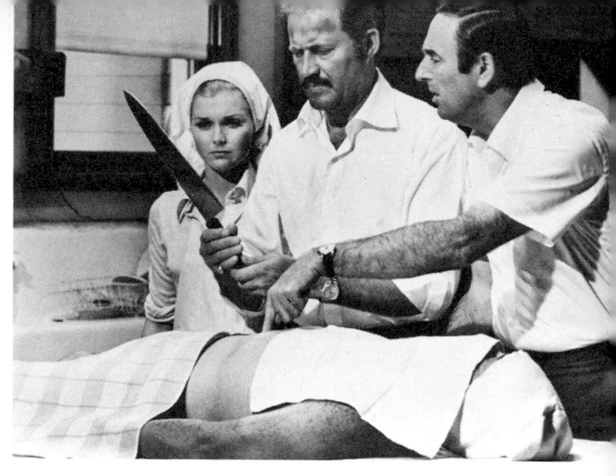

Carol Lynley, Dan Rowan, Dick Martin

DEATH OF A GUNFIGHTER

(UNIVERSAL) Producer, Richard Lyons; Director, Allen Smithee; Screenplay, Joseph Calvelli; Photography, Andy Jackson; Assistant Director, Joe Boston; In Technicolor; June release.

CAST

Frank Patch	Richard Widmark
Claire Quintana	Lena Horne
Lou Trinidad	John Saxon
Dan Joslin	Michael McGreevey
Hilda Jorgensen	Darleen Carr
Lester Locke	Carrol O'Connor
Will Oxley	Mercer Harris
Andy Oxley	Kent Smith
Mayor Chester Sayre	Larry Gates
Ivan Stanek	Morgan Woodward
Father Sweeney	James O'Hara
Rev. Rork	Harry Carey
Laurie Mills	Jacqueline Scott
Doc Adams	Dub Taylor
Luke Mills	Jimmy Lydon

Left Center: Richard Widmark, Lena Horne

CASTLE KEEP

(COLUMBIA) Producers, Martin Ransohoff, John Calley; Director, Sydney Pollack; Screenplay, Daniel Taradash, David Rayfiel; From novel by William Eastlake; Photography, Henri Decae; Assistant Directors, Marc Maurette, Pierre Roubaud; Costumes, Jacques Fonteray; Choreography, Dirk Sanders; In Panavision and Eastmancolor; July release.

CAST

Maj. Abraham Falconer	Burt Lancaster
Sgt. Orlando Rossi	Peter Falk
Capt. Lionel Beckman	Patrick O'Neal
Henri Tixier, Comte de Maldorais	Jean-Pierre Aumont
Therese, Comtesse de Maldorais	Astrid Heeren
Cpl. Ralph Clearboy	Scott Wilson
Lt. Adam Amberjack	Tony Bill
Sgt. Juan De Vaca	Michael Conrad
Lt. Billy Byron Bix	Bruce Dern
Pfc. Alistair Benjamin	Al Freeman, Jr.
Pvt. Henry Three Ears of an Elk	James Patterson
Baker's Wife	Bisera Vukotic
David	Ernest Clark
Dancing Soldier	Harry Baird
One-eared Soldier	Dave Jones
First Puerto Rican	Jean Gimello
The Red Queen	Caterina Boratto
Red Queen Girls	Karen Blanguernon, Maria Danube, Elizabeth Darius, Merja Allanen, Anne Marie Moscovenko, Elizabeth Teissier, Eya Tuuli

Burt Lancaster, Al Freeman, Jr., Tony Bill, Jean-Pierre Aumont.

EASY RIDER

(COLUMBIA) Producer, Peter Fonda; Director, Dennis Hopper; Executive Producer, Bert Schneider; Associate Producer, William Hayward; Screenplay, Peter Fonda, Dennis Hopper, Terry Southern; Photography, Lazlo Kovacs; Produced by Pando Company in association with Raybert Productions; In Color; July release.

CAST

Wyatt	Peter Fonda
Billy	Dennis Hopper
Jesus	Antonio Mendoza
Connection	Phil Spector
Body Guard	Mac Mashourian
Rancher	Warren Finnerty
Rancher's Wife	Tita Colorado
Stranger	Luke Askew
Commune:	
Lisa	Luanna Anders
Sarah	Sabrina Scharf
Joanne	Sandy Wyeth
Jack	Robert Walker
Mimes	Robert Ball, Carman Phillips, Ellie Walker, Michael Pataki
Jail:	
George Hanson	Jack Nicholson
Guard	George Fowler, Jr.
Sheriff	Keith Green
Cafe:	
Cat Man	Hayward Robillard
Deputy	Arnold Hess, Jr.
Customers	Buddy Causey, Jr., Duffy LaFont, Blase M. Dawson, Paul Guedry, Jr.
Girls	Suzie Ramagos, Elida Ann Hebert, Rose LeBlance, Mary Kay Hebert, Cynthia Grezaffi, Colette Purpera
House of Blue Lights:	
Mary	Toni Basil
Karen	Karen Marmer
Dancing Girl	Cathi Cozzi
Hookers	Thea Salerno, Ann McLain, Beatriz Monteil, Marcia Bowman
Pickup Truck	David C. Billodeau, Johnny David

Peter Fonda, Dennis Hopper, also above
Top: Peter Fonda

Jack Nicholson. Above: Peter Fonda

Dennis Hopper.
Top: Dennis Hopper, Peter Fonda, Jack Nicholson

Dennis Hopper, Jack Nicholson Peter Fonda,

Joanna Shimkus, Sidney Poitier, also above and top with Al Freeman, Jr.

THE LOST MAN

(UNIVERSAL) Producers, Edward Muhl, Melville Tucker; Direction and Screenplay, Robert Alan Aurthur; Associate Producer, Ernest B. Wehneyer; Photography, Jerry Finnerman; Music, Quincy Jones; Costumes, Edith Head; Assistant Director, Joseph Kenny; In Panavision and Technicolor; July release.

CAST

Jason Higgs	Sidney Poitier
Cathy Ellis	Joanna Shimkus
Dennis	Al Freeman, Jr.
Hamilton	Michael Tolin
Eddie	Leon Bibb
Barnes	Richard Dysart
Photographer	David Steinberg
Sally	Beverly Todd
Orville	Paul Winifeld
Reggie	Bernie Hamilton
Ronald	Richard Anthony Williams
Police Captain	Dolph Sweet
Terry	Arnold Williams
Theresa	Virginia Capers
Diane	Vonetta McGee
Warren	Frank Marth
Miss Harrison	Maxine Stuart
Plainclothesman	George Tyne
Grandma	Paulene Myers
Willie	Lee Weaver
Miller	Morris Erby
Teddy	Doug Johnson
Minister	Lincoln Kilpatrick

WHATEVER HAPPENED TO AUNT ALICE?

(CINERAMA) Producer, Robert Aldrich; Director, Lee H. Katzin; Screenplay, Theodore Apstein; From Novel by Ursula Curtiss; Executive Producer, Peter Nelson; Music, Gerald Fried; Costumes, Renie; Photography, Joseph Biroc; Assistant Director, Daisy Gerber; A Palomar Picture in MetroColor; July release.

CAST

Mrs. Marrable	Geraldine Page
Mrs. Dimmock	Ruth Gordon
Harriet Vaughn	Rosemary Forsyth
Mike Darrah	Robert Fuller
Miss Tinsley	Mildred Dunnock
Julia Lawson	Joan Huntington
George Lawson	Peter Brandon
Jim Vaughn	Michael Barbera
Mr. Bentley	Peter Bonerz
Sheriff Armijo	Richard Angarola
Elva	Claire Kelly
Dottie	Valerie Allen
Juan	Martin Garralaga
Olin	Jack Bannon
Warren	Seth Riggs
Telephone Man	Lou Kane

Ruth Gordon, Geraldine Page (also above and at top)

TRUE GRIT

(PARAMOUNT) Producer, Hal Wallis; Director, Henry Hathaway; Screenplay, Marguerite Roberts; Based on novel by Charles Portis; Associate Producer, Paul Nathan; Photography, Lucien Ballard; Assistant Director, William W. Gray; Music, Elmer Bernstein; Costumes, Dorothy Jeakins; Title Song, Don Black; In Technicolor; July release.

CAST

Rooster Cogburn ---------- John Wayne
La Boeuf ---------- Glen Campbell
Mattie Ross ---------- Kim Darby
Emmett Quincy ---------- Jeremy Slate
Ned Pepper ---------- Robert Duvall
Moon ---------- Dennis Hopper
Goudy ---------- Alfred Ryder
Colonel Stonehill ---------- Strother Martin
Tom Chaney ---------- Jeff Corey
Capt. Boots Finch ---------- Ron Soble
Lawyer Daggett ---------- John Fiedler
Judge Parker ---------- James Westerfield
Sheriff ---------- John Doucette
Barlow ---------- Donald Woods
Mrs. Floyd ---------- Edith Atwater
Dirty Bob ---------- Carlos Rivas
Mrs. Bagby ---------- Isabel Boniface
Chen Lee ---------- H. W. Gim
Frank Ross ---------- John Pickard
Mrs. Ross ---------- Elizabeth Harrower
Yarnell ---------- Ken Renard
Harold Parmalee ---------- Jay Ripley
Farrell Parmalee ---------- Kenneth Becker

John Wayne, also top with Kim Darby, Glen Campbell

Glen Campbell, Kim Darby

John Wayne, Kim Darby, also at top
(For his performance, John Wayne received
1969 Academy Award)

Alfred Ryder (C), John Wayne (R). Above:
Kim Darby, Glen Campbell, John Wayne

THE CHAIRMAN

(20th CENTURY-FOX) Producer, Mort Abrahams; Director, J. Lee Thompson; Screenplay, Ben Maddow; From novel by Jay Richard Kennedy; Music, Jerry Goldsmith; Photography, John Wilcox; Associate Producer, Pepi Lenzi; Assistant Director, Ferdinand Fairfax; Costumes, Anna Duse; An Arthur P. Jacobs Production in Panavision and DeLuxe Color; July release.

CAST

John Hathaway	Gregory Peck
Kay Hanna	Anne Heywood
Shelby	Arthur Hill
Benson	Alan Dobie
The Chairman	Conrad Yama
Ting Ling	Zienia Merton
Shertov	Ori Levy
Yin	Eric Young
Chang Shou	Burt Kwouk
Gardner	Alan White
Prof. Soong Li	Keye Luke
Soong Chu	Francisca Tu
Stewardess	Mai Ling
First Girl Student	Janet Key
Air Force Sergeant	Gordon Sterne
Hotel Night Manager	Robert Lee
Susan Wright	Helen Horton
Chinese Officer	Keith Bonnard
Soldier (Baggage)	Cecil Cheng
Russian Guard	Lawrence Herder
Signals Captain	Simon Cain
Chinese Officer	Anthony Chinn
Audio Room Technician	Edward Cast

Top: Francisca Tu, Keye Luke, Gregory Peck
Below: Anne Heywood, Gregory Peck

Gregory Peck, Francisca Tu. Above: Conrad Yama, Eric Young, Gregory Peck

Top: Alan Dobie, Arthur Hill

James Farentino, Patty Duke. Above: Patty Duke. Top: Elsa Lanchester, Patty Duke (also right)

ME, NATALIE

(NATIONAL GENERAL) Producer, Stanley Shapiro; Director, Fred Coe; Screenplay, A. Martin Zweiback; Based on story by Stanley Shapiro; Photography, Arthur J. Ornitz; Associate Producer, Kurt Newmann; Music, Henry Mancini; Lyrics, Rod McKuen; July release.

CAST

Natalie Miller .... Patty Duke
David Harris .... James Farentino
Uncle Harold .... Martin Balsam
Miss Dennison .... Elsa Lanchester
Shirley Norton .... Salome Jens
Mrs. Miller .... Nancy Marchand
Mr. Miller .... Phil Sterling
Betty Simon .... Deborah Winters
Stanley Dexter .... Ronald Hale
Morris .... Bob Balaban
Harvey Belman .... Matthew Cowles
Mrs. Schroder .... Ann Thomas
Tony .... Al Pacino
Hester .... Catherine Burns
Natalie at 7 .... Robyn Morgan
Surviving Brother .... Dan Keyes
Attorney .... Peter Turgeon
Plastic Surgeon .... Milt Kamen
Arnold .... Ross Charap
Mrs. Simon .... Dortha Duckworth
Mr. Simon .... Milo Boulton
Max .... Dennis Allen
Freddie .... Robert Frink
Betty Simon at 10 .... Melinda Blachley

SLAVES

(CONTINENTAL) Producer, Philip Langner; Associate Producer, Marshall Young; Director, Herbert J. Biberman; Screenplay, Herbert J. Biberman, John O. Killen, Alida Sherman; Music, Bobby Scott; Photography, Joseph Brun; Costumes, Robert Magahay, Laurence Gross; A Theatre Guild Films Production in Movielab Color; July release.

CAST

Luke	Ossie Davis
Madame Stillwell	Nancy Coleman
Zacharious	Oscar Paul Jones
Jericho	Robert Kya-Hill
Esther	Barbara Ann Teer
Holland	David Huddleston
Stillwell	Sheppard Strudwick
MacKay	Stephen Boyd
Emmeline	Adline King
Dame de New Orleans	Gale Sondergaard
Julia	Eva Jessye
Cassy	Dionne Warwick
Madame Bennet	Marilyn Clark
Luther	James Heath
Shadrach	Julius Harris

Right: Dionne Warwick, Stephen Boyd

Barbara Ann Teer, Ossie Davis. Above: Barbara Ann Teer, Ossie Davis, Robert Kya-Hill, Sheppard Strudwick

Ossie Davis, Stephen Boyd, Robert Kya-Hill
Above: Stephen Boyd, Ossie Davis

PUTNEY SWOPE

(CINEMA V) Directed and Written by Robert Downey; Associate Producer, Ronald Sullivan; Photography, Gerald Cotts; Music, Charley Cuva; Costumes, New Breed Inc.; Produced by Herald Productions in black and white and EastmanColor; July release.

CAST

Stanley Gottlieb (Nathan), Allen Garfield (Elias, Jr.), Archie Russell (Joker), Ramon Gordon (Bissinger), Bert Lawrence (Hawker), Joe Engler (Mr. Syllables), Arnold Johnson (Putney), David Kirk (Elias, Sr.), Don George (Mr. Cards), Buddy Butler (Putney's Bodyguard), Vincent Hamill (Man in white suit), Tom Odachi (Wing), Ching Yeh (Wing, Jr.), Spunky-Funk Johnson (Mr. Major), Joe Fields (Pittsburgh Willie), Norman Schreiber (Messenger), Bob Staats (War Toys), Alan Abel (Mr. Lucky), Sol Brawerman (Dinkleberry), Ben Israel (Pit Stop), Mel Brooks (Forget It), Louise Heath (Secretary), Barbara Clarke (Secretary), Catherine Lojacono (Lady Beaver), Johnjohn Robinson (Wayne), Charles Buffum (Director), Ron Palombo (Assistant Director), Wendy Appel (Script Girl), Antonio Fargas (Arab), Geegee Brown (Secretary), Vance Amaker (Wall Man), Al Green (Cowboy 1), Chuck Ender (Cowboy 2), Anthony Chisholm (Cowboy 3), Walter Jones (Jim Keranga), Khaula Bakr (Mrs. Keranga), Laura Greene (Mrs. Swope), Ed Gordon (Victrola Cola), Eric Krupnik (Mark Focus), George Morgan (Token), Abdul Hakeim (Bouncer), Allan Arbus (Bad News), Jesse McDonald (Young Militant), C. Robert Scott, Leopoldo Mandeville (Militants), Vince Morgan, Jr. (West Indian), Al Browne (Moderate), Marie Claire (Eugenie), Eileen Peterson (Narrator), William H. Boesen (Bert), Carol Farber (Secretary), Cerves McNeil (Youngblood), Carolyn Cardwell (Borman Six Girl), Charles Green (Myron X), Pepi Hermine (President), Ruth Hermine (First Lady), Paul Storob (Secret Service), Larry Wolfe (Borman Six), Jeff Lord (Bald), Tom Boya (O'Dinga), Major Cole, David Butts, Franklin Scott, Paul Alladice (Idea Men), Ronald Dyson (Face Off Boy), Shelley Plimpton (Face Off Girl), Elzbleta Czyzewska (Maid), Peter Maloney (Chauffeur), Peter Benson (Jingle).

Ruth Hermine, Pepi Hermine (R)
Top: Arnold Johnson (C)

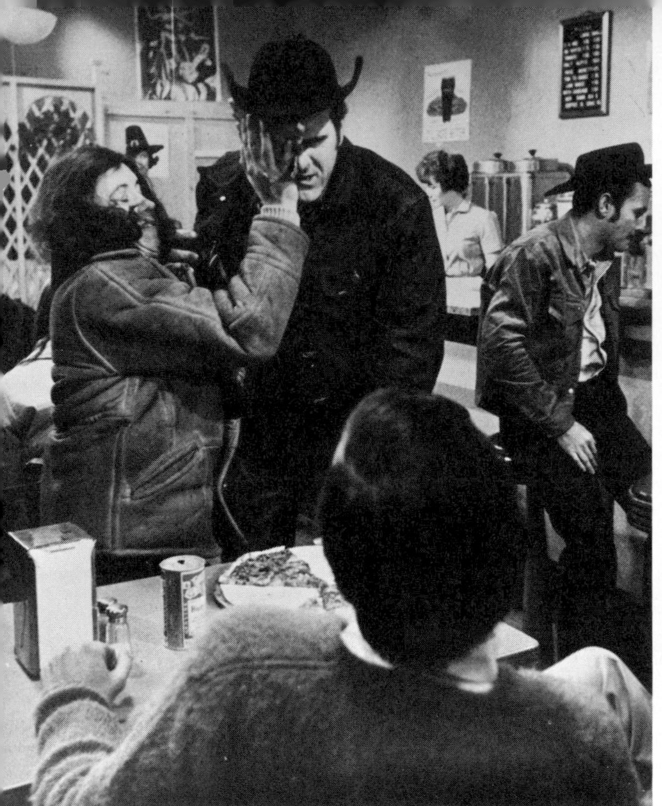

Arlo Guthrie (also top left). Top Right: William Obanhein, Pat Quinn

ALICE'S RESTAURANT

(UNITED ARTISTS) Producers, Hillard Elkins, Joe Manduke; Director, Arthur Penn; Screenplay, Venable Herndon, Arthur Penn; Based on "The Alice's Restaurant Massacree" by Arlo Guthrie; Music, Arlo Guthrie and Garry Sherman; Photography, Michael Nebbia; Associate Producer, Harold Leventhal; Costumes, Anna Hill Johnstone; Assistant Directors, William Gerrity, Jr., Frank Simpson; A Florin Production in DeLuxe Color; August release.

CAST

Arlo	Arlo Guthrie
Alice	Pat Quinn
Ray	James Broderick
Shelly	Michael McClanathan
Roger	Geoff Outlaw
Mari-chan	Tina Chen
Karin	Kathleen Dabney
Officer Obie	William Obanhein
Evangelist	Seth Allen
Blueglass	Monroe Arnold
Woody	Joseph Boley
Lady Clerk	Vinnette Carroll
Marjorie	Sylvia Davis
Jacob	Simm Landres
Ruth	Eulalie Noble
Dean	Louis Beachner
Deconsecration Minister	MacIntyre Dixon
Second Deconsecration Minister	Pierce Middleton
Funeral Director	Donald Marye
Reenie	Shelley Plimpton
Group W Sergeant	M. Emmet Walsh
Cop #1	Ronald Weyand
Landlady	Eleanor Wilson
Medic	Simon Deckard
Waiter	Thomas DeWolfe
Himself	Judge James Hannon
Music Teacher	Graham Jarvis
Cop #2	John Quill
Sergeant	Frank Simpson
Themselves	Peter Seege, Lee Hays

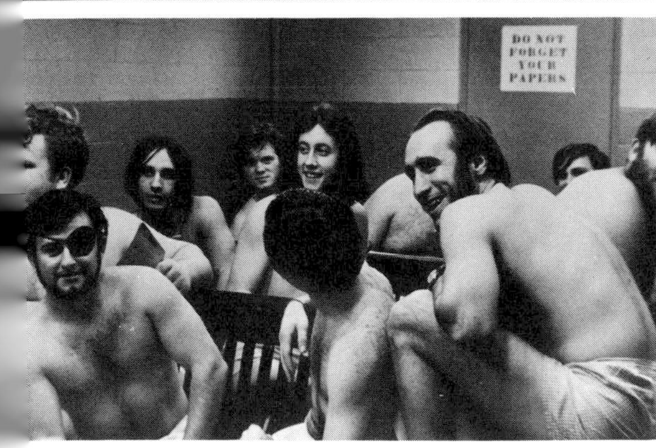

Arlo Guthrie (C). Above: Arlo Guthrie, Kathleen Dabney. Top: Tina Chen, James Broderick, Pat Quinn, Arlo Guthrie

Arlo Guthrie, Geoff Outlaw

TAKE THE MONEY AND RUN

(CINERAMA) Producer, Charles H. Joffe; Director, Woody Allen; Executive Producer, Sidney Glazier; Screenplay, Woody Allen, Mickey Rose; Music, Marvin Hamlisch; Associate Producer, Jack Grossberg; Photography, Lester Shorr; Assistant Director, Louis A. Stroller; August release.

CAST

Virgil Starkwell	Woody Allen
Louise	Janet Margolin
Fritz	Marcel Hillaire
Miss Blaire	Jacquelyn Hyde
Jake	Lonny Chapman
Al	Jan Merlin
Chain Gang Warden	James Anderson
Fred	Howard Storm
Vince	Mark Gordon
Frank	Micil Murphy
Joe Agneta	Minnow Moskowitz
Judge	Nate Jacobson
Farm House Lady	Grace Bauer
Mother Starkwell	Ethel Sokolow
Father Starkwell	Henry Leff
Psychiatrist	Don Frazier
Michael Sullivan	Mike O'Dowd
Narrator	Jackson Beck

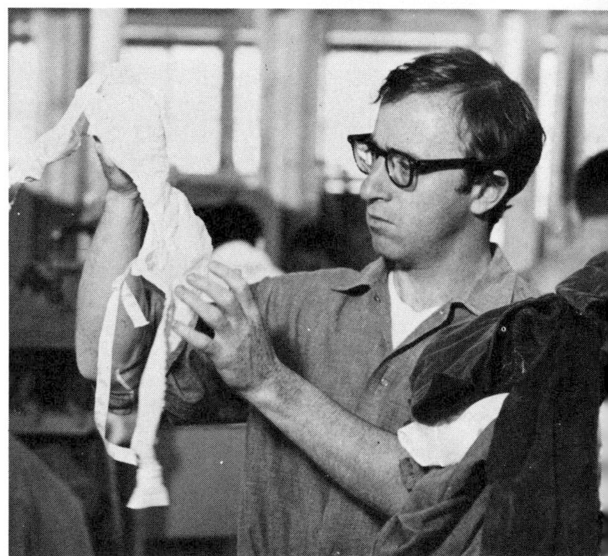

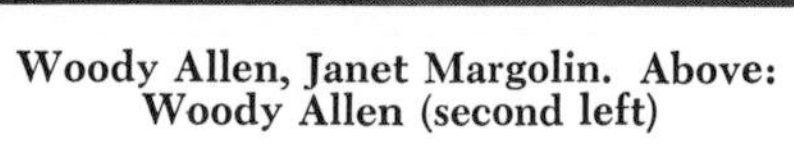

Woody Allen, Janet Margolin. Above: Woody Allen (second left)

Henry Leff, Ethel Sokolow. Above: Woody Allen. Top: Woody Allen (L)

NUMBER ONE

(UNITED ARTISTS) Producer, Walter Seltzer; Director, Tom Gries; Screenplay, David Moessinger; Music, Dominic Frontiere; Associate Producer, Frank Baur; Photography, Michel Hugo; Assistant Director, Phil Parslow; Costumes, Rita Riggs; In DeLuxe Color; August release.

CAST

Ron "Cat" Catlan	Charlton Heston
Julie Catlan	Jessica Walter
Richie Fowler	Bruce Dern
Coach Jim Southerd	John Randolph
Ann Marley	Diana Muldaur
Dr. Tristler	G. D. Spradlin
Kelly Williams	Richard Elkins
Walt Chaffee	Mike Henry
Deke Coleman	Ernie Barnes
Robin	Steve Franken
Ed Davis	Bart Burns
Attendant	Forrest Wood
Dr. Overstreet	George Sperdakos
Roy Nelson	Roy Jenson
Himself	Al Hirt
Themselves	The New Orleans Saints
Harvey Hess	Bobby Troup

John Randolph, Charlton Heston. Above: Diana Muldaur, Charlton Heston

Jessica Walter, Charlton Heston. Above: Bruce Dern, Jessica Walter. Top: Richard Elkins (L), Charlton Heston (C)

THE GYPSY MOTHS

(MGM) Producers, Hal Landers, Bobby Roberts; Director, John Frankenheimer; Executive Producer, Edward Lewis; Screenplay, William Hanley; Based on novel by James Drought; Photography, Philip Lathrop; Music, Elmer Bernstein; Assistant Director, Al Jennings; In Metrocolor; August release.

CAST

Mike Rettig	Burt Lancaster
Elizabeth Brandon	Deborah Kerr
Joe Browdy	Gene Hackman
Malcolm Webson	Scott Wilson
V. John Brandon	William Windom
Annie Burke	Bonnie Bedelia
Waitress	Sheree North
Pilot	Carl Reindel
Stand Owner	Ford Rainey
Dick Donford	John Napier

Scott Wilson, William Windom, Gene Hackman. Above: Burt Lancaster, Deborah Kerr

Scott Wilson, Bonnie Bedelia. Above: Sheree North, Gene Hackman. Top Left: Gene Hackman, Burt Lancaster, Scott Wilson

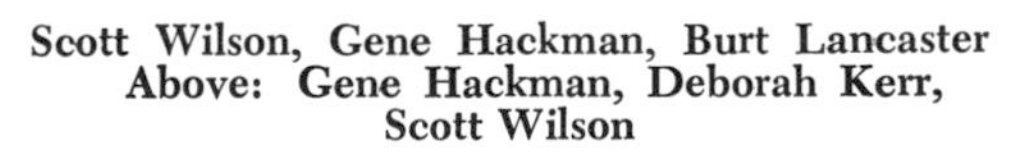

Scott Wilson, Gene Hackman, Burt Lancaster
Above: Gene Hackman, Deborah Kerr, Scott Wilson

Burt Lancaster, Scott Wilson. Above: Bonnie Bedelia, Gene Hackman

YOUNG BILLY YOUNG

(UNITED ARTISTS) Producer, Max E. Youngstein; Director, Burt Kennedy; Associate Producer, J. Paul Popkin; Screenplay, Burt Kennedy; Based on "Who Rides With Wyatt" by Will Henry; Music, Shelly Manne; Title Song, Shelly Manne, Ernie Sheldon; Sung by Robert Mitchum; Photography, Harry Stradling; Assistant Director, Maxwell O. Henry; A Talbot-Youngstein Production in DeLuxe Color; September release.

CAST

Kane	Robert Mitchum
Lily	Angie Dickinson
Billy	Robert Walker
Jesse	David Carradine
Behan	Jack Kelly
Boone	John Anderson
Charlie	Paul Fix
Doc Cushman	Willis Bouchey
Bell	Parley Baer
Gambler	Bob Anderson
Evvie	Deana Martin
Mexican Officer	Rodolfo Acosta

Robert Mitchum, Angie Dickinson, Robert Walker. Above: Robert Mitchum, Robert Walker. Top: Robert Walker, Deana Martin

Top: Jack Kelly, Angie Dickinson. Below: Robert Walker, David Carradine

THE LEARNING TREE

(WARNER BROS.-7 ARTS) Producer-Director, Gordon Parks; Screenplay, Gordon Parks; Based on his novel; Photography, Burnett Guffey; Title Song sung by O. C. Smith; Assistant Director, Jack Aldworth; A Winger Enterprises Production in Panavision and Technicolor; September release.

CAST

Newt	Kyle Johnson
Marcus	Alex Clarke
Sarah	Estelle Evans
Kirky	Dana Elcar
Arcella	Mira Waters
Uncle Rob	Joel Fluellen
Silas Newhall	Malcolm Atterbury
Booker Savage	Richard Ward
Judge Cavanaugh	Russell Thorson
Miss McClintock	Peggy Rea

Estelle Evans, Kevin Hagen, Kyle Johnson
Above: Kyle Johnson, Dana Elcar

Alex Clarke, Kyle Johnson. Above: Kyle Johnson, Mira Waters. Top: Felix Nelson, Estelle Evans, Kyle Johnson

MEDIUM COOL

(PARAMOUNT) Producers, Tully Friedman, Haskell Wexler; Directed and Written by Haskell Wexler; Executive Producer, Tully Friedman; Associate Producers, Michael Philip Butler, Steven North; Assistant Director, Wendell Franklin; Photography, Haskell Wexler; Music, Mike Bloomfield; In Technicolor; September release.

CAST

John .... Robert Forster
Eileen .... Verna Bloom
Gus .... Peter Bonerz
Ruth .... Marianne Hill
Harold .... Harold Blankenship
Frank Baker .... Sid McCoy
Dede .... Christine Bergstrom
Penny Baker .... Robert McAndrew
News Director Karlin .... William Sickinger
Rich Lady .... Beverly Younger
Social Worker .... Marrian Walters
Plainclothesman .... Edward Croke
Blonde .... Sandra Ann Roberts
Newscaster .... Doug Kimball
Gun Clinic Manager .... Peter Boyle
Secretary .... Georgia Tadda
Buddy .... Charles Geary
Black Militants .... Jeff Donaldson, Richard Abrams, Felton Perry, Val Grey, Bill Sharp, Robert Paige, Walter Bradford, Russell Davis, Livingston Lewis, Barbara Jones, John Jackson
Reporters and Photographers .... Simone Zorn, Madeleine Maroou, Mickey Pallas, Lynn Erlich, Lester Brownlee, Morris Bleckman, Wally Wright, Sam Ventura, George Boulet
Kennedy Students .... James Jacobs, Spence Jackson, Dorien Suhr, Kenneth Whitener, Connie Fleischauer, Mary Smith, Nancy Noble
Gun Glinic Ladies .... Linda Handelman, Moira Friedman, Kathryn Schubert, Barbara Brydenthal, Elizabeth Moisant, Rose Bormacher

Peter Bonerz, Robert Forster (R)
Top: Robert Forster

Verna Bloom, Harold Blankenship, Robert Forster. Above: Sid McCoy, Peter Bonerz, Robert Forster, Jeff Donaldson

Robert Forster, Sandra Ann Roberts, Peter Bonerz
Top: Robert Forster, Verna Bloom

THE RAIN PEOPLE

(WARNER BROS.- 7 ARTS) Producers, Bart Patton, Ronald Colby; Direction and Screenplay, Francis Ford Coppola; Photography, Wilmer Butler; Assistant Directors, Richard Bennett, Jack Cunningham; Music, Ronald Stein; In Technicolor; September release.

CAST

Kilgannon	James Caan
Natalie	Shirley Knight
Gordon	Robert Duvall
Rosalie	Marya Zimmet
Mr. Alfred	Tom Aldredge
Ellen	Laurie Crewes
Artie	Andrew Duncan
Marion	Margaret Fairchild
Beth	Sally Gracie
Lou	Alan Manson
Vinny	Robert Modica

Shirley Knight, James Caan. Above: Robert Duvall, Shirley Knight

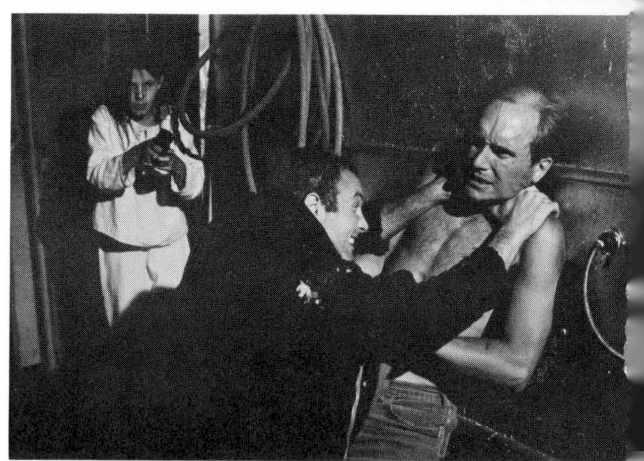

Marya Zimmet, James Caan, Robert Duvall
Above: James Caan. Top: Shirley Knight, Robert Duvall

THE CHRISTMAS TREE

(CONTINENTAL) Producer, Robert Dorfmann; Directed and Written by Terence Young; Based on novel by Michel Bataille; Music, Georges Auric; Photography, Henri Alekan; Assistant Director, Paul Feyder; A Walter Reade Presentation in Color by Movielab; September release.

CAST

Laurent	William Holden
Catherine	Virna Lisi
Verdun	Andre Bourvil
Pascal	Brook Fuller
Narinette	Madeleine Damien
Vernet	Friedrich Ledebur
Doctor	Mario Feliciani

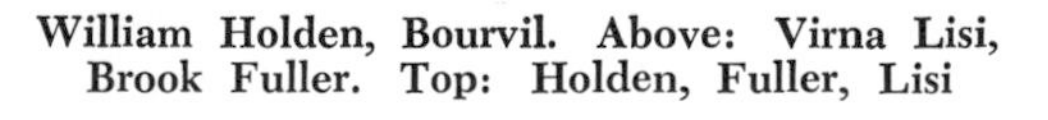

William Holden, Bourvil. Above: Virna Lisi, Brook Fuller. Top: Holden, Fuller, Lisi

Brook Fuller, Bourvil. Above: Brook Fuller

Katharine Hepburn

THE MADWOMAN OF CHAILLOT

(WARNER BROS.-7 ARTS) Producer, Ely Landau; Director, Bryan Forbes; Screenplay, Edward Anhalt; Based on play by Jean Giraudoux; Adapted by Maurice Valency; Photography, Claude Renoir, Burnett Guffey; Executive Producer, Henry T. Weinstein; Associate Producer, Anthony B. Unger; Music, Michael J. Lewis; Costumes, Rosine Delamare; Assistant Directors, Louis-Alain Pitzele, Alain Bonnot; In Technicolor; October release.

CAST

Countess Aurelia .... Katharine Hepburn
The Broker .... Charles Boyer
Dr. Jadin .... Claude Dauphin
Josephine .... Edith Evans
The Reverend .... John Gavin
The General .... Paul Henreid
The Commissar .... Oscar Homolka
Constance .... Margaret Leighton
Gabrielle .... Giulietta Masina
Irma .... Nanette Newman
Roderick .... Richard Chamberlain
The Chairman .... Yul Brynner
The Prospector .... Donald Pleasence
The Ragpicker .... Danny Kaye
Police Sergeant .... Fernand Gravet
The Folksinger .... Gordon Heath
Julius .... Gerald Sim

Oscar Homolka, Paul Henreid, Charles Boyer, Yul Brynner, Donald Pleasence, Katharine Hepburn. Above: Richard Chamberlain, Nanette Newman

Katharine Hepburn, Charles Boyer. Above: Danny Kaye. Top: Katharine Hepburn, Giulietta Masina, Edith Evans, Margaret Leighton

Donald Pleasence, Richard Chamberlain Above: Oscar Homolka, Danny Kaye, Yul Brynner, John Gavin, Paul Henreid

BUTCH CASSIDY AND THE SUNDANCE KID

(20th CENTURY-FOX) Executive Producer, Paul Monash; Producer, John Foreman; Director, George Roy Hill; Screenplay, William Goldman; Music, Burt Bacharach; Costumes, Edith Head; Photography, Conrad Hall; Assistant Director, Steven Bernhardt; A Newman-Foreman Presentation in Panavision and DeLuxe Color; October release.

CAST

Butch Cassidy	Paul Newman
Sundance Kid	Robert Redford
Etta Place	Katharine Ross
Percy Garris	Strother Martin
Bike Salesman	Henry Jones
Sheriff Bledsoe	Jeff Corey
Woodcock	George Furth
Agnes	Cloris Leachman
Harvey Logan	Red Cassidy
Marshal	Kenneth Mars
Macon	Donnelly Rhodes
Large Woman	Jody Gilbert
News Carver	Timothy Scott
Fireman	Don Keefer
Flat Nose Curry	Charles Dierkop
Bank Manager	Francisco Cordova
Photographer	Nelson Olmstead
Card Players	Paul Bryar, Sam Elliott
Bank Teller	Charles Akins
Tiffany's Salesman	Eric Sinclair

Paul Newman, Katharine Ross, Robert Redford
Top: Tim Scott, Robert Redford, Ted Cassidy, Paul Newman, Dave Dunlap, Charlie Dierkop

Paul Newman, Katharine Ross
Top: Paul Newman, Robert Redford

Paul Newman, Timothy Scott

PAUL NEWMAN and ROBERT REDFORD
in "Butch Cassidy and The Sundance Kid"

MARLOWE

(MGM) Producers, Gabriel Katzka, Sidney Beckerman; Director, Paul Bogart; Screenplay, Stirling Silliphant; Based on novel "The Little Sister" by Raymond Chandler; Photography, William H. Daniels; Music, Peter Matz; Assistant Director, Bud Grace; "Little Sister" sung by Orpheus; Produced by Katzka-Berne Productions and Cherokee Productions in association with Beckerman Productions; October release.

CAST

Philip Marlowe	James Garner
Mavis Wald	Gayle Hunnicutt
Lt. Christy French	Carroll O'Connor
Dolores Gonzales	Rita Moreno
Orfamay Quest	Sharon Farrell
Mr. Crowell	William Daniels
Sonny Steelgrave	H. M. Wynant
Grant W. Hicks	Jackie Coogan
Sgt. Fred Beifus	Kenneth Tobey
Winslow Wong	Bruce Lee
Chuck	Christopher Cary
Oliver Hady	George Tyne
Julie	Corinne Camacho
Dr. Vincent Lagardie	Paul Stevens
Orrin Quest	Roger Newman
Gumpshaw	Read Morgan
Haven Clausen	Warren Finnerty

James Garner, Jackie Coogan. Above: James Garner, Kenneth Tobey, Carroll O'Connor

James Garner, Gayle Hunnicutt. Above: Gayle Hunnicutt, Sharon Farrell, James Garner
Top: James Garner, Rita Moreno

Sergio Franchi, Virna Lisi. Above: Anna Magnani, Anthony Quinn. Right: Anthony Quinn, Eduardo Cianelli, Renato Rascel

THE SECRET OF SANTA VITTORIA

(UNITED ARTISTS) Producer-Director, Stanley Kramer; Associate Producer, George Glass; Screenplay, William Rose, Ben Maddow; From novel by Robert Crichton; Photography, Giuseppe Rotunno; Assistant Directors, Ray Gosnell, Franco Cirino; Costumes, Joe King; Music, Ernest Gold; In Panavision and Technicolor; October release.

CAST

Italo Bombolini	Anthony Quinn
Rosa Bombolini	Anna Magnani
Caterina Malatesta	Virna Lisi
Sepp Von Prum	Hardy Kruger
Tufa	Sergio Franchi
Babbaluche	Renato Rascel
Fabio	Giancarlo Giannini
Angela	Patrizia Valturri
Gabriella	Valentina Cortese
Luigi Lunghetti	Eduardo Ciannelli
Vittorini	Leopoldo Trieste
Padre Polenta	Gigi Ballista
Copa	Quinto Parmeggiani
Giovanni Pietrosanto	Carlo Caprioli
Francocci	Francesco Mule
Sgt. Zopf	Wolfgang Jansen
"Old Vines"	Aldo De Carellis
Mazzola	Marco Tulli
Cpl. Heinsick	Chris Anders
Sgt. Traub	Peter Kuiper
Hans	Dieter Wilken
Otto	Karlo Otto Alberty
Benedetti	Gigi Bonos
Julietta	Clelia Matania
Pulci	Pippo Lauricella
Capoferro	Carlo Capannelle
Bracolini	Renato Chiantoni
Dr. Bara	Pino Ferrara
Col. Scheer	Curt Lowens
Pvt. Holtzmann	Tim Donnelly

Anthony Quinn. Above: Hardy Kruger, Anthony Quinn. Top: Virna Lisi

Anthony Quinn, Anna Magnani (also at top) Above: Sergio Franchi, Virna Lisi, Anthony Quinn

THE STERILE CUCKOO

(PARAMOUNT) Producer-Director, Alan J. Pakula; Screenplay, Alvin Sargent; Based on novel by John Nichols; Music, Fred Karlin; Photography, Milton Krasner; Associate Producer, David Lange; Assistant Director, Don Kranze; "Come Saturday Morning" performed by The Sandpipers; In Technicolor; October release.

CAST

"Pookie" Adams	Liza Minnelli
Jerry Payne	Wendell Burton
Schumacher	Tim McIntire
Landlady	Elizabeth Harrower
Pookie's Father	Austin Green
Nancy Putnam	Sandra Faison
Roe	Chris Bugbee
Helen Upshaw	Jawn McKinely

Liza Minnelli, Wendell Burton (C)
(also above and at top)

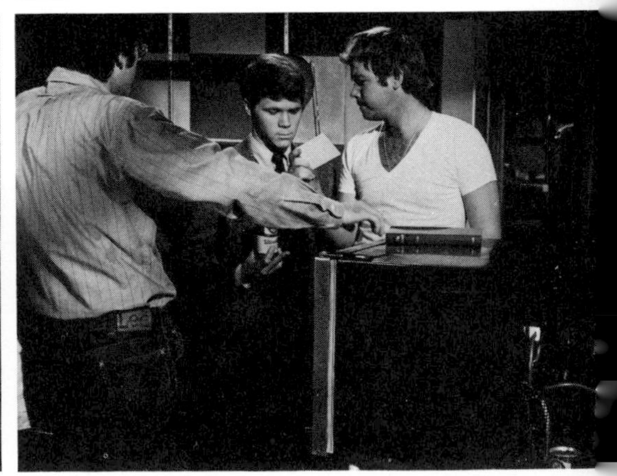

Wendell Burton, Tim McIntire. Above:
Wendell Burton, Liza Minnelli

Liza Minnelli, Wendell Burton (also at top)

CHANGE OF MIND

(CINERAMA) Producers, Seeleg Lester, Richard Wesson; Executive Producer, Henry S. White; Director, Robert Stevens; Screenplay, Seeleg Lester, Richard Wesson; Music, Duke Ellington; Photography, Arthur Ornitz; Assistant Director, Kris Paterson; A Sagittarius Production in Color; October release.

CAST

David Rowe .... Raymond St. Jacques
Margaret Rowe .... Susan Oliver
Elizabeth Dickson .... Janet MacLachlan
Sheriff Webb .... Leslie Nielsen
Roger Morrow .... Donnelly Rhodes
Tommy Benson .... David Bailey
Scupper .... Andre Womble
Rose Landis .... Clarisse Taylor
Bill Chambers .... Jack Creley
Angela Rowe .... Cosette Lee
Judge Forrest .... Larry Reynolds
Nancy .... Hope Clarke
Howard Culver .... Rudy Challenger
Chief Enfield .... Henry Ramer
Mayor Farrell .... Franz Russell
Governor LaTourette .... Joseph Shaw
Attorney Nash .... Sydney Brown
Dr. Bornear .... Tony Kamreither
Dr. Kelman .... Ron Hartmann
Judge Stanton .... Murray Westgate
Reporters .... Guy Sanvido, Chuck Shamata, Dan MacDonald, Joseph Wynn
Mako .... Charles Elder
Moorland .... Horace Bailey
Officer .... Buddy Ferens
Callicot .... Don Crawford
Mrs. Robinson .... Pat Collins
Mr. Robinson .... Sean Sullivan
Gloria .... Vivian Reis
Butler .... Clarence Haynes

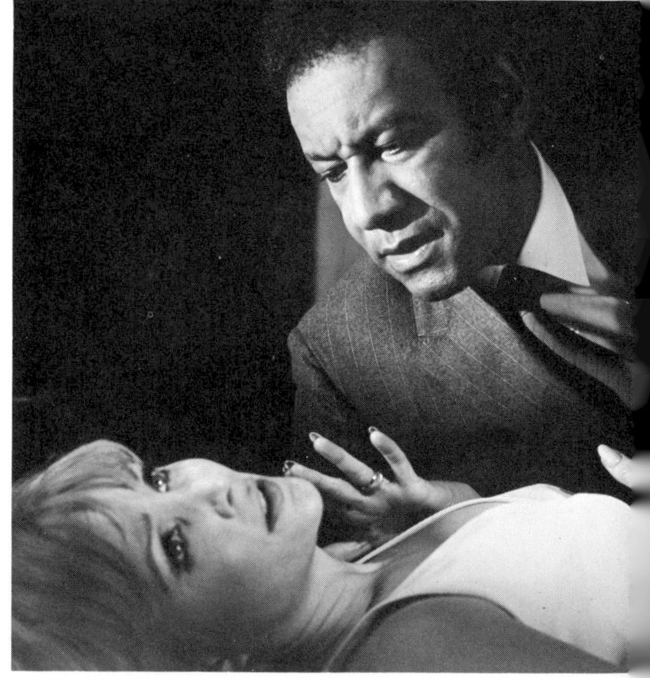

Raymond St. Jacques, Susan Oliver. Top: Janet MacLachlan, Raymond St. Jacques, Susan Oliver

Arthur Kennedy, Michael Douglas, Deborah Winters. Above: Michael Douglas, Louise Latham. Top: Michael Douglas, Deborah Winters

HAIL, HERO!

(NATIONAL GENERAL) Producer, Harold D. Cohen; Director, David Miller; Screenplay, David Manber; From novel by John Weston; Photograpny, Robert Hauser; Music, Jerome Moross; Songs, Gordon Lightfoot; Costumes, Don MacDonald, Dorothy Rodgers; A Halcyon Production; October release.

CAST

Carl Dixon .... Michael Douglas
Albert Dixon .... Arthur Kennedy
Santha Dixon .... Teresa Wright
Mr. Conklin .... John Larch
Senator Murchiston .... Charles Drake
Jimmy .... Mercer Harris
Becky .... Deborah Winters
Frank Dixon .... Peter Strauss
Congressman Arcado .... Mario Alcalde
Rhetha .... Amy Stuart
Tinky .... Rene Tetro
Miss Mirabel .... Louise Latham
Billy Hurd .... John Qualen
Juana .... Carmen Zapata
Eleanor Murchiston .... Virginia Christine
Molly Adams .... Heather Menzies
Carl's Aunts .... Dorothy Newman, Marjorie Eaton

Michael Douglas

PAINT YOUR WAGON

(PARAMOUNT) Producer, Alan Jay Lerner; Director, Joshua Logan; Screenplay and Lyrics, Alan Jay Lerner; Adaptation, Paddy Chayefsky; Music, Frederick Loewe; Additional Songs, Andre Previn; Associate Producer, Tom Shaw; Photography, William A. Fraker; Costumes, John Truscott; Choreography, Jack Baker; Assistant Directors, Jack Roe, Al Murphy; Based on Broadway musical; In Panavision and Technicolor; October release.

CAST

Ben Rumson	Lee Marvin
Pardner	Clint Eastwood
Elizabeth	Jean Seberg
Rotten Luck Willie	Harve Presnell
Mad Jack Duncan	Ray Walston
Horton Fenty	Tom Ligon
Parson	Alan Dexter
Horace Tabor	William O'Connell
Haywood Holbrook	Ben Baker
Mr. Fenty	Alan Baxter
Mrs. Fenty	Paula Trueman
Atwell	Robert Easton
Foster	Geoffrey Norman
Steve Bull	H. B. Haggerty
Joe Mooney	Terry Jenkins
Schermerhorn	Karl Bruck
Jacob Woodling	John Mitchum
Sarah Woodling	Sue Casey
Indian	Eddie Little Sky
Higgins	Harvey Parry
Wong	H. W. Gim
Frock-Coated Man	William Mims
Hennessey	Roy Jenson
Clendennon	Pat Hawley

Jean Seberg, John Mitchum, Sue Casey. Above: Lee Marvin, Clint Eastwood (also top)

Harve Presnell (C), Lee Marvin, Clint Eastwood. Above: Lee Marvin, Jean Seberg

Ray Walston, Lee Marvin. Above: Jean Seberg, Tom Ligon, Clint Eastwood, Alan Baxter, Paula Trueman. Top: Alan Dexter, Jean Seberg, Lee Marvin, Clint Eastwood

Lee Marvin, Clint Eastwood
Above: Lee Marvin, Jean Seberg

DON'T DRINK THE WATER

(AVCO EMBASSY) Executive Producer, Joseph E. Levine; Producer, Charles H. Joffe; Director, Howard Morris; Screenplay, R. S. Allen, Harvey Bullock; Based on play by Woody Allen; Associate Producer, Jack Grossberg; Assistant Director, Louis Stroller; Photography, Harvey Genkins; Costumes, Gene Coffin; Music, Pat Williams; A Jack Rollins and Charles H. Joffe Production in Color; November release.

CAST

Walter Hollander	Jackie Gleason
Marion Hollander	Estelle Parsons
Axel Magee	Ted Bessell
Susan Hollander	Joan Delaney
Krojack	Michael Constantine
Ambassador Magee	Howard St. John
Kilroy	Danny Meehan
Father Drobney	Richard Libertini
Chef	Pierre Olaf
Sultan	Avery Schrieber
Sam	Phil Leeds
Mirik	Mark Gordon
Donald	Dwayne Early
Airline Clerk	Joan Murphy
Mishkin	Martin Danzig
Organgrinder	Rene Constantineau
Getaway Pilot	Howard Morris

Riehard Libertini, Jackie Gleason. Above: Michael Constantine, Jackie Gleason, Estelle Parsons, Ted Bessell

Estelle Parsons, Jackie Gleason, Howard Morris Above: Estelle Parsons, Joan Delaney, Ted Bessell. Top: Jackie Gleason, Estelle Parsons

THE DOWNHILL RACER

(PARAMOUNT) Producer, Richard Gregson; Director, Michael Ritchie; Screenplay, James Salter; Photography, Brian Probyn; Music, Kenyon Hopkins; Assistant Directors, Kip Gowans, Walter Coblenz; A Wildwood International Production in Technicolor; November release.

CAST

David Chappellet	Robert Redford
Eugene Claire	Gene Hackman
Carole Stahl	Camilla Sparv
Machet	Karl Michael Vogler
Creech	Jim McMullan
Brumm	Christian Doermer
American Newspaperwoman	Kathleen Crowley
Mayo	Dabney Coleman
D. K.	Kenneth Kirk
Kipsmith	Oren Stevens
Engel	Jerry Dexter
David's father	Walter Stroud
Lena	Carole Carle
Devore	Rip McManus
Tommy	Joe Jay Jalbert
Stiles	Tom J. Kirk
Gabriel	Robin Hutton-Potts
Meier	Heini Schuler
Boyriven	Peter Rohr
Hinsch	Arnold Alpiger
Haas	Eddie Waldburger
Istel	Marco Walli

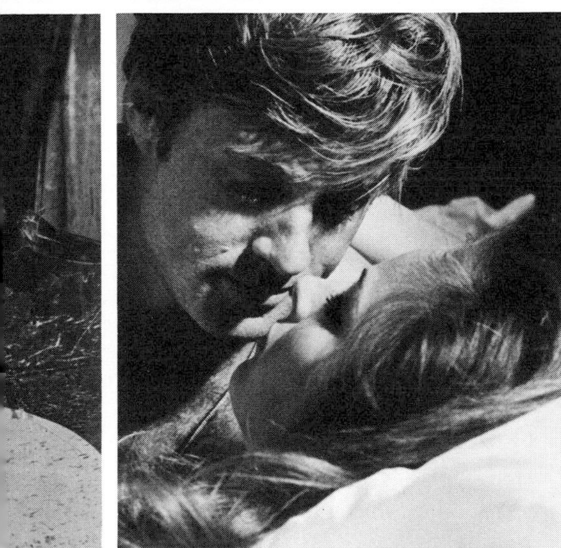

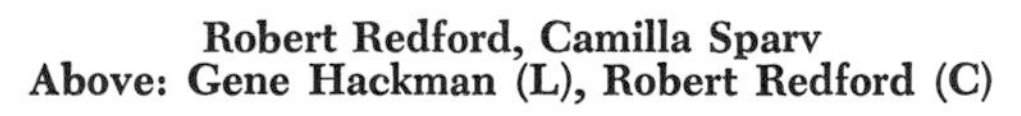

Robert Redford, Camilla Sparv
Above: Gene Hackman (L), Robert Redford (C)

Camilla Sparv, Robert Redford
Top: Gene Hackman, Robert Redford

Mildred Natwick, Susan Dunfee. Above: Donnie Melvin, Geraldine Page. Right: Maureen Stapleton, Martin Balsam

TRILOGY

(ALLIED ARTISTS) Producer-Director, Frank Perry; Screenplay, Truman Capote, Eleanor Perry; Based on stories by Truman Capote; Narrated by Truman Capote; Music, Meyer Kupferman; Photography, Joseph Brun, Harry Sunby; Costumes, Anna Hill Johnstone, Frank Thompson; Assistant Directors, Stan Ackerman, Dan Eriksen, George Goodman; November release.

CAST

"Miriam"

Miss Miller	Mildred Natwick
Miriam	Susan Dunfee
Miss Lake	Carol Gustafson
Emily	Robin Ponterio
Nina	Beverly Ballard
Mrs. Connolly	Jane Connell
Man in theatre	Frederic Morton
Man in automat	Richard Hamilton
Woman in automat	Phyllis Eldridge
Mr. Connolly	Brooks Rogers

"Among the Paths to Eden"

Mary O'Meaghan	Maureen Stapleton
Ivor Belli	Martin Balsam

"A Christmas Memory"

Woman	Geraldine Page
Buddy	Donnie Melvin
Aunts	Lavinia Cassels, Christine Marler
Haha	Josip Elic
Woman in car	Lynn Forman
Storekeeper	Win Forman

SOME KIND OF A NUT

(UNITED ARTISTS) Producer, Walter Mirisch; Director, Garson Kanin; Screenplay, Garson Kanin; Associate Producer, Allen K. Wood; Photography, Burnett Guffey, Gerald Hirschfeld; Music, Johnny Mandel; Costumes, Anthea Sylbert; Assistant Directors, John Chulay, Chris Seitz; In DeLuxe Color; November release.

CAST

Fred Amidon	Dick Van Dyke
Rachel	Angie Dickinson
Pamela	Rosemary Forsyth
Bunny	Zohra Lampert
Gardner	Elliot Reid
Baxter	Steve Roland
Otis Havemeyer	Dennis King
Dr. Sara	Pippa Scott
Mr. Suzumi	Peter Brocco
George Toyota	Robert Ito
Defoe	Peter Turgeon
Dr. Ball	Harry Davis
Cab Driver	Benny Baker
Samantha	Lucy Saroyan
First Vice President	Roy Roberts
Second Vice President	Jonathan Hale
Larry	Ned Wertimer
Dr. Abrams	Danny Crystal
Mrs. Boland	Connie Gilchrist
Himself	Heywood Hale Broun

Steve Boland, Elliot Reid, Rosemary Forsyth, Dick Van Dyke. Above: Dick Van Dyke

Dick Van Dyke, Angie Dickinson, Zohra Lampert. Above: Rosemary Forsyth, Dick Van Dyke

BOB & CAROL & TED & ALICE

(COLUMBIA) Executive Producer, M. J. Frankovich; Producer, Larry Tucker; Director, Paul Mazursky; Screenplay, Paul Mazursky, Larry Tucker; Music, Quincy Jones; Costumes, Moss Mabry; Photography, Charles E. Lang; Assistant Director, Anthony Ray; Choreography, Miriam Nelson; A Frankovich Production in Technicolor; November release.

CAST

Carol	Natalie Wood
Bob	Robert Culp
Ted	Elliott Gould
Alice	Dyan Cannon
Horst	Horst Ebersberg
Emelio	Lee Bergere
Psychiatrist	Donald F. Muhich
Sean	Noble Lee Holderread, Jr.
Phyllis	K. T. Stevens
Susan	Celeste Yarnall
Cutter	Lynn Borden
Stewardess	Linda Burton
Dave	John Brent
Bert	Garry Goodrow
Sue	Carol O'Leary
Norma	Constance Egan
Institute Group:	
Leader	Gregg Mullavey
Myrna	Diana Berghoff
Oscar	Andre Philippe
Conrad	John Halloran
Toby	Susan Merin
Roger	Jeffrey Walker
Jane	Vicki Thal
Wendy	Joyce Easton
Howard	Howard Dayton
Alida	Alida Ihle

Robert Culp, Elliott Gould
Above: Natalie Wood, Robert Culp

Elliott Gould, Dyan Cannon

Elliott Gould, Natalie Wood, Robert Culp, Dyan Cannon (also above)

Michele Lee, Dick Van Dyke
also above, and Right with Mickey Rooney

THE COMIC

(COLUMBIA) Produced and Written by Carl Reiner and Aaron Ruben; Director, Carl Reiner; Photography, W. Wallace Kelley; Assistant Director, Rusty Meek; Costumes, Guy Verhille; Music, Jack Elliott; An Acre Enterprises Production in Berkey Pathe Color, November release.

CAST

Billy Bright	Dick Van Dyke
Mary Gibson	Michele Lee
Cockeye	Mickey Rooney
Frank Powers	Cornel Wilde
Sybil	Nina Wayne
Mama	Pert Kelton
Steve Allen	Himself
Ginger	Barbara Heller
Edwin G. Englehardt	Ed Peck
Lorraine	Jeannine Riley
First Director	Gavin MacLeod
Miguel	Jay Novello
Doctor	Craig Huebing
Phoebe	Paulene Myers
Armand	Fritz Feld
Lawrence	Jerome Cowan
Woman	Isabell Sanford
Nurse	Jeff Donnell
At Schilling	Carl Reiner

THE UNDEFEATED

(20th CENTURY-FOX) Producer, Robert L. Jacks; Director, Andrew V. McLaglen; Screenplay, James Lee Barrett; Based on story by Stanley L. Hough; Music, Hugo Montenegro; Costumes, Bill Thomas; Photography, William Clothier; Assistant Director, Jack Cunningham; In Panavision and DeLuxe Color; November release.

CAST

Col. John Henry Thomas .... John Wayne
Col. James Langdon .... Rock Hudson
General Rojas .... Tony Aguilar
Blue Boy .... Roman Gabriel
Ann .... Marian McCargo
Margaret .... Lee Meriwether
Big George .... Merlin Olsen
Charlotte .... Melissa Newman
Jeff Newby .... Bruce Cabot
Bubba Wilkes .... Michael Vincent
Short Grub .... Ben Johnson
Anderson .... Edward Faulkner
Webster .... Harry Carey, Jr.
General Joe Masters .... Paul Fix
Major Sanders .... Royal Dano
Dan Morse .... Richard Mulligan
Diaz .... Carlos Rivas
Christian .... John Agar
Giles .... Guy Raymond
Goodyear .... Don Collier
Mudlow .... Big John Hamilton
McCartney .... Dub Taylor
Thad Benedict .... Henry Beckman
Major Tapia .... Victor Junco
Judd Mailer .... Robert Donner
Escalante .... Pedro Armendariz, Jr.
Jamison .... James Dobson
Sanchez .... Rudy Diaz
Petain .... Richard Angarola
Jimmy Collins .... James McEachin
Parker .... Gregg Palmer
Colonel Gomez .... Juan Garcia
Union Runner .... Kiel Martin
Joe Hicks .... Bob Gravage

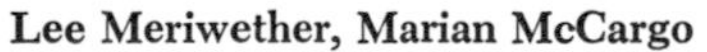

Lee Meriwether, Marian McCargo

Rock Hudson, John Wayne (also above)

CHANGE OF HABIT

(UNIVERSAL) Producer, Joe Connelly; Associate Producer, Irving Paley; Director, William Graham; Music, William Goldenberg; Costumes, Helen Colvig; Assistant Director, Phil Bowles; In Technicolor; November release.

CAST

Dr. John Carpenter	Elvis Presley
Sister Michelle	Mary Tyler Moore
Sister Irene	Barbara McNair
Sister Barbara	Jane Elliot
Mother Joseph	Leora Dana
Lt. Moretti	Edward Asner
The Banker	Robert Emhardt
Father Gibbons	Regis Toomey
Rose	Doro Merande
Lily	Ruth McDevitt
Bishop Finley	Richard Carlson
Julio Hernandez	Nefti Millet
Desiree	Laura Figueroa
Amanda	Lorena Kirk
Miss Parker	Virginia Vincent
Colom	David Renard
Hawk	Ji-Tu Cumbuka
Robbie	Bill Elliott
Mr. Hernandez	Rodolfo Hoyos

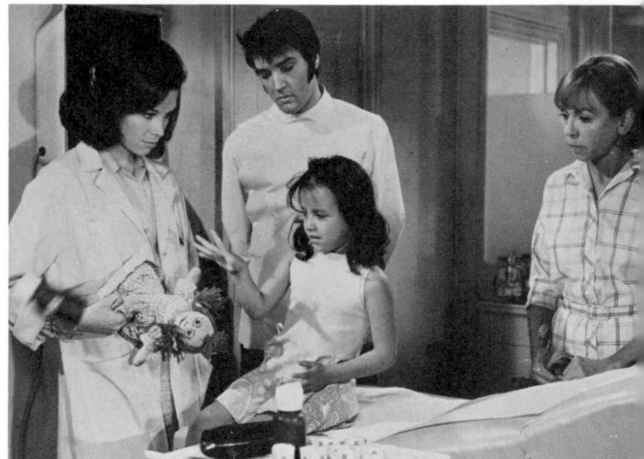

Elvis Presley, Jane Elliot. Above: Bill Elliott, Barbara McNair, Ji-Tu Cumbuka

Elvis Presley. Above: Mary Tyler Moore, Elvis Presley, Lorena Kirk, Virginia Vincent
Top: Elvis Presley, Mary Tyler Moore

THE GOOD GUYS AND THE BAD GUYS

(WARNER BROS.-7 ARTS) Executive Producer, Robert Goldstein; Written and Produced by Ronald M. Cohen, Dennis Shryack; Director, Burt Kennedy; Photography, Harry Stradling, Jr.; Associate Producer, Stan Jolley; Music, William Lava; Assistant Director, Richard Bennett; Song "The Ballad of Marshal Flagg" by William Lava, Ned Washington; Sung by Glenn Yarbrough; In Panavision and Technicolor; November release.

CAST

Flagg	Robert Mitchum
McKay	George Kennedy
Waco	David Carradine
Carmel	Tina Louise
Grundy	Douglas V. Fowley
Mary	Lois Nettleton
Mayor Wilker	Martin Balsam
Deuce	John Davis Chandler
Ticker	John Carradine
Polly	Marie Windsor
Boyle	Dick Peabody
Mrs. Stone	Kathleen Freeman
Buckshot	Jimmy Murphy
Hawkins	Garrett Lewis
Engineer #2	Nick Dennis

Tina Louise, Martin Balsam. Above: Lois Nettleton, Robert Mitchum, George Kennedy Top: Robert Mitchum, Douglas Fowley

Robert Mitchum, George Kennedy. Above: Robert Mitchum, Martin Balsam, Dick Peabody

THE ARRANGEMENT

(WARNER BROS.-7 ARTS) Produced, Directed, and Written by Elia Kazan; From his novel of the same name; Photography, Robert Surtees; Music, David Amram; Associate Producer, Charles Maguire; Costumes, T. Van Runkle; Assistant Director, Burtt Harris; An Athena Enterprises Production in Panavision and Technicolor; November release.

CAST

Eddie and Evangelos	Kirk Douglas
Gwen	Faye Dunaway
Florence Anderson	Deborah Kerr
Sam Anderson	Richard Boone
Arthur	Hume Cronyn
Michael	Michael Higgins
Charles	John Randolph Jones
Gloria	Carol Rossen
Thomna	Anne Hegira
Dr. Weeks	William Hansen
Finnegan	Charles Drake
Dr. Liebman	Harold Gould
Uncle Joe	E. J. Andre
Father Draddy	Michael Murphy
Judge Morris	Philip Bourneuf
Ellen	Dianne Hull

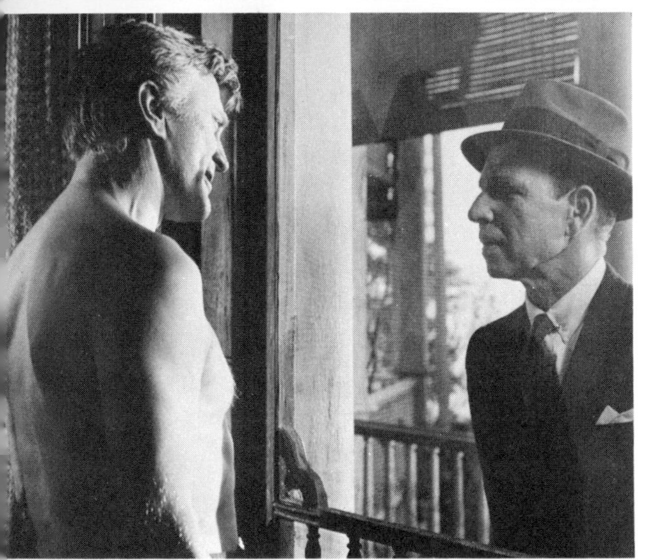

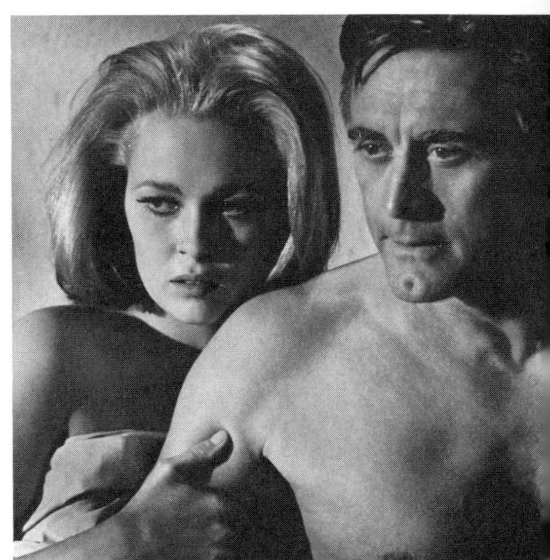

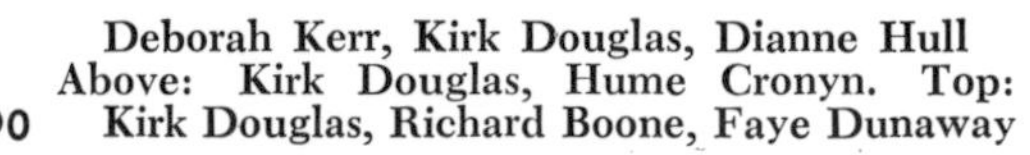

Deborah Kerr, Kirk Douglas, Dianne Hull
Above: Kirk Douglas, Hume Cronyn. Top: Kirk Douglas, Richard Boone, Faye Dunaway

Kirk Douglas, above with Faye Dunaway

A BOY NAMED CHARLIE BROWN

(NATIONAL GENERAL) Producers, Lee Mendelson, Bill Melendez; Director, Bill Melendez; Screenplay, Charles M. Schulz; Words and Music, Rod McKuen; Original Music Score, Vince Guaraldi; A Cinema Center Presentation; In Technicolor; December release.

CAST

	Voices of
Charlie Brown	Peter Robbins
Lucy Van Pelt	Pamelyn Ferdin
Linus Van Pelt	Glenn Gilger
Schroeder	Andy Pforsich
Patty	Sally Dryer
Violet	Anne Altieri
Sally	Erin Sullivan
Frieda	Linda Mendelson
Pig Pen	Chrisopher DeFaria
Second Boy	David Carey
Third Boy	Guy Pforsich
Snoopy	Bill Melendez

Steve McQueen, Mitch Vogel, Dub Taylor, Sharon Farrell. Top: Steve McQueen, Rupert Crosse, Mitch Vogel. Right: Steve McQueen, Sharon Farrell

THE REIVERS

(NATIONAL GENERAL) Executive Producer, Robert E. Relyea; Producer, Irving Ravetch; Director, Mark Rydell; Associate Producer, Rick Rosenberg; Screenplay, Irving Ravetch, Harriet Frank, Jr.; Photography, Richard Moore; Music, John Williams; Assistant Director, Tim Zinnemann; An Irving Ravetch-Arthur Kramer Production in Panavision and Technicolor; December release.

CAST

Boon Hoggenbeck	Steve McQueen
Corrie	Sharon Farrell
Boss McCaslin	Will Geer
Mr. Binford	Michael Constantine
Ned McCaslin	Rupert Crosse
Lucius McCaslin	Mitch Vogel
Maury McCaslin	Lonny Chapman
Uncle Possum	Juano Hernandez
Butch Lovemaiden	Clifton James
Miss Reba	Ruth White
Dr. Peabody	Dub Taylor
Alison McCaslin	Allyn Ann McLerie
Hannah	Diane Shalet
Phoebe	Diane Ladd
Sally	Ellen Geer
May Ellen	Pat Randall
Edmonds	Charles Tyner
Aunt Callie	Vinnette Carroll
Minnie	Gloria Calomee
Sarah	Sara Taft
Otis	Lindy Davis
Uncle Ike	Raymond Guth
Cousin Zack	Shug Fisher
Walter Clapp	Logan Ramsey
Joe Poleymus	Jon Shank
Mrs. Possum	Ella Mae Brown
Mary Possum	Florence St. Peter
Van Tosch	John McLiam
Doyle	Lou Frizzell
Ed	Roy Barcroft

Mitch Vogel, Steve McQueen, Ruth White
Above: Juano Hernandez, Clifton James, Sharon Farrell

Allyn Ann McLerie, Mitch Vogel, Will Geer
Top: Mitch Vogel, Steve McQueen, Rupert Crosse

A DREAM OF KINGS

(NATIONAL GENERAL) Producer, Jules Schermer; Director, Daniel Mann; Screenplay, Harry Mark Petrakis, Ian Hunter; Based on novel by Harry Mark Petrakis; Assistant Directors, James A. Rosenberger, Charles Dismukes, Joe Nayfack; Photography, Richard Kline; Music, Alex North; In Technicolor; December release.

CAST

Matsoukas	Anthony Quinn
Caliope	Irene Papas
Anna	Inger Stevens
Cicero	Sam Levene
Stavros	Radames Pera
Mother-in-law	Tamara Daykarhanova
Fatsas	Val Avery
Falconis	Peter Mamakos
Fig King	Alan Reed, Sr.
Turk	H. B. Haggerty
Telecles	Chris Marks
Aristotle	Alberto Morin
Javaras	Peter Xantho
Zenoitis	Zvee Scooler
Apollo	George Savalas
Toundas	Ernest Sarracino
Herman	Tol Avery
Uncle Louie	Tony Jochim
Hope	Effi Columbus
Faith	Sandra Damato
Young Doctor	James Dobson
Manulis	James Fortunes
Mrs. Cournos	Katherine Theodore
Doctor in church	George Michaelides
Nurses	Lisa Pera, Lisa Moore

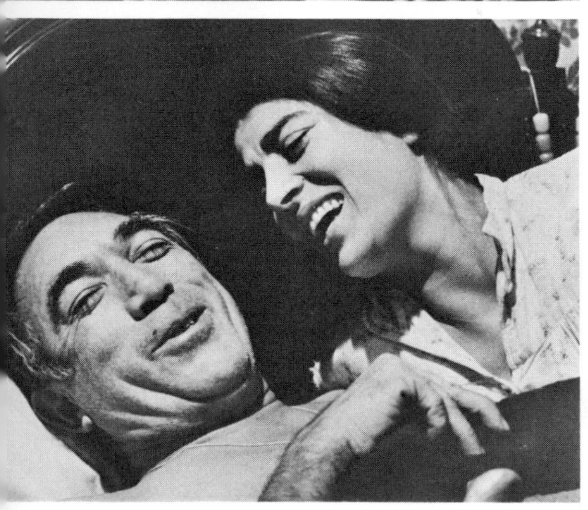

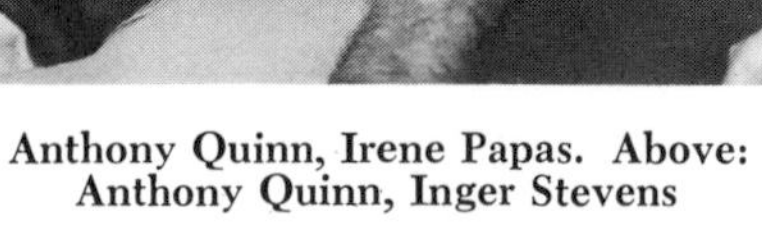

Anthony Quinn, Irene Papas. Above: Anthony Quinn, Inger Stevens

Anthony Quinn, Radames Pera. Above: Anthony Quinn, Val Avery, Sam Levene Top: Irene Papas, Anthony Quinn

Jon Voight, Barry Gordon, Lada Edmund, Jr.

Lada Edmund, Jr., Jon Voight. Above: Barry Gordon, Gretchen Corbett. Top: Jon Voight, Peter Grad

OUT OF IT

(UNITED ARTISTS) Producer, Edward Rambach Pressman; Directed and Written by Paul Williams; Photography, John C. Auildsen; Music, Michael Small; Assistant Director, Nyles Gradus; Songs, Michael Benedikdt, Michael Small; Associate Directors, David Feldshuh, Elizabeth Rosenwald; Associate Producer, John G. Auildsen, Thomas Sand; December release.

CAST

Paul .... Barry Gordon
Russ .... Jon Voight
Christine .... Lada Edmund, Jr.
Barbara .... Gretchen Corbett
Steve .... Peter Grad

THE HAPPY ENDING

(UNITED ARTISTS) Produced, Directed, and Written by Richard Brooks; Photography, Conrad Hall; Music, Michel Legrand; Lyrics, Alan and Marilyn Bergman; Assistant Director, Tom Shaw; A PaxFilms Production in Panavision and Technicolor; December release.

CAST

Mary Wilson	Jean Simmons
Fred Wilson	John Forsythe
Sam	Lloyd Bridges
Flo	Shirley Jones
Mrs. Spencer	Teresa Wright
Harry Spencer	Dick Shawn
Agnes	Nanette Fabray
Franco	Robert Darin
Helen Bricker	Tina Louise
Marge Wilson	Kathy Fields
Divorcee	Karen Steele
Betty	Gail Hensley

Jean Simmons, Kathy Fields. Above: Nanette Fabray, Jean Simmons, Teresa Wright
Top: Jean Simmons, John Forsythe

Jean Simmons, John Forsythe
Above: Jean Simmons

Robert Darin, Jean Simmons. Above: Jean Simmons. Top: Shirley Jones, Lloyd Bridges

John Forsythe, Jean Simmons. Above: Shirley Jones, Lloyd Bridges, Jean Simmons. Top: Dick Shawn, Karen Steele

THREE

(UNITED ARTISTS) Producer, Bruce Becker; Directed and Written by James Salter; From story by Irwin Shaw "Then There Were Three"; An Obelisk Production in DeLuxe Color; December release.

CAST

Marty	Charlotte Rampling
Bert	Robie Porter
Taylor	Sam Waterston
Claude	Pascale Roberts
Liz	Edina Ronay
Ann	Gilliam Hills
Silvano	Mario Cotone
Gloria	Patrizia Giammei

Sam Waterston, Charlotte Rampling, Robie Porter

Sam Waterston, Charlotte Rampling. Top:
Robie Porter, Charlotte Rampling,
Sam Waterston

Robie Porter, Edina Ronay

GAILY, GAILY

(UNITED ARTISTS) Producer-Director, Norman Jewison; Associate Producer, Hal Ashby; Screenplay, Abram S. Ginnes; Based on Ben Hecht's "Gaily, Gaily"; Music, Henry Mancini; Photography, Richard Kline; Costumes, Ray Aghayan; Assistant Directors, Mike Moder, Phil Parslow; A Mirisch-Cartier Production in DeLuxe Color; December release.

CAST

Ben Harvey	Beau Bridges
Queen Lil	Melina Mercouri
Francis X. Sullivan	Brian Keith
Axel P. Johanson	George Kennedy
"Honest" Tim Grogan	Hume Cronyn
Adeline	Margot Kidder
The Governor	Wilfrid Hyde-White
Lilah	Melodie Johnson
Kitty	Joan Huntington
Father Harvey	John Randolph
Mother Harvey	Claudie Bryar
Virgil Harvey	Eric Shea
Grandma Harvey	Merie Earle
Frankie	James Christy
Dr. Lazarus	Charles Tyner
The Stranger	Harry Holcombe
Dunne	Roy Poole
Wally Hill	Clark Gordon
Swami	Peter Brocco
Mrs. Krump	Maggie Oleson
Chauffeur	Nikita Knatz

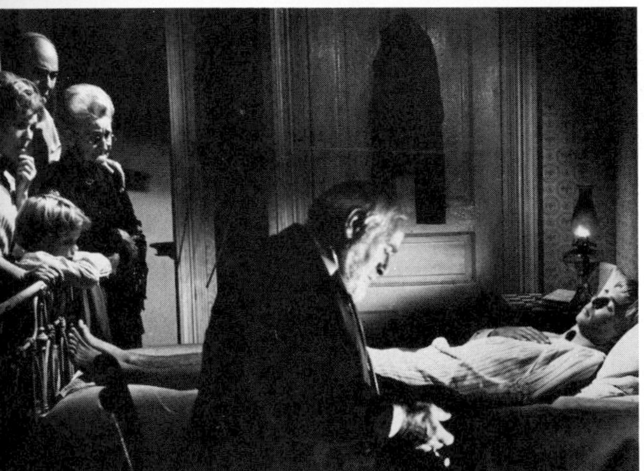

Brian Keith, James Christy, Beau Bridges
Above: Eric Shea, Claudie Bryar, John Randolph, Merie Earle, Roy Barcroft, Beau Bridges

Beau Bridges. Top Left: Maggie Oleson, Beau Bridges

Beau Bridges, Margot Kidder. Above: Brian Keith, Hume Cronyn, Roy Poole. Top: Brian Keith, Melina Mercouri, George Kennedy

Brian Keith, Melina Mercouri. Above: John Randolph, Claudie Bryar, Merie Earle, Melina Mercouri, George Kennedy. Top: Beau Bridges, Melodie Johnson

Mia Farrow, Dustin Hoffman
also above and at top

JOHN AND MARY

(20th CENTURY-FOX) Producer, Ben Kadish; Director, Peter Yates; Screenplay, John Mortimer; Based on novel by Mervyn Jones; Music, Quincy Jones; Photography, Gayne Rescher; Costumes, Anthea Sylbert; Assistant Director, Stephen Barnett; Lyrics, Alan and Marilyn Bergman; A Debrod Production in DeLuxe Color; December release.

CAST

John	Dustin Hoffman
Mary	Mia Farrow
James	Michael Tolan
Ruth	Sunny Griffin
Ernest	Stanley Beck
Hilary	Tyne Daly
Jane	Alix Elias
Fran	Julie Garfield
Dean	Marvin Lichterman
Mags Elliot	Marian Mercer
Minnie	Susan Taylor
John's Mother	Olympia Dukakis
Tennis Player	Carl Parker
Charlie	Richard Clarke
Film Director	Cleavon Little
His Wife	Marilyn Chris
Imaginary Film Director	Alexander Cort
Boy Scout	Kristoffer Tabori

Dustin Hoffman, Mia Farrow

THEY SHOOT HORSES, DON'T THEY?

(**ABC**) Producers, Irwin Winkler, Robert Chartoff, Sydney Pollack; Director, Sidney Pollack; Screenplay, James Poe, Robert E. Thompson; Based on novel by Horace McCoy; Music, John Green; Photography, Philip H. Lathrop; Assistant Director, Al Jennings; A Palomar Picture in Panavision and DeLuxe Color; December release.

CAST

Gloria .... Jane Fonda
Robert .... Michael Sarrazin
Alice .... Susannah York
Rocky .... Gig Young
Sailor .... Red Buttons
Ruby .... Bonnie Bedelia
James .... Bruce Dern
Joel .... Robert Fields
Shirl .... Allyn Ann McLerie
and Michael Conrad, Al Lewis, Severn Darden, Jacquelyn Hyde, Felice Orlandi, Art Metrano, Gail Billings, Maxine Greene, Mary Gregory, Robert Dunlap, Paul Mantee, Tim Herbert, Tom McFadden, Noble "Kid" Chissell

Red Buttons. Above: Gig Young

Jane Fonda, Michael Sarrazin (also above)

Bonnie Bedelia, Bruce Dern, Jane Fonda, Red Buttons
Top Center: Michael Sarrazin, Jane Fonda

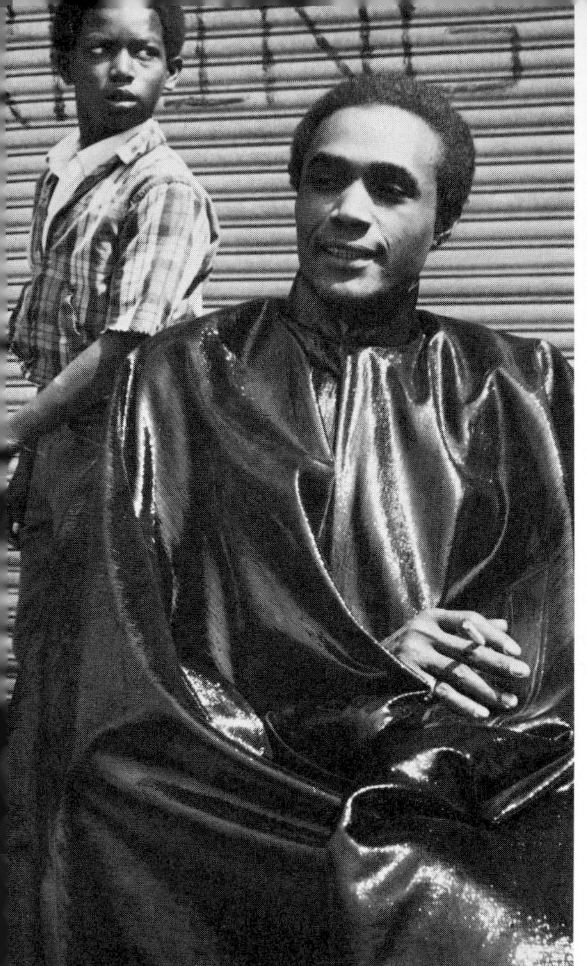

COTTON COMES TO HARLEM

(UNITED ARTISTS) Producer, Samuel Goldwyn, Jr.; Director, Ossie Davis; Screenplay, Ossie Davis, Arnold Perl; Based on novel by Chester Himes; Photography, Gerald Hirschfeld; Music, Galt MacDermot; Costumes, Anna Hill Johnstone; Assistant Directors, Dom D'Antonio, John Kates, Sam Bennerson; In DeLuxe Color; December release.

CAST

Coffin Ed Johnson	Raymond St. Jacques
Grave Digger Jones	Godfrey Cambridge
Rev. Deke O'Malley	Calvin Lockhart
Iris	Judy Pace
Uncle Bud	Redd Foxx
Bryce	John Anderson
Mabel	Emily Yancy
Calhoun	J. D. Cannon
Billie	Mabel Robinson
Jerema	Dick Sabol
Barry	Theodore Wilson
Anderson	Eugene Roche
Casper	Frederick O'Neal
Reba	Vinnette Carroll
Luddy	Gene Lindsey
Early Riser	Van Kirksey
Lo Boy	Cleavon Little
Church Sister	Helen Martin
Dum Dum	Turk Turpin
44	Tom Lane
Hi Jenks	Arnold Williams

Emily Yancy, Calvin Lockhart. Above: Godfrey Cambridge, Raymond St. Jacques
Left: Calvin Lockhart

GENERATION

(AVCO EMBASSY) Executive Producer, Leanard Lightstone; Producer, Frederick Brisson; Director, George Schaefer; Screenplay, William Goodhart; Based on his play; Photography, Lionel Linden; Music, Dave Grusin; Assistant Director, Fred Gammon; Costumes, Noel Taylor; Title Song, Dino Fekaris, Nick Zesses, Bea Verdi; Sung by The Rare Earth; In Color; December release.

CAST

Jim Bolton	David Janssen
Doris Bolton Owen	Kim Darby
Stan Herman	Carl Reiner
Walter Owen	Pete Duel
Winn Garand	Andrew Prine
Mr. Blatto	James Coco
Desmond	Sam Waterston
Arlington	David Lewis
Gilbert	Don Beddoe
Airline Policeman	Jack Somack
Hey Hey	Lincoln Kilpatrick

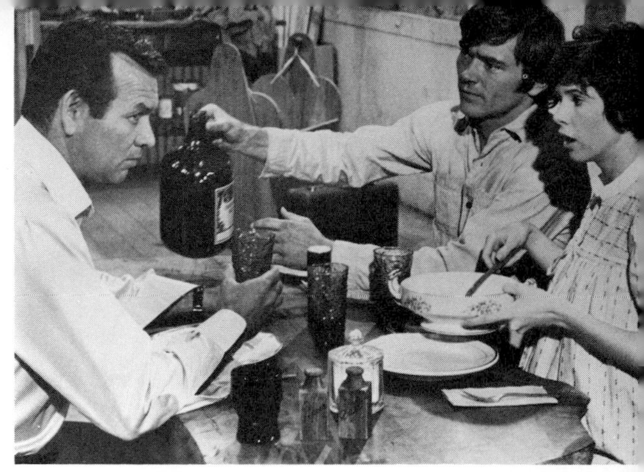

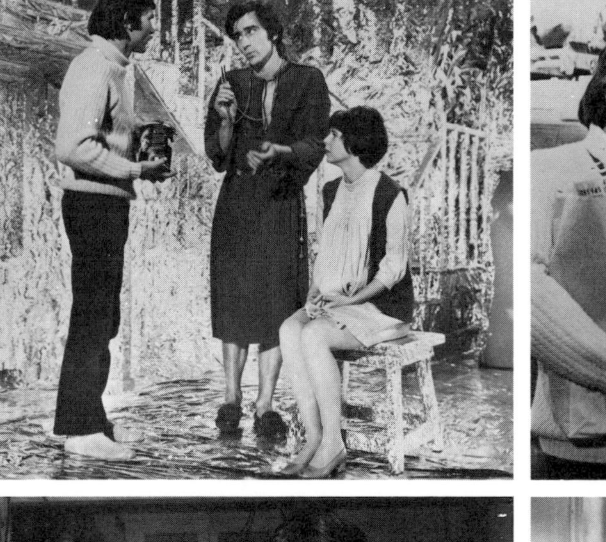

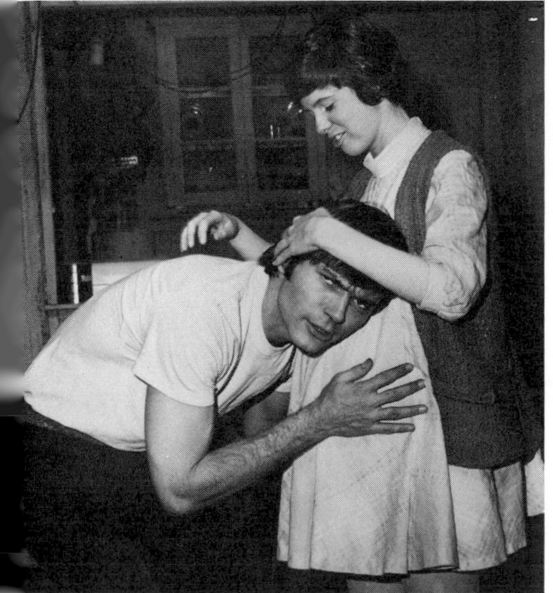

Pete Duel, Kim Darby. Above: Pete Duel, Sam Waterston, Kim Darby. Top Right: David Janssen, Pete Duel, Kim Darby

David Janssen, Carl Reiner, Andrew Prine
Above: Pete Duel, Kim Darby, James Coco

HELLO, DOLLY!

(20th CENTURY-FOX) Produced and Written by Ernest Lehman; Director, Gene Kelly; Associate Producer, Roger Edens; Dances and Musical Numbers Staged by Michael Kidd; Music and Lyrics, Jerry Herman; Based on musical by Jerry Herman and Michael Stewart, and play "The Matchmaker" by Thornton Wilder; Photography, Harry Stradling; Costumes, Irene Sharaff; Assistant Director, Paul Helmick; Assistant Choreographer, Shelah Hackett; A Chenault Production in Todd-AO R and DeLuxe Color; December release.

CAST

Dolly Levi .... Barbra Streisand
Horace Vandergelder .... Walter Matthau
Cornelius Hackl .... Michael Crawford
Orchestra Leader .... Louis Armstrong
Irene Molloy .... Marianne McAndrew
Minnie Fay .... E. J. Peaker
Barnaby Tucker .... Danny Lockin
Ermengarde .... Joyce Ames
Ambrose Kemper .... Tommy Tune
Gussie Granger .... Judy Knaiz
Rudolph Reisenweber .... David Hurst
Fritz .... Fritz Feld
Vandergilder's Barber .... Richard Collier
Policeman in park .... J. Pat O'Malley

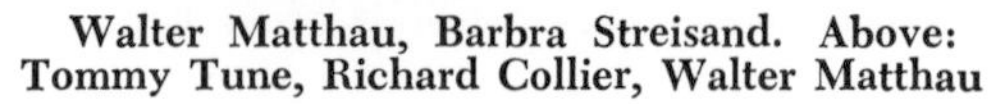

Walter Matthau, Barbra Streisand. Above: Tommy Tune, Richard Collier, Walter Matthau

Danny Lockin, Michael Crawford. Above: (C) Joyce Ames, Tommy Tune, Barbra Streisand

Judy Knaiz, Walter Matthau. Above: E. J. Peaker, Danny Lockin, Marianne McAndrew, Michael Crawford. Top: Walter Matthau, Barbra Streisand, Marianne McAndrew

Walter Matthau, Barbra Streisand (also at top) Above: Barbra Streisand (C)

VIVA MAX!

(COMMONWEALTH UNITED) Producer, Mark Carliner; Director, Jerry Paris; Screenplay, Elliott Baker; Based on novel by James E. Lehrer; Photography, Henri Persin; Music, Hugo Montenegro, Ralph Dino, John Sembello; Played by Al Hirt; Assistant Directors, Claude Binyon, Jr., Neil T. Maffeo; In EastmanColor; December release.

CAST

General Maximilian De Santos	Peter Ustinov
Paula Whitland	Pamela Tiffin
Gen. Billy Joe Hallson	Jonathan Winters
Sgt. Valdez	John Astin
General Lacomber	Keenan Wynn
Police Chief Sylvester	Harry Morgan
Hattie	Alice Ghostley
Dr. Sam Gillison	Kenneth Mars
Edna Miller	Ann Morgan Guilbert
Desmond Miller	Bill McCutcheon
Contreras	Gino Conforti
Gomez	Chris Ross
Romero	Larry Hankin
Moreno	Paul Sand
Hernandez	Don Diamond
Garcia	Jack Colvin
Mrs. Dodd	Jessica Myerson
Custom Guard Collins	Ted Gehring
Custom Guard Michaels	Jim B. Smith
Quincy	Eldon Quick
Policeman Milton	Jack Wakefield
Captain Harris	Glenn Tucker
Sentry Bus Briver	Lee Brandt

Pamela Tiffin, Peter Ustinov
Above: Peter Ustinov

Paul Sand, Peter Ustinov. Above: Peter Ustinov, John Astin. Top: Peter Ustinov, Jonathan Winters

MAROONED

(COLUMBIA) Producer, M. J. Frankovich; Director, John Sturges; Associate Producer, Frank Capra, Jr.; Screenplay, Mayo Simon; Based on novel by Martin Caidin; Assistant Director, Daniel J. McCauley; Photography, Daniel Fapp; In Panavision and Technicolor; December release.

CAST

Charles Keith .... Gregory Peck
Jim Pruett .... Richard Grenna
Ted Dougherty .... David Janssen
Clayton Stone .... James Franciscus
Buzz Lloyd .... Gene Hackman
Celia Pruett .... Lee Grant
Teresa Stone .... Nancy Kovack
Betty Lloyd .... Mariette Hartley
Public Affairs Officer .... Scott Brady
Flight Director .... Craig Huebing
Flight Surgeon .... John Carter
Mission Director .... George Gaynes
Houston Cap-Com .... Tom Stewart
Titan Specialist .... Duke Hobbie
Network Commentator .... Walter Brooke
Launch Director .... Dennis Robertson

Top: Gregory Peck, David Janssen. Below: James Franciscus, Gene Hackman, Richard Crenna

David Janssen (R). Above: Lee Grant, Nancy Kovack, Mariette Hartley. Top: Gregory Peck

CACTUS FLOWER

(COLUMBIA) Producer, M. J. Frankovich; Director, Gene Saks; Screenplay, I. A. L. Diamond; From play by Abe Burrows; Based on French play by Barillet and Gredy; Photography, Charles E. Lang; Music, Quincy Jones; Choreography, Miriam Nelson; "A Time For Love Is Anytime" sung by Sarah Vaughan; Assistant Director, Anthony Ray; Costumes, Moss Mabry; A Frankovich Production in Technicolor; December release.

CAST

Julian Winston .... Walter Matthau
Stephanie Dickinson .... Ingrid Bergman
Toni Simmons .... Goldie Hawn
Harvey Greenfield .... Jack Weston
Igor Sullivan .... Rick Lenz
Senor Sanchez .... Vito Scotti
Mrs. Durant .... Irene Hervey
Georgia .... Eve Bruce
Store Manager .... Irwin Charone
Nephew .... Matthew Saks

Rick Lenz, Goldie Hawn. Above: Goldie Hawn, Walter Matthau. Top: Walter Matthau, Ingrid Bergman

Vito Scotti, Ingrid Bergman. Above: Ingrid Bergman, Irene Hervey

Ingrid Bergman, Walter Matthau. Top: (L) Goldie Hawn, Walter Matthau, Jack Weston, Ingrid Bergman, (R) Goldie Hawn, Ingrid Bergman

TELL THEM WILLIE BOY IS HERE

(**UNIVERSAL**) Producer, Philip Waxman; Directed and Written by Abraham Polonsky; From novel "Willie Boy . . . A Desert Manhunt" by Harry Lawton; Photography, Conrad Hall; Assistant Director, Joe Kenny; Music, David Grusin; A Jennings Lang Production in Technicolor; December release.

CAST

Coop	Robert Redford
Lola	Katharine Ross
Willie Boy	Robert Blake
Liz Arnold	Susan Clark
Calvert	Barry Sullivan
Frank Wilson	Charles McGraw
Benby	Charles Aidman
Hacker	John Vernon
Finney	Shelly Novack
Tom	Ned Romero
Sam Wood	John Daheim
Meathead	Lee DeBroux
Le Marie	George Tyne
Johnny Hyde	Steve Shemayme
Third Man	John Hudkins
Chino	Jerry Velasco
Dr. Mills	Gary Walberg
Station Agent	Lou Frizzell
Newman	John Wheeler
Digger	Eric Holland
Harry	Wayne Sutherlin
Old Mike	Mikel Angel
Salesman	Jerome Raphel
Cody	Spencer Lyons

Barry Sullivan, Robert Redford
Top: Robert Redford, Susan Clark

Susan Clark, Katharine Ross, Robert Redford
Top: Robert Blake, Katharine Ross

Robert Blake

Janis Joplin in "Monterey Pop"

Jan Sterling, James MacArthur in "The Angry Breed"

MONTEREY POP (Leacock Pennebaker) Producers, John Phillips, Lou Adler; Filmed by James Desmond, Barry Feinstein, Richard Leacock, Albert Maysles, Roger Murphy, D. A. Pennebaker, Nick Proferes; Titles, Tomi Ungerer; Filmed in color at the Monterey International Pop Festival; January release. CAST: Otis Redding, Mamas and Papas, The Who, Janis Joplin with Big Brother and The Holding Company, Jimi Hendrix, Country Joe and The Fish, Scott McKenzie, Hugh Masekela, Canned Heat, Grack Slick with Jefferson Airplane, The Animals, Ravi Shankar.

STRATEGY OF TERROR (Universal) Producer, Arthur H. Nadel; Director, Jack Smight; Executive Producer, Frank P. Rosenberg; Screenplay, Robert L. Joseph; Photography, Budd Thackeray; Music, Lyn Murray; In Color; January release. CAST: Hugh O'Brian (Matt), Barbara Rush (Karen), Neil Hamilton (Mr. Harkin), Frederick O'Neal (Jacques) Will Corry (Wally).

THE EXTRAORDINARY SEAMAN (MGM) Producers, Edward Lewis, John H. Cushingham; Director, John Frankenheimer; Screenplay, Philip Rock, Hal Dresner; Based on story by Philip Rock; Photography, Lionel Linden; Music, Maurice Jarre; Assistant Director, Enrico Isacco; In Panavision and MetroColor; January release. CAST: David Niven (Finchhaven), Faye Dunaway (Jennifer), Alan Alda (Krim), Mickey Rooney (Oglethorpe), Jack Carter (Toole), Juano Hernandez (Ali Shar), Manu Tupou (Lightfoot).

THE TAMING (Times) Producer-Director, Robert Arkless; Photography, Julianna Wang; Music, Marcel Aimee; Released by Victoria Films. January release. CAST: Lindsey Bowen (Tom), Liz Stevens (Rita), Sharon Church (Barbra), Sam Stewart (Marco).

THE ANGRY BREED (Commonwealth United) Producer, David Commons; Executive Producers, Frank Brandt, Fred Maisel; Directed and Written by David Commons; In Color; January release. CAST: Jan Sterling (Gloria), James MacArthur (Deek), William Windom (Vance), Jan Murray (Mori), Murray McLeod (Johnny), Lori Martin (Diane Patton), Melody Patterson (April), Karen Malouf (Jade), Suzi Kaye (Ginny).

THE YOUNG REBEL (Commonwealth) Producer, Miguel Salkind; Executive Producer, Henry Weinstein; Director, Vincent Sherman; Screenplay, David Karp; In Colorscope; January release. CAST: Horst Buchholz (Cervantes), Gina Lollobrigida (Julis), Jose Ferrer (Hassam Bey), Louis Jourdan (Cardinal Acquaviva), Francisco Rabal, Fernando Rey.

ME AND MY BROTHER (New Yorker) Producer, Helen Silverstein; Directed and Photographed by Robert Frank; Screenplay, Sam Sheppard, Robert Frank; In color and black and white; February release. CAST: Joseph Chaikin (Julius), Julius Orlovsky (Julius), John Coe (Psychiatrist), Allen Ginsberg (Himself), Peter Orlovsky (Himself), Virginia Kiser (Social Worker), Nancy Fish (Herself), Cynthia McAdams (Actress), Roscoe Lee Browne (Photographer).

THE HANGING OF JAKE ELLIS (Hollywood Cinemart) Produced, Directed, and Written by J. van Hearn; Photography, John Koester; Music, Elsa Singman; Assistant Director, Paul Wilmoth; In EastmanColor; February release. CAST: Charles Napier (Jake), Deborah Downey (Kathy), Bambi Allen (Isabel), Jim Lemp (Frank), Louis Ojena (Don), Don Derby (Cattlebuyer), Rod Wilmoth (Sheriff), Chuy Castro (Pablo), Sol Bar (Bartender), Mike MacDonald (Ellen), Gerry Patterson (Her husband), Larry Martinelli (Driskill), Don Angelo (Henchman), Melvin Wilmoth (Stuntman).

Hugh O'Brian, Mort Mills in "Strategy Of Terror"

David Niven, Faye Dunaway, Alan Alda in "The Extraordinary Seaman"

"The Taming"

Ralph Meeker, Leslie Parrish, Christopher George in "The Devil's 8"

THE VIXENS (International Film Artists) Producer, Sande N. Johnson; Director, Harvey Cort; Screenplay, Al Rosati; Photography, Harri Petricek; A Trio Films Presentation; February release. CAST: Anne Linden (Betty), Mary Kahn (Ann), Peter Burns (Bob), Steven Harrison (Alan), Claudia Bach (Judy), Robert Raymond (Harold), Hector Elizando (Inspector).

THE OUTDOORSMAN (Theatre Management) Producers, Bill Bryant, Ned Payne; In Color; February release. A documentary on a safari to a sportsman's paradise throughout the world.

CHANGES (Cinerama) Producer-Director, Hall Bartlett; Screenplay, Bill E. Kelly, Hall Bartlett; Photography, Richard Moore; Songs, Tim Buckley; Sung by Judy Collins; February release. CAST: Michele Carey (Julie), Kent Lane (Kent), Manuela Thiess (Bobbi), Marcia Strassman (Kristine), Jack Albertson (Father), Bill Kelly (Sammy), Tom Fielding (Roommate), Kenneth Washington (Negro) and Kim Weston, Sam Chew, Jr., Doug Dowell, Doug Bell, Buddy Hart, Cindy Mitchum, Monica Petersen, Christopher Hayden, Clarice Gillis, Katherine Victory, Sherri Mitchel, Sammy Vaughn, Grant Conroy, Terry Garr, Sammy Tanner, Jesus Alonzo, Jr., John Moio, Vincent George.

THIS IS MY ALASKA (Alaskan Adventures) Produced, Directed, Photographed, and Narrated by Leroy "Buster" Shebal; In DeLuxe Color; February release. A documentary on hunting in the Far North.

SAPPHO, DARLING (Cambist) Producer, Hal Senter; Executive Producer, Donald E. Leon; Director, Gunnar Steele; Screenplay, Albert Zugsmith; In Color; March release. CAST: Carol Young (Sappho), Yvonne D'Angers (Brigitte), Alan Darnay (Sven), Sally Sanford (Luana), Julia Blackburn (Britt).

THE DEVIL'S 8 (American International) Producer-Director, Burt Topper; Screenplay, James Gordon White, Willard Huyck, John Milius; Story, Larry Gordon; Photography, Richard C. Glouner; Music, Mike Curb; Associate Producer, Jack Cash; Assistant Directors, James Petch, Lew Borzage; In Pathe Color; March release. CAST: Christopher George (Faulkner), Fabian (Sonny), Tom Nardini (Billy Joe), Leslie Parrish (Cissy), Ross Hagen (Frank), Larry Bishop (Chandler), Cliff Osmond (Bubba), Robert Doqui (Henry), Ron Rifkin (Martin), Baynes Barron (Bureau Chief), Joseph Turkell (Sam), Lada Edmund, Jr. (Inez), Marjorie Dayne (Hallie), Ralph Meeker (Burl).

CHARRO! (National General) Executive Producer, Harry Caplan; Writer-Producer-Director, Charles Marquis Warren; Story, Frederic Louis Fox; Associate Producer-Assistant Director, Dink Templeton; Photography, Ellsworth Fredericks; Assistant Directors, W. Les Sheldon, Joe Nayfack; Music, Hugo Montenegro; Lyrics, Alan and Marilyn Bergman; In Panavision and Technicolor; March release. CAST: Elvis Presley (Jess Wade), Ina Balin (Tracy), Victor French (Vince), Lynn Kellogg (Marcie), Barbara Werle (Sara), Solomon Sturges (Billy Roy), Paul Brinegar (Opie), James Sikking (Gunner), Harry Landers (Heff), Tony Young (Lt. Rivera), James Almanzar (Sheriff), Charles H. Gray (Mody), Rodd Redwing (Lige), Garry Walberg (Martin), Duane Grey (Gabe), J. Edward McKinley (Henry), John Pickard (Jerome), Robert Luster (Will), Christa Lang (Christa), Robert Karnes (Harvey).

WHITE FURY (Dubs) Produced, Directed, Written, Photographed, and Narrated by A. R. Dubs; March release. A documentary on game hunting in Alaska.

Horst Buchholz, Gina Lollobrigida in "The Young Rebel"

Kent Lane, Michele Carey in "Changes"

Terry-Thomas (C)
in "2000 Years Later"

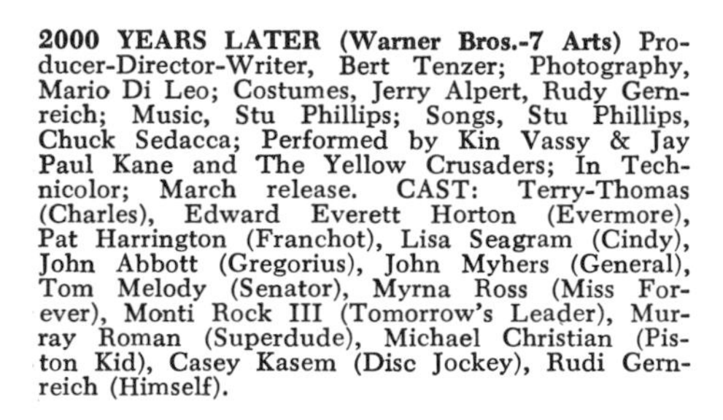

2000 YEARS LATER (Warner Bros.-7 Arts) Producer-Director-Writer, Bert Tenzer; Photography, Mario Di Leo; Costumes, Jerry Alpert, Rudy Gernreich; Music, Stu Phillips; Songs, Stu Phillips, Chuck Sedacca; Performed by Kin Vassy & Jay Paul Kane and The Yellow Crusaders; In Technicolor; March release. CAST: Terry-Thomas (Charles), Edward Everett Horton (Evermore), Pat Harrington (Franchot), Lisa Seagram (Cindy), John Abbott (Gregorius), John Myhers (General), Tom Melody (Senator), Myrna Ross (Miss Forever), Monti Rock III (Tomorrow's Leader), Murray Roman (Superdude), Michael Christian (Piston Kid), Casey Kasem (Disc Jockey), Rudi Gernreich (Himself).

SKI FEVER (Allied Artists) Producers, Wolfgang Schmidt, Mark Cooper; Director, Curt Siodmak; Screenplay, Curt Siodmak, Robert Joseph; Based on story by Frank Agrama, Edward Zatlyn; Photography, Jan Stallich; Songs, Guy Hemric, Jerry Styner; Sung by Jerry Styner; Assistant Director, Vladimir Zelenka; In Color; March release. CAST: Martin Milner (Brian), Claudia Martin (Susan), Vivi Bach (Karen), Dietmar Schoenherr (Toni), Toni Sailor (Franz), Dorit Dom (Dominique), Kurt Grosskurth (Max), Curt Bock (MacDoodle).

MORE DEAD THAN ALIVE (United Artists) Executive Producer, Aubrey Schenck; Producer, Hal Klein; Director, Robert Sparr; Screenplay, George Schenck; Assistant Director, Morris R. Abrams; In DeLuxe Color; April release. CAST: Clint Walker (Killer Cain), Vincent Price (Ruffalo), Anne Francis (Monica), Paul Hampton (Billy), Mike Henry (Luke), Craig Littler (Karma), Beverly Powers (Sheree), Clarke Gordon (Carson).

Clint Walker, Anne Francis
in "More Dead Than Alive"

Claudia Martin, Martin Milner
in "Ski Fever"

THE HOOKED GENERATION (Allied Artists) Producer-Director, William Grefe; Screenplay, Quinn Morrison, Ray Preston, William Grefe; Photography, Gregory Sandor; A Film Artists International Production in EastmanColor; April release. CAST: Jeremy Slate (Daisey), Steve Alaimo (Mark), John Davis Chandler (Acid), Willie Pastrano (Dum Dum), Cece Stone (Kelly).

KING, MURRAY (Iconographic) Producer, Amram Nowak; Directors, David Hoffman, Jonathan Gordon; Photography, David Hoffman; In Color; April release. CAST: Murray Ramsey King (King, Murray), Laura Kaye (Girl for trip), George Koski (masseur), and Barbara Linden, Addie Pezzotta, Gloria Riegger, Jackie Morris, Noga Lord.

RUN, ANGEL, RUN (Fanfare) Producer, Joe Solomon; Director, Jack Starrett; Screenplay, Jerry Wish, V. A. Furlong; Photography, John Stephens; Music, Stu Phillips; In Color; April release. CAST: William Smith (Angel), Valerie Starrett (Laurie), Gene Shane (Ron), Lee DeBroux (Pappy), Eugene Cornelius (Space), Paul Harper (Chic), Earl Finn (Turk), Bill Bonner (Duke), Dan Kemp (Dan) Ann Fry (Flo), Margaret Markov (Meg).

A BOY . . . A GIRL (Jack Hanson) Producer, Jack Hanson; Directed, Written, and Photographed by John Derek; Music, Joe Greene; Lyrics, John Derek; A Cinema J Production in Color; April release. CAST: Dino Martin, Jr. (Boy), Airion Fromer (Girl), Karen Steele (Elizabeth), Kerwin Mathews (Mr. Christian).

HIGH (Joseph Brenner) Directed and Written by Larry Kent; Photography, Paul Van Der Linden; Music, Side Tracks; April release. CAST: Astri Throvik (Vicky), Lanny Beckman (Tom), Peter Matthews, Joyce Cay, Dennis Payque, Carol Epstein, Doris Cowan, Mortie Golub, Al Mayoff, Melinda McCracken, Janet Amos, Paul Kirby, Jack Epstein, Peter Pyper.

Elvis Presley, Ina Balin
in "Charro!"

Wes Stern, Wink Roberts, Rick Kelman, Jacqueline Bisset in "The First Time"

THE FIRST TIME (**United Artists**) Producers, Roger Smith, Allan Carr; Director, James Neilson; Screenplay, Jo Heims, Roger Smith; Story, Bernard Bassey; Photography, Ernest Laszlo; Music, Kenyon Hopkins; Assistant Director, David Salven; A Mirisch Productions-Rogallan Presentation in DeLuxe Color; April release. CAST: Jacqueline Bisset (Anna), Wes Stern (Kenny), Rick Kelman (Mike), Wink Roberts (Tommy), Gerard Parkes (Charles), Sharon Acker (Pamela), Cosette Lee (Grandmother), Vincent Marino (Frankie), Eric Lane (Joe), Murray Westgate (Customs Officer), Leslie Yeo (Bartender), Guy Sanvido (Stranger), William Barringer (Elevator Man).

HELL'S BELLES (**American International**) Producer-Director, Maury Dexter; Associate Producer, Hank Tani; Assistant Director, Robert Jones; Screenplay, James Gordon White, R. G. McMullen; Photography, Ken Peach; Color by Berkey Pathe; April release. CAST: Jeremy Slate (Dan), Adam Roarke (Tampa), Jocelyn Lane (Cathy), Angelique Pettyjohn (Cherry), Michael Walker (Tony), Astrid Warner (Piper), William Lucking (Gippo), Eddie Hice (Red Beard), Dick Bullock (Meatball), Jerry Randall (Crazy John), Jerry Brutsche (Rabbit), Kristian Van Buren (Zelda), Elaine Gefner (Big Sal).

THE CORPORATE QUEEN (**Victoria**) Produced, Directed, and Written by John and Lem Amero; Photography, John Amero; Costumes, John Brock Benson; Music, Firth DeMule; April release. CAST: Renay Claire (Crystal), Marie Brent (Edna), Tony Vito (Chino).

AFRICAN SAFARI (**Crown International**) Produced, Directed, Written, and Photographed by Ron Shanin; In DeLuxe Color; April release. A documentary and travelogue through Africa.

Jeremy Slate, Jocelyn Lane in "Hell's Belles"

George Maharis, Jack Palance, Christian Roberts in "The Desperados"

THE DESPERADOS (**Columbia**) Producer, Irving Allen; Director, Henry Levin; Screenplay, Walter Brough; Story, Clarke Reynolds; Associate Producer, Andrew Donally; Music, David Whitaker; Photography, Sam Leavitt; Assistant Director, Pedro Vidal; In Color; April release. CAST: Vince Edwards (David Galt), Jack Palance (Parson Galt), George Maharis (Jacob Galt), Neville Brand (Sheriff), Sylvia Syms (Laura), Christian Roberts (Adam Galt), Kate O'Mara (Adah).

THE WEDDING PARTY (**Powell Productions Plus-Ondine**) Produced, Directed, Written, and Edited by Wilford Leach, Cynthia Munroe, Brian de Palma; April release. CAST: Jill Clayburgh (Bride), Charles Pfluger (Groom), Valda Setterfield (Mrs. Fish), Raymond McNally (Mr. Fish), Jennifer Salt (Phoebe), John Braswell (Rev. Oldfield), Judy Thomas (Organist), Sue Ann Converse (Nanny), Robert DeNero (Cecil), William Finley (Alistair), Helmuth Pfluger (Groom's father), R. Kollmar, Jr. (Jean-Claude, Hindu, Klaus).

GUNS OF THE MAGNIFICENT SEVEN (**United Artists**) Producer, Vincent M. Fennelly; Director, Paul Wendkos; Screenplay, Herman Hoffman; Photography, Antonio Macasoli; Assistant Director, Jose Maria Ochoa; A Mirisch Productions Presentation in Panavision and Eastmancolor; May release. CAST: George Kennedy (Chris), Monte Markham (Keno), James Whitmore (Levi), Reni Santoni (Max), Bernie Casey (Cassie), Joe Don Baker (Slater), Scott Thomas (P. J.), Michael Ansara (Col. Diego), Frank Silvera (Lovero), Tony Davis (Emile), Wende Wagner (Tina), Luis Rivera (Prensa), Fernando Rey (Quintero), Sancho Gracia (Miguel), Jorge Rigaud (Gabriel), Ramon Serrano (Cesar), Vicente Sangiovani (Manuel).

Reni Santoni, George Kennedy in "Guns of the Magnificent 7"

Michael Sarrazin, Tony Franciosa
in "A Man Called Gannon"

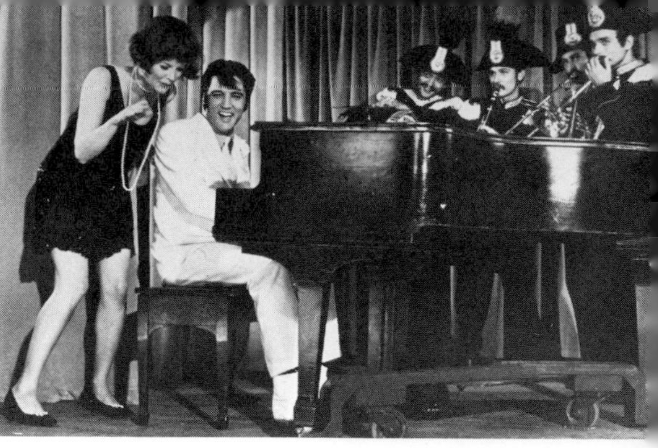

Marlyn Mason, Elvis Presley
in "The Trouble With Girls"

A MAN CALLED GANNON (Universal) Producer, Howard Christie; Director, James Goldstone; Screenplay, Gene Kearney, Borden Chase, D. D. Beauchamp; Based on novel "Man Without A Star" by Dee Linford; Photography, William Margulies; Music, Dave Grusin; Costumes, Helen Colvig; Assistant Director, Earl J. Bellamy; In Technicolor; May release. CAST: Tony Franciosa (Gannon), Michael Sarrazin (Jess), Judi West (Beth), Susan Oliver (Matty), John Anderson (Capper), David Sheiner (Sheriff), James Westerfield (Amos), Gavin MacLeod (Lou), Eddie Firestone (Maz), Ed Peck (Delivery Rider), Harry Davis (Harry), Robert Sorrells (Goff), Terry Wilson (Cass), Eddra Gale (Louisa), Harry Basch (Ben), James Callahan (Bo), Cliff Potter (Ike), Jason Evers (Mills).

HOOK, LINE & SINKER (Columbia) Producer, Jerry Lewis; Director, George Marshall; Associate Producer, Joe E. Stabile; Screenplay, Rod Amateau; Story, Rod Amateau, David Davis; Music, Dick Stabile; Assistant Director, Hal Bell; Photography, W. Wallace Kelley; In Technicolor; May release. CAST: Jerry Lewis (Peter Ingersoll), Peter Lawford (Dr. Carter), Anne Francis (Nancy) Pedro Gonzalez Gonzalez (Perfecto), Jimmy Miller (Jimmy), Jennifer Edwards (Jennifer), Eleanor Audley (Mrs. Durham), Henry Corden (Kenyon Hammercher), Sylvia Lewis (Karlotta Hammercher), Phillip Pine (Head Surgeon), Felipe Turich (Mortician), Kathleen Freeman (Baby Sitter).

FIVE THE HARD WAY (Fantascope) Producers, Jon Hall, Ross Hagen; Director, Gus Trikonis; Screenplay, Tony Huston, Larry Billman; Story, Larry Billman; Photography, Jon Hall; Music, Mike Curb, Jerry Steiner; Assistant Director, Tony Lorea; In EastmanColor; May release. CAST: Ross Hagen, Diane McBain, Michael Pataki, Claire Polan, Richard Merrifield, Edward Parrish, Michael Graham, Hoke Howell.

THE TROUBLE WITH GIRLS (MGM) Producer, Lester Welch; Director, Peter Tewksbury; Screenplay, Arnold and Lois Peyser; Story, Mauri Grashin; From novel by Day Keene and Dwight Babcock; Photography, Jacques Marquette; Assistant Director, John Clark Bowman; Music, Billy Strange; In MetroColor; May release. CAST: Elvis Presley (Walter Hale), Marlyn Mason (Charlene), Nicole Jaffe (Betty), Sheree North (Nita), Edward Andrews (Johnny), John Carradine (Drewcott), Anissa Jones (Caro), Vincent Price (Morality), Joyce Van Patten (Maude), Pepe Brown (Willy), Dabney Coleman (Harrison), Bill Zuckert (Mayor), Pitt Herbert (Perper), Anthony Teague (Clarene), Med Flory (Constable), Robert Nichols (Smith), Helene Winston (Olga), Kevin O'Neal (Yale), Frank Welker (Rutgers), John Rubinstein (Princeton), Chuck Briles (Amherst), Patsy Garrett (Mrs. Gilchrist), Linda Sue Risk (Lily-Jean), Charles P. Thompson (Cabbie), Leonard Rumery (Farmhand), William M. Paris (Farmhand), Kathleen Rainey (Farmhand), Hal James Pederson (Soda Jerk), Mike Wagner (Chowderhead), Brett Parker (Iceman), Duke Snider (Cranker), Pacific Palisades High School Madrigals.

THE FANTASTIC PLASTIC MACHINE (Crown International) Produced, Directed and Written by Eric and Lowell Blum; Photography, John M. Stephens; Music, Harry Betts; In Techniscope and Technicolor; May release. A documentary on surf boarding.

RUSS MEYER'S VIXEN (Eve) Produced, Directed, and Photographed by Russ Meyer; Screenplay, Robert Rudelson; May release. CAST: Erica Gavin (Vixen), Harrison Page (Niles), Jon Evans (Jud), Michael O'Donnell (O'Bannion), Garth Pillsbury (Tom), Vincene Wallace (Janet), Robert Aiken (Dave).

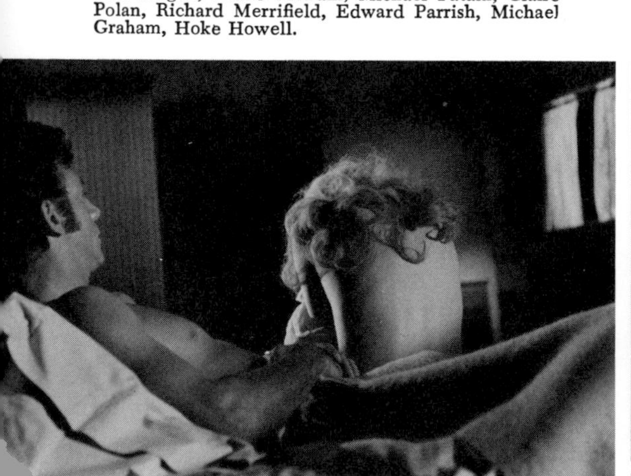

Tony Franciosa, Judi West
in "A Man Called Gannon"

Anne Francis, Peter Lawford
in "Hook, Line & Sinker"

Edward Andrews, Sheree North, Elvis Presley in "The Trouble With Girls"

Jerry Lewis, Anne Francis in "Hook, Line & Sinker"

PIT STOP (Distributors International) Producer, Lee Stonsnider; Directed and Written by Jack Hill; Photography, Austin McKinney; May release. CAST: Brian Donlevy (Grant), Dick Davalos (Rick), Ellen McRae (Ellen), Sid Haig (Hawk), Beverly Washburn (Jolene), George Washburn (Ed).

THE WITCHMAKER (Excelsior) Produced, Directed, and Written by William O. Brown; Photography, John Arthur Morrill; Music, Jaime Mendoza-Nava; In Techniscope and Technicolor; May release. CAST: John Lodge (Luther), Alvy Moore (Dr. Hayes), Thordis Brandt (Tasha), Anthony Eisley (Victor), Shelby Grant (Maggie), Robyn Millan (student), Tony Benson (student), Helene Winston (Jessie #1), Warene Ott (Jessie #2), Burt Mustin (Boatman), Kathy Lynn (Patty), Sue Bernard (Felicity), Howard Viet (San Blas), Nancy Crawford (Goody), Patty Wymer (Hag of Devon), Carolyn Rhodimer (Marta), Diane Webber (Nautch), Larry Vincent (Amos), Del Kaye (Le Singe), Gwen Lipscomb (Fong), Valya Garanda (El A Haish Ma).

NAKED ANGELS (Favorite) Producer, David R. Dawdy; Directed and Written by Bruce Clark; Photography, Robert Eberlein, Bill Kaplan; Assistant Director, Marc Siegler; In Pathe Color; May release. CAST: Art Jenoff, Felicia Guy, Leonard Coates, Tedd King, Bruce Sunkees, Cory Fischer, Sahn Berti, Howard Lester, Joe Kasey, Glenn Lee, Penelope Sprerris, Carol Ries.

THE ASTRO-ZOMBIES (Geneni) Executive Producers, Kenneth Altose, Wayne Rogers; Director, Ted V. Mikels; Screenplay, Ted V. Mikels, Wayne Rogers; Photography, Robert Maxwell; Music, Nico Karaski; A Ram Ltd. Presentation in EastmanColor; May release. CAST: Wendell Corey, John Carradine, Tom Pace, Joan Patrick, Rafael Campos, Tura Satana, Joseph Hoover, Vincent Barbi, Victor Izay.

FLOWER THIEF (Film-Makers) Produced, Directed, and Written by Ron Rice; May release. CAST: Taylor Mead, Turk, Ella, Mikey, Ted, Eric Nord, Bob Kauffman, Phil McKenna.

HIGH SCHOOL (Osti) Produced, Directed, and Edited by Frederick Wiseman; Photography, Richard Leiterman; May release. A documentary on a big-city high school (Philadelphia) and its students.

THE TREE (Guenette) Produced, Directed, and Written by Robert Guenette; Music, Kenyon Hopkins; Photography, Jess Paley; May release. CAST: Jordan Christopher (Bucky), Eileen Heckart (Sally), George Rose (Stuey), James Broderick (Det. McCarthy), Ruth Ford (Mrs. Gagnon), Fred J. Scollay (Alex), Kathy Ryan (Terry), Alan Landers (Jim), Gale Dixon (Lorry), Ed Griffith (Det. Gorman).

MIDAS RUN (Cinerama) Executive Producer, Selig J. Seligman; Producer, Raymond Stross; Director, Alf Kjellin; Screenplay, James Buchanan, Ronald Austin; Story, Berne Giler; Photography, Ken Higgins; Assistant Directors, Luciano Sacripanti, Luciano Palermo; Title Song, Don Black, Elmer Bernstein; Sung by Anne Heywood; A Selmur Pictures Production in Color; May release. CAST: Richard Crenna (Warden), Anne Heywood (Sylvia), Fred Astaire (Pedley), Roddy McDowall (Wister), Ralph Richardson (Henshaw), Cesar Romero (Dodero), Adolfo Celi (Ferranti), Maurice Denham (Crittenden), John LeMesurier (Wells), Aldo Bufi Landi (Carabinieri), Fred Astaire, Jr. (Co-Pilot), Jacques Sernas (Giroux), Karl Otto Alberty (Dietrich), George Hartman (Pfeiffer), Caroline de Fonseca (Mrs. Pfeiffer), Stanley Baugh (Pilot), Bruce Beeby (Gordon), Robert Henderson (Dean).

John Mony in "The Fantastic Plastic Machine"

Anne Heywood, Richard Crenna in "Midas Run"

"Follow Me"

FOLLOW ME (Cinerama) Executive Producer, Robert L. Dellinger; Producer-Director, Gene McCabe; Associate Producer, Ric Eyrich; Screenplay, Stanley Ralph Ross; Photography, Mike Margulies, Jim Freeman, Greg MacGillivray; Music, Stu Phillips; Songs performed by Dino, Desi and Billy; A Robert E. Petersen Presentation in Eastmancolor; May release. A documentary of three surfing champions searching the world for big waves, with Claude Codgen, Mary Lou McGinnis, Bob Purvey, Bonnie Hill, Andrea Kermot, Deborah Lee, Ava Zamora.

BACKTRACK (Universal) Producer, David J. O'Connel; Director, Earl Bellamy; Screenplay, Borden Chase; Photography, Richard H. Kline, John Russell, Andrew Jackson; Music, Jack Marshall; In Color; June Release. CAST: James Drury (Ramrod), Neville Brand (Reese), Doug McClure (Trampas), Peter Brown (Chad), William Smith (Riley), Philip Carey (Capt. Parmelee), Fernando Lamas (Capt. Estrada), Rhonda Fleming (Carmelita), Ida Lupino (Dolores), Royal Dano (Faraway), Gary Clark (Steve), Randy Boone (Randy).

THE HELLCATS (Crown International) Producer, Anthony Cardoza; Co-Producer, Herman Tomlin; Director, Robert F. Slatzer; Screenplay, Tony Houston, Robert F. Slatzer; Based on story by James Gordon White, John Zila, Jr.; Photography, Gil Hubbs; Assistant Director, Tony Houston; A Gemini American Production in EastmanColor; June release. CAST: Ross Hagen (Monte), Dee Duffy (Linda), Sharyn Kinzie (Sheila), Sonny West (Snake), Bob Slatzer (Mr. Adrian), Eric Lidberg (Hiney), Shannon Summers (Rita), Bro Beck (David), Diane Ryder (Candy), Nick Raymond (Pepper), Dick Merrifield (Dean), Hildegard Wendt (Hildy).

Anthony Perkins
in "The Fool Killer"

THE FOOL KILLER (Dreyfus-Landau) Producer, David Friedkin; Executive Producer, Worthington Miner; Director, Servando Gonzalez; Screenplay, Morton Fine, David Friedkin; Based on novel by Helen Eustis; Photography, Alex Phillips; Music, Gustavo C. Carreon; Associate Producers, Harrison Starr, Alfred Markim; Costumes, Dorothy Jeakins; June release. CAST: Anthony Perkins (Milo), Dana Elcar (Dodd), Edward Albert (George), Henry Hull (Dirty Jim), Salome Jens (Milo), Dana Elcar (Dodd), Edward Albert (George), Henry Hull (Dirty Jim), Salome Jens (Mrs. Dodd), Charlotte Jones (Ova), Arnold Moss (Rev. Spotts), Sindee Anne Richards (Blessing), Frances Gaar (Old Crab), Wendell Phillips (Old Man).

THE GAY DECEIVERS (Fanfare) Producer, Joe Solomon; Director, Bruce Kessler; Screenplay, Jerome Wish; Based on story by Abe Polsky, Gil Lasky; Associate Producer, Paul Rapp; Photography, Dick Glouner; Assistant Director, Chris Morgan; Costumes, Norman Saling; Music, Stu Phillips; June release. CAST: Kevin Coughlin (Danny), Brooke Bundy (Karen), Larry Casey (Eliot), Jo Ann Harris (Leslie), Michael Greer (Malcolm), Sebastian Brook (Craig), Jack Starrett (Dixon), Richard Webb (Devlin), Eloise Hardt (Mrs. Devlin), Jeanne Baird (Mrs. Conway), Marishka (Carolyn), Mike Kopscha (Psychiatrist), Joe Tornatori (Sgt. Kravits), Robert Reese (Real Estate Agent), Christopher Riordan (Duane), Doug Hume (Corporal), Dave Osterhout (Stern), Marilyn Wirt (Sybil), Ron Gans (Freddie), Rache Romen (Dorothy), Tom Grubbs (Paul), Louise Williams (Bunny), Randee Lynne (Sheryl), Meridith Williams (Phil), Harry Sodoni (Georgette), Lenore Stevens (Laverne), Trigg Kelly (Jackie), Tony Epper (Vince).

Ida Lupino, Neville Brand
in "Backtrack"

Philip Carey, Doug Mc Clure,
Rhonda Fleming in "Backtrack"

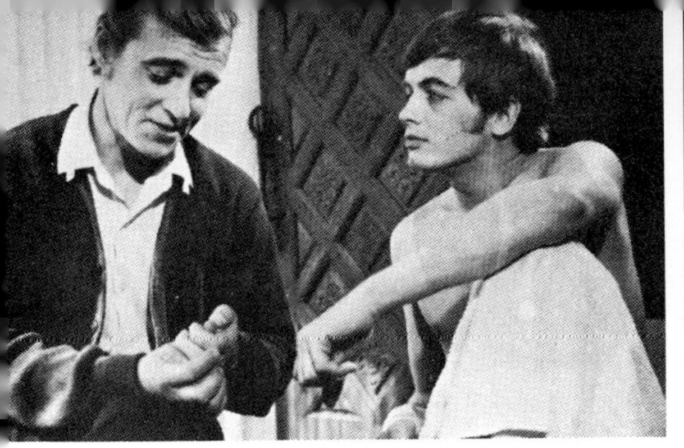

Wayne Douglas, Gary Yuma
in "The Stud Farm"

Bob Hope, Jackie Gleason
in "How To Commit Marriage"

CHILDISH THINGS (Filmworld) Produced and Written by Don Murray; Directed and Photographed by John Derek; Assistant Director, Jonathan Haze; In EastmanColor; June release. CAST: Don Murray (Tom), Linda Evans (Pat), David Brian (Jennings), Angelique Pettyjohn (Angelique), Don Joslyn (Kelly), Gypsy Boots (Gypsy), Rod Lauren (Rod), LeRoy Jenkins (Preacher), Logan Ramsey (Simmons), Erik Holland (Fighter), Jack Griffin (Jack), Valerie Brooke (Girl), Gene LaBelle (Peanut Man), Ed Bennett (Carousel Man), Seaman Glass (Ex-Fighter), George Atkinson (Last Fighter), Peter Tenen (Gene), Claire Kelly (Sharon).

THE STUD FARM (McAbee) Produced and Written by Ian Ogilvie, M. J. Margolis; Director, Jac Zacha; Photography, Manuel Conde; Music, David Hayward; In EastmanColor; June release. CAST: Gary Yuma (Gary), Wayne Douglas (Wayne), Paul Daniels (Sam), Joe Dante (Clarence), Ken Craig (House Manager) Jac Zacha (Sheldon).

THE FABULOUS BASTARD FROM CHICAGO (Walnut International) Producer, Jay Fineberg; Director, Greg Corarito; Screenplay, Richard Compton; Photography, Gary Graver; Music, Gregor Saint-Sanez; Narration, Reed Hadley; In Eastmancolor; June release. CAST: John Alderman (Steve), Maria Lease (Nancy), James Meyers (Fats), Victoria Carbe (Maria), Daryl Colinot (Danny), Bambi Allen, Jimmie Johnson, Mike Stringer, Geretta Taylor, Pony Tobias.

CHARLES LLOYD—JOURNEY WITHIN (Sherman) Produced, Directed, Photographed, Edited, and Recorded by Eric Sherman; Music, Charles Lloyd; June release. A Documentary attempt to get the essence of the man, Charles Lloyd, and his jazz music.

HOW TO COMMIT MARRIAGE (Cinerama) Producer, Bill Lawrence; Director, Norman Panama; Screenplay, Ben Starr, Michael Kanin; Photography, Charles Lang; Music, Joseph J. Lilley; Assistant Director, Arthur Jacobson; Costumes, Nolan Miller; Choreography, Jack Baker; Music performed by The Comfortable Chair; A Naho Production in Technicolor; June release. CAST: Bob Hope (Frank), Jackie Gleason (Oliver), Jane Wyman (Elaine), Maureen Arthur (Lois), Leslie Nielsen (Phil), Tina Louise (LaVerne), Paul Stewart (Attorney), Irwin Corey (BabaZiba), Joanna Cameron (Nancy), Tim Matthieson (David).

DADDY'S GONE A-HUNTING (NATIONAL GENERAL) Director-Producer, Mark Robson; Screenplay, Larry Cohen, Lorenzo Semple, Jr.; Photography, Ernest Laszlo; Music, John Williams; Title Song sung by Lyn Roman; Costumes, Travilla; Assistant Director, Fred Simpson; In Technicolor; July release. CAST: Carol White (Cathy), Paul Burke (Jack), Scott Hylands (Kenneth), Mala Powers (Meg), Rachel Ames (Nurse), Barry Cahill (FBI Agent), Matilda Calnan (Ilsa), Andrea King (Brenda), Gene Lyons (Doctor), Ron Masak (Paul), Dennis Patrick (Dr. Parkington), James Sikking (FBI Agent).

HELL'S ANGELS '69 (American International) Producer, Tom Stern; Director, Lee Madden; Executive Producer, Pat Rooney; Screenplay, Don Tait; Story, Tom Stern, Jeremy Slate; Photography, Paul Loman; Music, Tony Bruno; In Color by Berkey Pathe; July release. CAST: Conny Van Dyke (Betsy), Tom Stern (Chuck), Jeremy Slate (Wes), Steve Sandor (Apache), J. D. Spradlin (Detective), Sonny Barger (Oakland), and Terry The Tramp and the Original Oakland Hell's Angels.

Scott Hylands, Carol White
in "Daddy's Gone A-Hunting"

Tom Stern, Jeremy Slate, Conny Van Dyke
in "Hell's Angels '69"

Zero Mostel, Kim Novak in "The Great Bank Robbery"

Jordan Christopher, Jennifer Jones in "Angel, Angel, Down We Go"

THE GREAT BANK ROBBERY (Warner Bros.-7 Arts) Producer, Malcolm Stuart; Director, Hy Averback; Screenplay, William Peter Blatty; Based on novel by Frank O'Rourke; Associate Producer, Richard Freed; Music, Nelson Riddle; Assistant Director, Jack Cunningham; Photography, Fred J. Koenekamp; Costumes, Moss Mabry; Choreography, Miriam Nelson; Songs, Sammy Kahn, James Van Heusen; In Panavision and Technicolor; July release. CAST: Zero Mostel (Pious Blue), Kim Novak (Lyda Kabanov), Clint Walker (Ben Quick), Claude Akins (Slade), Akim Tamiroff (Papa), Larry Storch (Juan), John Anderson (Kincaid), Sam Jaffe (Brother Lilac), Mako (Secret Service Agent), Elisha Cook (Jeb), Ruth Warrick (Mrs. Applebee), John Fiedler (Brother Dismas), John Larch (Sheriff), Peter Whitney (Brother Jordan), Norman Alden (The Great Gregory).

THE THOUSAND PLANE RAID (United Artists) Producer, Lewis J. Rachmil; Director, Boris Sagal; Screenplay, Donald S. Sanford; Story, Robert Vincent Wright; Based on book by Ralph Barker; Photography, Bill Spencer; Music, James Haskell; Assistant Director, Erich von Stroheim, Jr.; A Mirisch Films Presentation in DeLuxe Color; July release. CAST: Christopher George (Col. Greg Brandon), Laraine Stephens (Wac Lt. Gabrielle Ames), J. D. Cannon (Gen. Cotten Palmer), Gary Marshall (RAF Wing Commander Trafton Howard), Michael Evans (Leslie Hardwicke), Ben Murphy (Lt. Archer), James Gammon (Maj. Varga), Gavin MacLeod (Sgt. Kruger), Scott Thomas (Richman), Tim McIntire (Quimby), Bo Hopkins (Douglas), Henry Jaglom (Worchek), Noam Pitlik (Jacobi), Barry Atwater (Gen. Conway), John Carter (Middleton), Charles Dierkop (Railla), Mac McLaughlin (Waist Gunner), Wayne Sutherlin (Waist Gunner), Philip Proctor (Turret Gunner), Larry Perkins (Navigator), Carl Reindel (Bombardier).

ANGEL, ANGEL, DOWN WE GO (American International) Producer, Jerome F. Katzman; Directed and Written by Robert Thom; Executive Producer, Sam Katzman; Associate Producer, Arthur Dreifuss; Assistant Director, John Wilson; Photography, Jack Warren; Music, Fred Karger; Songs, Barry Mann, Cynthia Weil; Choreographer, Wilda Taylor; A Four Leaf Production in Color; August release. CAST: Jennifer Jones (Astrid), Jordan Christopher (Bogart), Roddy McDowall (Santoro), Holly Near (Tara), Lou Rawls (Joe), Charles Aidman (Willy), Davey Davison (Anna), Marty Brill (Maitre D').

STILETTO (AVCO Embassy) Producer, Norman Rosemont; Director, Bernard Kowalski; Screenplay, A. J. Russell; From novel by Harold Robbins; A Joseph E. Levine presentation in Color; August release. CAST: Alex Cord (Cesare), Britt Ekland (Illeana), Patrick O'Neal (Baker), Joseph Wiseman (Matteo), Barbara McNair (Ann), John Dehner (Simpson), Titos Vandis (Tonio), Eduardo Ciannelli (Don Andrea), Roy Scheider (Bennett), Lincoln Kilpatrick (Hannibal).

THIS SAVAGE LAND (Universal) No credits. August release. CAST: Barry Sullivan (Ben Pride), Brenda Scott (Midge), Andrew Prine (Timothy), Kelly Corcoran (Kip), Katherine Squire (Grandma), Charles Seel (Grandpa), Kathryn Hayes (Elizabeth), Roy Roberts (Elizabeth's father), John Drew Barrymore (Stacey), Glenn Corbett (Chance).

WILD WHEELS (Fanfare) Producer, Bud Deil; Director, Kent Osborne; Screenplay, Kent Osborne, Ralph Luce; In Color; August release. CAST: Don Epperson, Robert Dix, Casey Casem, Dovi Beams, Terry Stafford, Johenne Lemont, Bruce Kimble.

Christopher George, Laraine Stephens in "The 1000 Plane Raid"

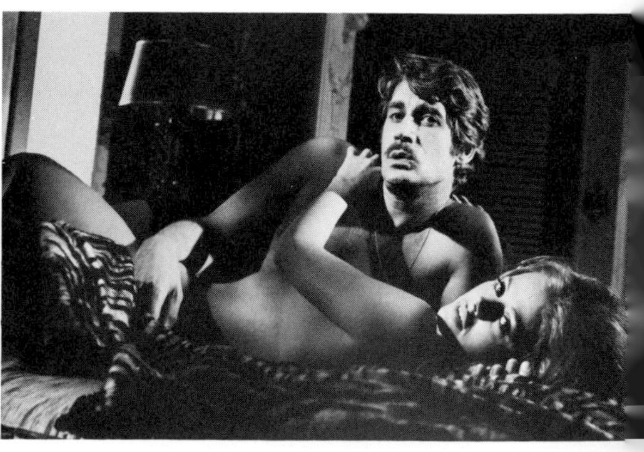

Alex Cord, Britt Ekland in "Stiletto"

Don Knotts (C)
in "The Love God?"

Viva, Louis Waldon
in "Blue Movie"

THE LOVE GOD? (Universal) Producer, Edward J. Montagne; Directed and Written by Nat Hiken; Photography, William Margulies; Assistant Director, Phil Bowles; Associate Producer, Billy Sands; Costumes, Helen Colvig; Choreographer, Wilda Taylor; Music, Vic Mizzy; In Technicolor; August release. CAST: Don Knotts (Abner), Anne Francis (Lisa), Edmond O'Brian (Osborn), James Gregory (Hughes), Maureen Arthur (Eleanor), Maggie Peterson (Rose), Jesslyn Fax (Miss Love), Jacques Aubuchon (Carter), Marjorie Bennett (Miss Pickering), Jim Boles (Amos), Ruth McDevitt (Miss Keezy), B. S. Pully (J. Charles Twilight).

THE RIBALD TALES OF ROBIN HOOD (Adam) Producers, Edward A. Paramore, John Harvey; Directed and Written by Richard Kanter; Based on story by Lawrence Morse; Photography, Paul Hipp; A Mondo Film in Eastmancolor; August release. CAST: Ralph Jenkins (Robin), Danielle Carver (Lady Sallyforth), Dee Lockwood (Maid Marian), Lawrence Adams (Prince John), C. S. Poole (Sheriff), James Brand, Wendel Swink, Eddie Nova, Bambi Allen, Paul Smith, Terry Sands, Scott Sizemore, Barbara Sanders.

IT TAKES ALL KINDS (Commonwealth) Executive Producer, Reginald Goldsworthy; Producer-Director, Eddie Davis; Screenplay, Eddie Davis, Charles E. Savage; Produced by Goldsworthy Productions in association with Commonwealth United Productions; In Color; August release. CAST: Robert Lansing (Tony), Vera Miles (Laura), Barry Sullivan (Orville), Sid Melton (Benji), Penny Sugg (J. P.).

AMERICAN REVOLUTION 2 (Cannon) Producers, The Film Group; September release. A documentary dealing with the racial and poverty tensions that came to the fore in 1968 at the National Democratic Convention.

CHERRY, HARRY AND RAQUEL (Eve) Produced, Directed, and Photographed by Russ Meyer; Screenplay, Tom Wolfe, Russ Meyer; Story, Russ Meyer; Music, Igo Kantor, William Loose; In DeLuxe Color; September release. CAST: Larissa Ely (Raquel), Linda Ashton (Cherry), Charles Napier (Harry), Bert Santos (Enrique), Franklin H. Bolger (Franklin), Astrid Lillimor (Soul), Michele Grand (Millie), John Milo (Apache), Robert Aiken (Tom), Michaelani (Dr. Lee), John Koester (Gas attendant), Daniel Roberts (Delivery boy).

BLUE MOVIE, OR FUCK (Factory) Produced, Directed, and Photographed by Andy Warhol; Executive Producer, Paul Morrissey; In Eastman-Color; September release. CAST: Viva, Louis Waldon.

WALL OF FLESH (Provocative) Producer, K. D. Dietz; Directed and Written by Joe Sarno; Photography, Steve Silverman; Music, Pir Marini; October release. CAST: Dan Machuen, Lita Coleman, Marianne Provost.

COMING APART (Kaleidoscope) Producers, Israel Davis, Andrew J. Kuehn; Direction and Screenplay, Milton Moses Ginsberg; Photography, Jack Yager; Costumes, Francesca Davis; Music, Jefferson Airplanes; October release. CAST: Rip Torn (Joe), Megan McCormick (Joy), Lois Markle (Burn Lady), Lynn Swann (Girl with baby carriage), Viveca Lindfors (Monica), Sally Kirkland (JoAnn), Phoebe Dorin (Friend's wife), Nancy MacKay (Amy), Julie Garfield (Second McCarthy Worker), Kevin O'Connor (Armand), Robert Blankshine (Sarabell), Michael McGuire, Darlene Cotton (Couple at party), Joanna Vischer (Dancing lady), Jane Marla Robbins (Wife).

Vera Miles, Robert Lansing
in "It Takes All Kinds"

Rip Torn, Lynn Swann
in "Coming Apart"

Susan Oliver, Guy Stockwell in "The Monitors"

Raquel Welch, James Stacy in "Flare Up"

THE MONITORS (Commonwealth United) Producer, Bernard Sahlins; Director, Jack Shea; Screenplay, Myron J. Gold; From novel by Keith Laumer; Photography, William Zsigmund; Music, Fred Kaz; Songs sung by Odetta, Sandy Holt; Narrators, Mel Zellman, Tom Erhart; Assistant Director, Rusty Meek; A Wilding/Second City Production in Technicolor; October release. CAST: Guy Stockwell (Harry), Susan Oliver (Barbara), Avery Schreiber (Max), Sherry Jackson (Mona), Shepperd Strudwick (Tersh), Keenan Wynn (General), Ed Begley (President), Larry Storch (Col. Stutz), with cameos by Alan Arkin, Adam Arkin, Xavier Cugat, Barbara Dana, Everett Dirkson, Stubby Kaye, Fred Kaz, Lynn Lipton, Jackie Vernon.

FINNEY (Gold Coast) Produced, Directed, and Written by Bill Hare; Photography, Jack Richards; Music, Dick Reynolds, Les Hooper, Eli Wolf; In Color and Black and White; October release. CAST: Robert Kilcullen (Jim Finney), Bill Levinson (Billy), Joan Sundstrom (Joyce).

LIONS LOVE (Raab) Produced, Directed, and Written by Agnes Varda; Executive Producer, Max L. Raab; Photography, Stefan Larner; Music, Joseph Byrd; In Technicolor; October release. CAST: Viva, Jerome Ragni, James Rado, Shirley Clarke, Carlos Clarens, Billie Dixon, Richard Bright, Eddie Constantine.

ALL THE LOVING COUPLES (U-M) Producer, Harold Nevenzal; Director, Mack Bing; Screenplay, Leo V. Golden; Photography, Carl F. Marquard; Music, Casanova; A Milo O. Frank Production presented by Cottage Films in Color; October release. CAST: Barbara Blake (Kathy), Lynn Cartwright (Natalie), Paul Comi (Mike Corey), Scott Graham (Dale), Paul Lambert (Irv), Gloria Mannon (Liz), Jackie Russell (Thelma), Norman Alden (Mitch).

FLAREUP (MGM) Producer, Leon Fromkess; Director, James Neilson; Screenplay, Mark Rodgers; Associate Producer, Erna Lazarus; Photography, Andrew J. McIntyre; Music, Les Baxter; Assistant Directors, Gilbert P. Mandelik, Jack R. Berne; A GMF Picture Corp. Production; November release. CAST: Raquel Welch (Michele), James Stacy (Joe), Luke Askew (Alan), Don Chastain (Lt. Manion), Ron Rifkin ("Sailor"), Jeane Byron (Jerri), Kay Peters (Lee), Pat Delany (Iris), Sandra Giles (Nikki), Joe Billings (Lloyd), Carol-Jean Thompson (Jackie), Mary Wilcox (Tora), Carl Byrd (Sgt. Newcomb), Steve Conte (Lt. Franklin), Tom Fadden (Willows), Michael Rougas (Dr. Connors), David Moses (Technician), Will J. White (Sgt. Stafford), Doug Rowe (Gas Station Attendant), Gordon Jump (Security Guard), Ike Williams (Policeman).

FUTZ (Commonwealth United) Producers, Ben Shapiro, Alan Stroh; Director, Tom O'Horgan; Screenplay, Joseph Stefano; Based on play by Rochelle Owens; Photography, Vilmos Zsigmond; Music, Tom O'Horgan; Executive Producer, Leon Mirell; A Guvnor Production in DeLuxe Color; November release. CAST: Seth Allen (Oscar), John Bakos (Cyprus), Mari-Claire Charba (Ann), Peter Craig (Sheriff), Jerry Own Cunliffe (Buford), Johnny Dodd (Riordon), Beth Porter (Marjorie), Jeannette Ertelt (Mother Satz), Fred Forrest (Sugford), Clay Haney (Jeffrey), Jane Holzer (Emily), Sally Kirkland (Merry), Victor Lipari (Ned), Michael Warren Powell (Bill), Marilyn Roberts (Mrs. Loop), Sean Shapiro (Clay), Rob Thirkield (Father Satz), Eric Wildwoode (Dorn).

"All the Loving Couples"

"Futz"

Ron Funk
in "The Last of the Ski Bums"

Cassius Clay in
"Float Like a Butterfly, Sting Like A Bee"

OTHER VOICES (DHS) Producer-Director, David Sawyer; Executive Producer, Mary W. Ellis; Photography, Robert Elfstrom; November release. CAST: Dr. Albert Honig, Emil Ondra, Dan Lieberman, Sylvia Honig. A documentary on the progress of four patients in a unique mental institution.

THE HONEYMOON KILLERS (Cinerama) Producer, Warren Steibel; Directed and Written by Leonard Kastle; Photography, Oliver Wood; Music, Gustave Mahler; A Roxanne Company Production; November release. CAST: Shirley Stoler (Martha), Tony LoBianco (Ray), Mary Jane Higby (Janet), Doris Roberts (Bunny), Kip McArdle (Delphine), Marilyn Chris (Myrtle), Barbara Cason (Evelyn), Ann Harris (Doris), Mary Breen (Rainelle), Mary Engel (Lucy), Guy Sorel (Dranoff), Diane Asselin (Severns), Elsa Raven (Matron).

THAT TENDER TOUCH (World Premiere) Produced, Directed, and Written by Russel Vincent; Photography, Robert Caramico; Music, David Saxon; In Color; November release. CAST: Sue Bernard (Terry), Bee Tompkins (Marsha), Rick Cooper (Ken), Phae Dera (Wendy), Margaret Read (Dodie), Victoria Hale (Jane), Richard St. John (Paul), Tania Lemani (Irene), Roger Helfond (Jim), Joe Castagna (Joe).

LAST OF THE SKI BUMS (U-M) Producer-Director, Photography, and Narration, Dick Barrymore; Associate Producer, Douglas Barrymore; Music, The Sandals; In Technicolor; November release. A documentary on skiing, featuring Ron Funk, Mike Zuettel, and Ed Ricks, as they tour the ski capitals of the world.

FLOAT LIKE A BUTTERFLY, STING LIKE A BEE (Grove) Produced, Directed and Photographed by William Klein; Music, Mickey Baker; A Delpire Production; November release. CAST: Cassius Clay (Muhammed Ali).

THE MINX (Cambist) Producers, Herbert Jaffey, Raymond Jacobs; Director, Raymond Jacobs; Screenplay, Raymond Jacobs, Herbert Jaffey; November release. CAST: Jan Sterling (Louise), Robert Rodan (Henry), Michael Beirne (John), Ned Cary (Benjamin), Shirley Parker (Terry).

THE GIRL WHO KNEW TOO MUCH (Commonwealth) Producer, Earle Lyon; Associate Producer, Bill Welch; Director, Francis D. Lyon; Screenplay, Charles Wallace; In Color; November release. CAST: Adam West (Johnny), Nancy Kwan (Revel), Robert Alda (Allardice), Buddy Greco (Lucky), Nehemiah Persoff (Lt. Crawford), David Brian (Had).

ONCE YOU KISS A STRANGER (Warner Bros.-7 Arts) Executive Producer, Robert Goldstein; Producer, Harold A. Goldstein; Director, Robert Sparr; Screenplay, Frank Tarloff, Norman Katov; Based on novel by Patricia Highsmith; Photography, Jacques Marquette; Associate Producer, Mann Rubin; Music, James Fagas; Title Song, James Fagas, Ken Darby; Sung by Dick Addrisi; Assistant Director, Howard Kazanjian; Color by Perfect; December release. CAST: Paul Burke (Jerry), Carol Lynley (Diana), Martha Hyer (Lee), Peter Lind Hayes (Peter), Philip Carey (Mike), Stephen McNally (Lt. Gavin), Whit Bissell (Dr. Haggis), Elaine Devry (Sharon), Kathryn Givney (Aunt Margaret), Jim Raymond (Johnny), George Fenneman (Announcer), Orville Sherman (Raymond), Maura McGiveney (Harriet), Ann Doran (Lee's Mother).

Nancy Kwan, Adam West
in "The Girl Who Knew Too Much"

Paul Burke, Martha Hyer
in "Once You Kiss A Stranger"

Michael Smith (C)
in "The Activist"

Rick Jason, Patricia Connolly, Tom Tryon
in "Color Me Dead"

TROIKA (Emerson) Directed and Written by Fredric Hobbs; Collaborating Director, Gordon Mueller; Photography, William Heick; An Inca Films Production in EastmanColor; December release. CAST: Fredric Hobbs, Nate Thurmond, Gloria Rossi, Morgan Upton, Richard Faun, Parra O'Siochain, San Francisco Art Center Ensemble.

THE ACTIVIST (Regional) Produced and Written by Art and Jo Napoleon; Director, Art Napoleon; Music, Ed Norton, Ron E. Grant; A Jana-Film Enterprises Production in Color; December release. CAST: Michael Smith (Mike), Lesley Gilbrun (Lee), Tom Maier (Prof. Williams), Benbow Ritchie (Home Owner), Patricia Ritchie (His Wife), Steering Committee: Brian Murphy, Naome Gilbert, Ben Schwartz, Charles Goldman, Wendel Brunner.

COLOR ME DEAD (Commonwealth) Producer-Director, Eddie Davis; Executive Director, Reginald Goldsworthy; Assistant Director, Warwick Freeman; Based on Screenplay by Russell Rouse, Clarence Greene; Photography, Mick Borneman; Music, Bob Young; In EastmanColor; December release. CAST: Tom Tryon (Frank), Carolyn Jones (Paula), Rick Jason (Bradley), Patricia Connolly (Marla), Tony Ward (Halliday), Penny Sugg (Miss Foster), Reg Gillam (Eugene), Margot Reid (Mrs. Phillips), Peter Sumner (Stanley), Michael Lawrence (George), Sandy Harbott (Chester).

TURN ON TO LOVE (Haven International) Producer, L. T. Kurtman; Director, John G. Avildsen; Screenplay, Atlas Geodesic; Based on story by Herman Worth; December release. CAST: Sharon Kent (Janice), Richard Michaels (Gerard), Luigi Mastoianni (Rico).

80 STEPS TO JONAH (Warner Bros.) Executive Producer, Steve Broidy; Producer-Director, Gerd Oswald; Screenplay, Frederic Louis Fox; Story, Frederic Louis Fox, Gerd Oswald; Photography, Joseph LaShelle; Music, George Shearing; A Motion Pictures International-El Tigre Production in Technicolor; December release. CAST: Wayne Newton (Jonah), Jo Van Fleet (Nonna), Keenan Wynn (Barney), Diana Ewing (Tracy), Slim Pickens (Scott), R. G. Armstrong (Mackray), Brandon Cruz (Little Joe), Teddy Quinn (Richard), Susan Mathews (Velma), Ira Angustain (Pepe), Dennis Cross (Maxon), Mickey Rooney (Wilfred), Sal Mineo (Taggart), James Bacon (Hobo), Erin Moran (Kim), Michele Tobin (Cathy), Lilly Martens (Nina), Butch Patrick (Brian), Frank Schuller (Whitney), Jackie Kahane (Self).

THE FUNNIEST MAN IN THE WORLD (Evergreen) Produced, Directed, and Written by Vernon P. Becker; Narrated by Douglas Fairbanks, Jr.; December release. A documentary compiled from excerpts of Charlie Chaplin's films with Chaplin, Mabel Normand, Chester Conklin, Fatty Arbuckle, Edna Purviance, Ben Turpin, Marie Dressler, Ford Sterling, Stan Laurel, and Oliver Hardy.

Wayne Newton, Sal Mineo
in "80 Steps To Jonah"

Georgia Hale, Charlie Chaplin
in "The Funniest Man In The World"

PROMISING PERSONALITIES OF 1969

BONNIE BEDELIA

RICHARD BENJAMIN

ROBERT BLAKE

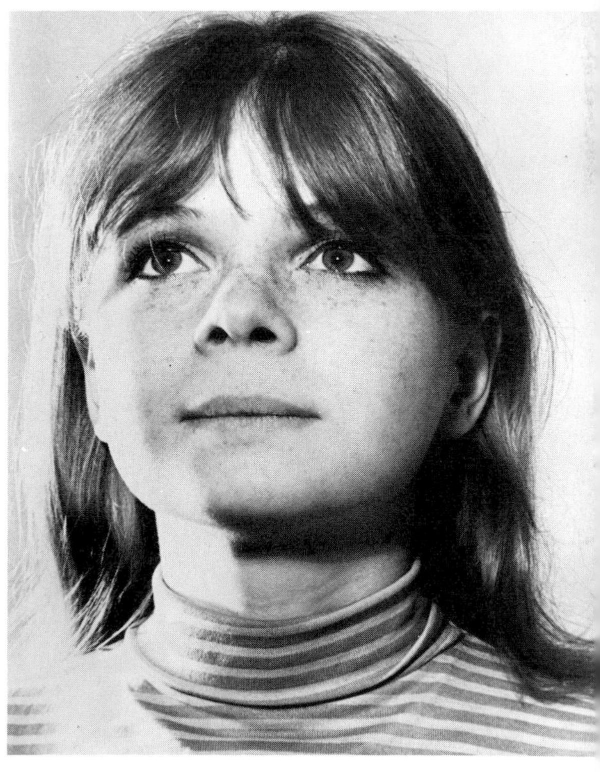

CATHERINE BURNS

DYAN CANNON

MICHAEL DOUGLAS

ROBERT DRIVAS

GOLDIE HAWN
Received 1969 Academy Award
for best supporting actress

ALI MacGRAW

ELLIOTT GOULD

BRENDA VACARRO

JACK NICHOLSON

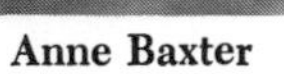

Anne Baxter

Ernest Borgnine

Joan Crawford

Walter Brennan

Celeste Holm

FORMER ACADEMY AWARD WINNERS

(1) Best Picture, (2) Actor, (3) Actress, (4) Supporting Actor, (5) Supporting Actress, (6) Director, (7) Special Award, (8) Best Foreign Language Film

1927-28: (1) "Wings", (2) Emil Jannings in "The Way Of All Flesh", (3) Janet Gaynor in "Seventh Heaven", (6) Frank Borzage for "Seventh Heaven", (7) Charles Chaplin.

1928-29: (1) "Broadway Melody", (2) Warner Baxter in "Old Arizona", (3) Mary Pickford in "Coquette", (6) Frank Lloyd for "The Divine Lady".

1929-30: (1) "All Quiet On The Western Front", (2) George Arliss in "Disraeli", (3) Norma Shearer in "The Divorcee", (6) Lewis Milestone for "All Quiet On The Western Front".

1930-31: (1) "Cimarron", (2) Lionel Barrymore in "A Free Soul", (3) Marie Dressler in "Min and Bill", (6) Norman Taurog for "Skippy".

1931-32: (1) "Grand Hotel", (2) Fredric March in "Dr. Jekyll and Mr. Hyde", (3) Helen Hayes in "The Sin of Madelon Claudet", (6) Frank Borzage for "Bad Girl".

1932-33: (1) "Cavalcade", (2) Charles Laughton in "The Private Life of Henry VIII", (3) Katharine Hepburn in "Morning Glory", (6) Frank Lloyd for "Cavalcade".

1934: (1) "It Happened One Night", (2) Clark Gable in "It Happened One Night", (3) Claudette Colbert in "It Happened One Night", (6) Frank Capra for "It Happened One Night", (7) Shirley Temple.

1935: (1) "Mutiny On The Bounty", (2) Victor McLaglen in "The Informer", (3) Bette Davis in "Dangerous", (6) John Ford for "The Informer", (7) D. W. Griffith.

1936: (1) "The Great Ziegfeld", (2) Paul Muni in "The Story of Louis Pasteur", (3) Luise Rainer, in "The Great Ziegfeld", (4) Walter Brennan in "Come and Get It", (5) Gale Sondergaard in "Anthony Adverse", (6) Frank Capra for "Mr. Deeds Goes To Town".

1937: (1) "The Life of Emile Zola", (2) Spencer Tracy in "Captains Courageous", (3) Luise Rainer in "The Good Earth", (4) Joseph Schildkraut in "The Life of Emile Zola", (5) Alice Brady in "In Old Chicago", (6) Leo McCarey for "The Awful Truth", (7) Mack Sennett, Edgar Bergen.

1938: (1) "You Can't Take It With You", (2) Spencer Tracy in "Boys' Town", (3) Bette Davis in "Jezebel", (4) Walter Brennan in "Kentucky", (5) Fay Bainter in "Jezebel", (6) Frank Capra for "You Can't Take It With You", (7) Deanna Durbin, Mickey Rooney, Harry M. Warner, Walt Disney.

1939: (1) "Gone With The Wind", (2) Robert Donat in "Goodbye, Mr. Chips", (3) Vivien Leigh in "Gone With The Wind", (4) Thomas Mitchell in "Stagecoach", (5) Hattie McDaniel in "Gone With The Wind", (6) Victor Fleming for "Gone With The Wind", (7) Douglas Fairbanks, Judy Garland.

1940: (1) "Rebecca", (2) James Stewart in "The Philadelphia Story", (3) Ginger Rogers in "Kitty Foyle", (4) Walter Brennan in "The Westerner", (5) Jane Darwell in "The Grapes of Wrath", (6) John Ford for "The Grapes of Wrath", (7) Bob Hope.

1941: (1) "How Green Was My Valley", (2) Gary Cooper in "Sergeant York", (3) Joan Fontaine in "Suspicion", (4) Donald Crisp in "How Green Was My Valley", (5) Mary Astor in "The Great Lie", (6) John Ford for "How Green Was My Valley", (7) Leopold Stokowski, Walt Disney.

1942: (1) "Mrs. Miniver", (2) James Cagney in "Yankee Doodle Dandy", (3) Greer Garson in "Mrs. Miniver", (4) Van Heflin in "Johnny Eager", (5) Teresa Wright in "Mrs. Miniver", (6) William Wyler for "Mrs. Miniver", (7) Charles Boyer, Noel Coward.

1943: (1) "Casablanca", (2) Paul Lukas in "Watch On The Rhine", (3) Jennifer Jones in "The Song of Bernadette", (4) Charles Coburn in "The More The Merrier", (5) Katina Paxinou in "For Whom The Bell Tolls", (6) Michael Curtiz for "Casablanca".

1944: (1) "Going My Way", (2) Bing Crosby in "Going My Way", (3) Ingrid Bergman in "Gaslight", (4) Barry Fitzgerald in "Going My Way", (5) Ethel Barrymore in "None But The Lonely Heart", (6) Leo McCarey for "Going My Way", (7) Margaret O'Brien, Bob Hope.

1945: (1) "The Lost Weekend", (2) Ray Milland in "The Lost Weekend", (3) Joan Crawford in "Mildred Pierce", (4) James Dunn in "A Tree Grows in Brooklyn", (5) Anne Revere in "National Velvet", (6) Billy Wilder for "The Lost Weekend", (7) Walter Wanger, Peggy Ann Garner.

1946: (1) "The Best Years of Our Lives", (2) Fredric March in "The Best Years of Our Lives", (3) Olivia de Havilland in "To Each His Own", (4) Harold Russell in "The Best Years of Our Lives", (5) Anne Baxter in "The Razor's Edge", (6) William Wyler for "The Best Years of Our Lives", (7) Laurence Olivier, Harold Russell, Ernst Lubitsch, Claude Jarman, Jr.

1947: (1) "Gentleman's Agreement", (2) Ronald Colman in "A Double Life", (3) Loretta Young in "The Farmer's Daughter", (4) Edmund Gwenn in "Miracle On 34th Street", (5) Celeste Holm in "Gentleman's Agreement", (6) Elia Kazan for "Gentleman's Agreement", (7) James Baskette, (8) "Shoe Shine."

1948: (1) "Hamlet", (2) Laurence Olivier in "Hamlet", (3) Jane Wyman in "Johnny Belinda", (4) Walter Huston in "The Treasure of The Sierra Madre", (5) Claire Trevor in "Key Largo", (6) John Huston for "The Treasure of The Sierra Madre", (7) Ivan Jandl, Sid Grauman, Adolph Zukor, Walter Wanger, (8) "Monsieur Vincent."

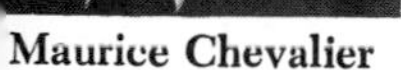

Maurice Chevalier

Claire Trevor

Bob Hope

Loretta Young

Harold Lloyd

1949: (1) "All The King's Men", (2) Broderick Crawford in "All The King's Men", (3) Olivia de Havilland in "The Heiress", (4) Dean Jagger in "Twelve O'Clock High", (5) Mercedes McCambridge in "All The King's Men", (6) Joseph L. Mankiewicz for "A Letter To Three Wives", (7) Bobby Driscoll, Fred Astaire, Cecil B. DeMille, Jean Hersholt, (8) "The Bicycle Thief."

1950: (1) "All About Eve", (2) Jose Ferrer in "Cyrano de Bergerac", (3) Judy Holliday in "Born Yesterday", (4) George Sanders in "All About Eve", (5) Josephine Hull in "Harvey", (6) Joseph L. Mankiewicz for "All About Eve", (7) George Murphy, Louis B. Mayer, (8) "The Walls of Malapaga."

1951: (1) "An American in Paris", (2) Humphrey Bogart in "The African Queen", (3) Vivien Leigh in "A Streetcar Named Desire", (4) Karl Malden in "A Streetcar Named Desire", (5) Kim Hunter in "A Streetcar Named Desire", (6) George Stevens for "A Place In The Sun", (7) Gene Kelly, (8) "Rashomon."

1952: (1) "The Greatest Show On Earth", (2) Gary Cooper in "High Noon", (3) Shirley Booth in "Come Back, Little Sheba", (4) Anthony Quinn in "Viva Zapata", (5) Gloria Grahame in "The Bad and the Beautiful", (6) John Ford for "The Quiet Man", (7) Joseph M. Schenck, Merian C. Cooper, Harold Lloyd, Bob Hope, George Alfred Mitchell, (8) Forbidden Games."

1953: (1) "From Here To Eternity", (2) William Holden in "Stalag 17", (3) Audrey Hepburn in "Roman Holiday", (4) Frank Sinatra in "From Here To Eternity", (5) Donna Reed in "From Here To Eternity", (6) Fred Zinnemann for "From Here To Eternity", (7) Pete Smith, Joseph Breen.

1954: (1) "On The Waterfront", (2) Marlon Brando in "On The Waterfront", (3) Grace Kelly in "The Country Girl", (4) Edmond O'Brien in "The Barefoot Contessa", (5) Eva Marie Saint in "On The Waterfront", (6) Elia Kazan for "On The Waterfront", (7) Greta Garbo, Danny Kaye, Jon Whitely, Vincent Winter, (8) "Gate of Hell."

1955: (1) "Marty", (2) Ernest Borgnine in "Marty", (3) Anna Magnani in "The Rose Tattoo", (4) Jack Lemmon in "Mister Roberts", (5) Jo Van Fleet in "East of Eden", (6) Delbert Mann for "Marty", (8) "Samurai."

1956: (1) "Around The World in 80 Days", (2) Yul Brynner in "The King and I", (3) Ingrid Bergman in "Anastasia", (4) Anthony Quinn in "Lust For Life", (5) Dorothy Malone in "Written On The Wind", (6) George Stevens for "Giant", (7) Eddie Cantor, (8) "La Strada."

1957: (1) "The Bridge On The River Kwai", (2) Alec Guinness in "The Bridge On The River Kwai", (3) Joanne Woodward in "The Three Faces of Eve", (4) Red Buttons in "Sayonara", (5) Miyoshi Umeki in "Sayonara", (6) David Lean for "The Bridge On The River Kwai", (7) Charles Brackett, B. B. Kahane, Gilbert M. (Broncho Billy) Anderson, (8) "The Nights of Cabiria."

1958: (1) "Gigi", (2) David Niven in "Separate Tables", (3) Susan Hayward in "I Want To Live", (4) Burl Ives in "The Big Country", (5) Wendy Hiller in "Separate Tables", (6) Vincente Minnelli for "Gigi", (7) Maurice Chevalier, (8) "My Uncle."

1959: (1) "Ben-Hur", (2) Charlton Heston in "Ben-Hur", (3) Simone Signoret in "Room At The Top", (4) Hugh Griffith in "Ben-Hur", (5) Shelley Winters in "The Diary of Anne Frank", (6) William Wyler for "Ben-Hur", (7) Lee de Forest, Buster Keaton, (8) "Black Orpheus."

1960: (1) "The Apartment", (2) Burt Lancaster in "Elmer Gantry", (3) Elizabeth Taylor in "Butterfield 8", (4) Peter Ustinov in "Spartacus", (5) Shirley Jones in "Elmer Gantry", (6) Billy Wilder for "The Apartment", (7) Gary Cooper, Stan Laurel, Hayley Mills, (8) "The Virgin Spring."

1961: (1) "West Side Story", (2) Maximilian Schell in "Judgment At Nuremberg", (3) Sophia Loren in "Two Women", (4) George Chakiris in "West Side Story", (5) Rita Moreno in "West Side Story", (6) Robert Wise for "West Side Story", (7) Jerome Robbins, Fred L. Metzler, (8) "Through A Glass Darkly."

1962: (1) 'Lawrence of Arabia", (2) Gregory Peck in "To Kill A Mockingbird", (3) Anne Bancroft in "The Miracle Worker", (4) Ed Begley in "Sweet Bird of Youth", (5) Patty Duke in "The Miracle Worker", (6) David Lean for "Lawrence of Arabia", (8) "Sundays and Cybele."

1963: (1) "Tom Jones", (2) Sidney Poitier in "Lilies of The Field", (3) Patricia Neal in "Hud", (4) Melvyn Douglas in "Hud", (5) Margaret Rutherford in "The V.I.P.'s", (6) Tony Richardson for "Tom Jones", (8) "8½".

1964: (1) "My Fair Lady", (2) Rex Harrison in "My Fair Lady", (3) Julie Andrews in "Mary Poppins", (4) Peter Ustinov in "Topkapi", (5) Lila Kedrova in "Zorba The Greek", (6) George Cukor for "My Fair Lady", (7) William Tuttle. (8) "Yesterday, Today and Tomorrow."

1965: (1) "The Sound Of Music", (2) Lee Marvin in "Cat Ballou", (3) Julie Christie in "Darling", (4) Martin Balsam in "A Thousand Clowns", (5) Shelley Winters in "A Patch Of Blue", (6) Robert Wise for "The Sound Of Music", (7) Bob Hope, (8) "The Shop On Main Street".

1966: (1) "A Man For All Seasons," (2) Paul Scofield in "A Man For All Seasons," (3) Elizabeth Taylor in "Who's Afraid Of Virginia Woolf?," (4) Walter Matthau in "The Fortune Cookie," (5) Sandy Dennis in "Who's Afraid of Virginia Woolf?," (6) Fred Zinnemann for "A Man For All Seasons," (8) "A Man and A Woman."

1967: (1) "In The Heat Of The Night," (2) Rod Steiger in "In The Heat Of The Night," (3) Katharine Hepburn in "Guess Who's Coming To Dinner," (4) George Kennedy in "Cool Hand Luke," (5) Estelle Parsons in "Bonnie and Clyde," (6) Mike Nichols for "The Graduate," (8) "Closely Watched Trains."

1968: (1) "Oliver!," (2) Cliff Robertson in "Charly," (3) Katharine Hepburn in "The Lion in Winter" and Barbra Streisand in "Funny Girl," (4) Jack Albertson in "The Subject Was Roses," (5) Ruth Gordon in "Rosemary's Baby," (6) Carol Reed for Oliver!," (7) Onna White for "Oliver!" choreography, John Chambers for "Planet of the Apes" make-up, (8) "War and Peace."

1968 ACADEMY AWARD WINNERS

OLIVER!

(COLUMBIA) Producer, John Woolf; Director, Carol Reed; Screenplay, Vernon Harris; Based on musical play with book, music, and lyrics by Lionel Bart; Choreography and Musical Sequences, Onna White; Photography, Oswald Morris; Costumes, Phyllis Dalton; Associate Choreographer, Tom Panko; Assistant Director, Colin Brewer; A Romulus Film in Panavision and Technicolor; December 1968 release.

CAST

Fagin .... Ron Moody
Bill Sikes .... Oliver Reed
Mr. Bumble .... Harry Secombe
Nancy .... Shani Wallis
Oliver .... Mark Lester
Artful Dodger .... Jack Wild
Magistrate .... Hugh Griffith
Bet .... Sheila White
Mr. Brownlow .... Joseph O'Conor
Widow Corney .... Peggy Mount
Mr. Sowerberry .... Leonard Rossiter
Mrs. Sowerberry .... Peggy Mount
Mrs. Bedwin .... Megs Jenkins
Noah Claypole .... Kenneth Cranham
Jessop .... James Hayter
Dr. Grimwig .... Wensley Pithey
Charlie Bates .... Clive Moss
Charlotte .... Elizabeth Knight
Oliver's Mother .... Veronica Page
Doctor .... Henry Kay
Maid Rose .... Jane Peach
Policeman Magistrate's Court .... Keith Roberts
Clerk of Court .... Peter Hoare
Chairman of Workhouse Governors .... Fred Emney
Workhouse Governors .... John Baskcombe, Norman Pitt, Arnold Locke, Frank Crawshaw
Fagin's Boys .... Robert Bartlett, Jeff Chandler, Chris Duff, Nigel Grice, Ronnie Johnson, Nigel Kingsley, Robert Langley, Peter Lock, Ian Ramsey, Billy Smith, Kim Smith, Freddie Stead, Raymond Ward, John Watters

Shani Wallis, Ron Moody, Oliver Reed
Above: Jack Wild, Shani Wallis, Mark Lester, Sheila White

Ron Moody. Top Left: Mark Lester, Jack Wild

BEST PICTURE: "OLIVER!"

CLIFF ROBERTSON
in "Charly"
BEST PERFORMANCE BY AN ACTOR

KATHARINE HEPBURN
in "The Lion In Winter"
BEST PERFORMANCE BY AN ACTRESS

BARBRA STREISAND
in "Funny Girl"
BEST PERFORMANCE BY AN ACTRESS
(first tie since 1932)

JACK ALBERTSON
in "The Subject Was Roses"
BEST SUPPORTING ACTOR

RUTH GORDON
in "Rosemary's Baby"
BEST SUPPORTING ACTRESS

WAR AND PEACE

(CONTINENTAL) Producer-Director, Sergei Bondarchuk; Screenplay, Sergei Bondarchuk, Vasily Solovyov; Based on novel by Leo Tolstoy; Photography, Anatoly Petritsky; Music, Vyacheslav Ovchinnikov; Choreography, V. Burmeister; Costumes, Mikhail Chikovany; Assistant Directors, Anatoly Golovanov, Anatoly Chemodurov, Adiba Shir-Akhmedova; A Mosfilm Production in Sovcolor; April 1968 release.

CAST

Natasha Rostova	Ludmila Savelyeva
Andrei Bolkonsky	Vyacheslav Tihonov
Countess Rostova	Hira Ivanov-Golovko
Sonya Rostova	Irina Gubanova
Maria Bolkonsky	Antonia Shuranova
Pierre Bezuhov	Sergei Bondarchuk
Count Rostova	Victor Stanitsin
Nikolai Rostova	Oleg Tabakov
Nikolai Bolkonsky	Anatoly Ktorov
Liza Bolkonsky	Anastasia Vertinskaya
Petya	Nikolai Kodin/Seryozha Yermilov
Prince Vasily	Boris Smirnov
Helene Kuragin	Irina Skobtseva
Anatole Kuragin	Vasily Lanovoi
Dolohov	Oleg Yefremov
Count Bezuhov	N. Tolkachev
Maria Ahrosimova	Yelena Tyapkina
Princess Anna Drubetskoy	K. Polivikova
Drubetskoy	Eduard Martsevich
Anna Scherer	Angelina Stepanova/D. Firsova
Julie Karagina	G. Kravtchenko
Kutuzov	Boris Zahava
Denisov	Nikolai Rybnikov
Tushin	Nikolai Trofimov
Bagratin	Giuli Chohonelidze
Uncle Mikhail Nikanori	Alexander Borisov
Alexander I	V. Murganov
Napoleon	Vladislav Strzhelchik
Francis II	V. Safronov

Vyacheslav Tihonov, Ludmila Savelyeva
Above: Irina Skobtseva, Vasily Lanovoi, Ludmila Savelyeva. Top: Boris Zahava (C)

Vyacheslav Tihonov, Sergei Bondarchuk

“WAR AND PEACE”
BEST FOREIGN LANGUAGE FILM OF 1968:

PLAY DIRTY

(UNITED ARTISTS) Producer, Harry Saltzman; Director, Andre De Toth; Screenplay, Lotte Colin, Melvyn Bragg; Story, George Marton; Music, Michele Legrand; Photography, Edward Scaife; Assistant Director, Roger Good; A Lowndes Production in Panavision and Technicolor; January release.

CAST

Captain Douglas .... Michael Caine
Cyril Leach .... Nigel Davenport
Colonel Masters .... Nigel Green
Brigadier Blore .... Harry Andrews
Sadok .... Aly Ben Ayed
German Nurse .... Vivian Pickles
Colonel Homerton .... Bernard Archard
Captain Attwood .... Daniel Pilon
Kostas Manou .... Takis Emmanouel
Kafkarides .... Enrique Avila
Boudesh .... Scott Miller
Assine .... Mohamed Kouka
Hassan .... Mohsen Ben Abdullah
Major Watkins .... Patrick Jordan
Captain Johnson .... Mike Stevens

Top Right: Michael Caine, Nigel Davenport

GRAZIE, ZIA

(AVCO EMBASSY) Producer, Enzo Doria; Director, Salvatore Samperi; Screenplay, Sergio Bazzini, Pier Giuseppe Murgia, Salvatore Samperi; Story, Salvatore Samperi; Photography, Aldo Scavarda; Music, Ennio Morricone; January release.

CAST

Lea .... Lisa Gastoni
Alvise .... Lou Castel
Stefano .... Gabriele Ferzetti

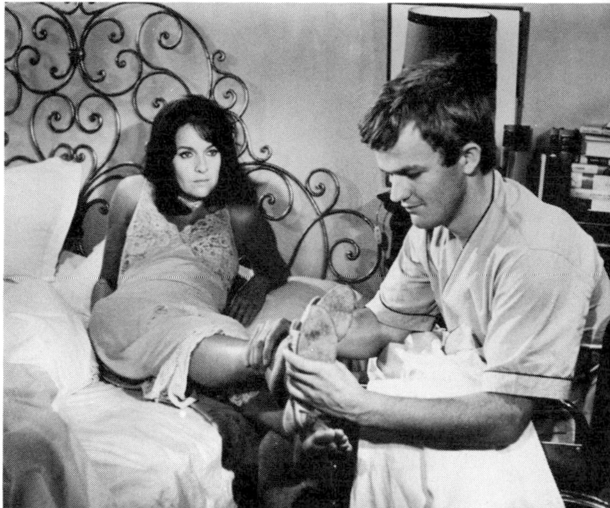

Right: Lisa Gastoni, Lou Castel

DECLINE AND FALL OF A BIRD WATCHER

(20th CENTURY-FOX) Producer, Ivan Foxwell; Director, John Krish; Adaptation, Ivan Foxwell; Additional Scenes, Alan Hackney, Hugh Whitmore; Music, Ron Goodwin; Associate Producer, Sydney Streeter; Photography, Desmond Dickinson; Assistant Directors, Douglas Hermes, Peter Bolton; Costumes, Julie Harris, Anna Duse; In DeLuxe Color; February release.

CAST

The Judge .... Felix Aylmer
Potts .... Rodney Bewes
Philbrick .... Colin Blakely
Flossie Fagan .... Patience Collier
Otto Silenus .... Roland Curram
Mr. Levy .... Kenneth Griffith
Prendergast .... Robert Harris
Sir Humphrey Maltravers .... Griffith Jones
Maniac .... Patrick Magee
Grimes .... Leo McKern
Margot Beste-Chetwynde .... Genevieve Page
Paul Pennyfeather .... Robin Phillips
Chief Warder .... Paul Rogers
Prison Governor .... Donald Sinden
Messenger Warder .... Kenneth J. Warren
Gallery Warder .... Jack Watson
Dr. Fagan .... Donald Wolfit

Robin Phillips, Donald Wolfit

BETTER A WIDOW

(UNIVERSAL) Producer, Turi Vasile; Director, Duccio Tessari; Screenplay, Ennio De Concini, Duccio Tessari; Story, Ennio De Concini; Photography, Ennio Guarnieri; Music, Carlo Rustichelli; Costumes, Adriana Berselli; Assistant Director, Mario Forges Davanzati; An Ultra Films Production in Color; February release.

CAST

Rosa	Virna Lisi
Tom Proby	Peter McEnery
Don Calogero	Gabriele Ferzetti
Baron Misceni	Jean Servais
Prostitute	Agnes Spaak
Carmelo	Nino Terzo
Rosa's Governess	Carla Calo
Don Santo	Salvatore Fucile
Orchestra Conductor	Roy Bosier
Hotel Manager	Bruno Lauzi
Chauffeur-Killer	Adriano Vitale

Top Left: Virna Lisi, Peter McEnery

THE WANDERER

(LEACOCK PENNEBAKER) Producer, Gilbert De Goldschmidt; Director, Jean-Gabriel Albicocco; Photography, Quinto Albicocco; Costumes, Sylvie Poulet; In Techniscope; February release.

CAST

Yvonne De. Galais	Brigitte Fossey
Augustin Meaulnes	Jean Blaise
Francois Seurel	Alain Libolt
Frantz De Galais	Alain Noury
Valentine Blondeau	Juliette Villard
Ganache	Christian De Tiliere
Monsieur Seurel	Marcel Cuvelier
Madame Seurel	Therese Quentin
Mouche Boeuf	Serge Spira
Delouche	Bruno Castan

Left Center: Brigitte Fossey, Jean Blaise

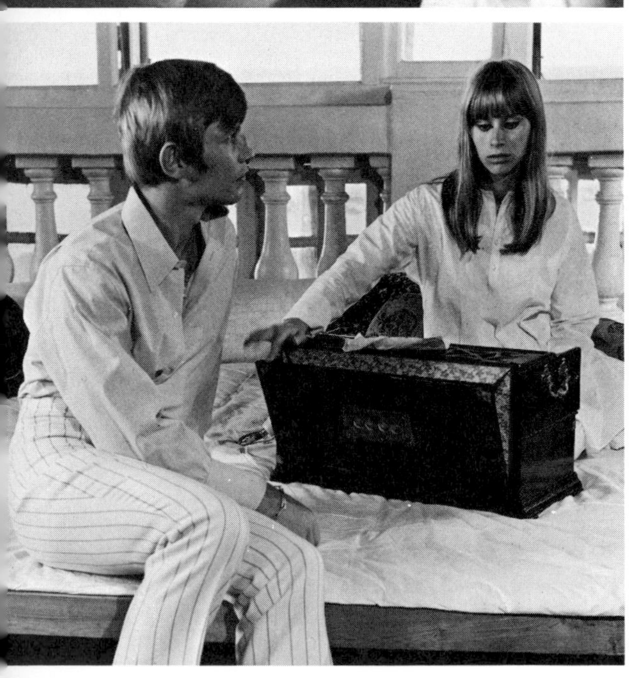

Michael York, Rita Tushingham

THE GURU

(20th CENTURY-FOX) Producer, Ismail Merchant; Director, James Ivory; Screenplay, R. Prawer Jhabvala, James Ivory; Photography, Subrata Mitra; Music, Ustad Vilayat Khan; An Arcadia Films in DeLuxe Color; February release.

CAST

Tom Pickle	Michael York
Murad	Saeed Jaffrey
Ustad Zafar Khan	Utpal Dutt
Begum Sahiba	Madhur Jaffrey
Lady Reporter	Usha Katrak
Jenny	Rita Tushingham
Howard	Fred Ohringer
Society Hostess	Nargis Cowasji
Girl at party	Leela Naidu
Snide Guest	Marcus Murch
Mustani	Zohra Seghal
Ghazala	Aparna Sen
Chris	Barry Foster
Tourist	Dorothy Strelsin
Master of Ceremonies	Ismail Merchant
Arnold D'Mello	Rafi Ameer
Miss Teen Queen	Soni Aurora
Guru's Guru	Nana Palsikar
Courtesan	Nadira
Murderer	Pincho Kapoor
Doctor	Shri Agarwal
Classical Singer	Prayag Raaj

MAYERLING

(**MGM**) Producer, Robert Dorfmann; Director, Terence Young; Screenplay, Terence Young; From novel by Claude Anet and historical documentation, and "The Archduke" by Michael Arnold; Photography, Henri Alekhan; Music, Francis Lai; In Panavision and Technicolor; February release.

CAST

Rudolf	Omar Sharif
Maria Vetsera	Catherine Deneuve
Franz-Josef	James Mason
Elizabeth	Ava Gardner
Prince of Wales	James Robertson Justice
Countess Larisch	Genevieve Page
Count Hoyos	Ivan Desny
Stephanie	Andrea Parisy
Mizzi Kaspar	Fabienne Dali
Szeps	Maurice Teynac
Bratfisch	Moustache
Loschek	Bernard Lajarrige
Lisl Stockau	Veronique Vendell

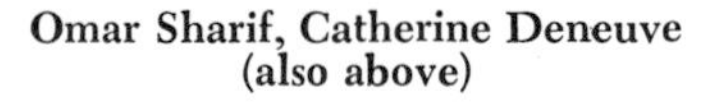

Omar Sharif, Catherine Deneuve (also above)

Omar Sharif, Ava Gardner. Above: Catherine Deneuve, Ava Gardner. Top: Ava Gardner, James Mason

MODEL SHOP

(COLUMBIA) Produced, Directed, and Written by Jacques Demy; Photography, Michel Hugo; Costumes, Rita Riggs, Gene Ashman; Assistant Director, Herbert Willis; Assistant Producer, Richard Roth; English Dialogue, Adrien Joyce; Songs composed and performed by Spirit; In Perfect Color, February release.

CAST

Lola	Anouk Aimee
George Matthews	Gary Lockwood
Gloria	Alexandra Hay
Barbara	Carol Cole
Portly Man	Severn Darden
Gerry	Tom Fielding
Fred	Neil Elliot
Model #1	Jacqueline Miller
Model #2	Anne Randall
David	Duke Hobbie
Rob	Craig Littler
Girl Hippie	Hilarie Thompson
Secretary	Jeanne Sorel
Tony	Jon Lawson

Gary Lockwood, Anouk Aimee. Above: Jacqueline Miller, Gary Lockwood,

Alexandra Hay, Gary Lockwood. Above: Gary Lockwood, Anouk Aimee. Top: Gary Lockwood, Tom Fielding, Alexandra Hay

Mike Marshall, Terry-Thomas. Above: Mike Marshall, Terry-Thomas, Luis De Funes, Bourvil. Top: (R) Terry-Thomas

DON'T LOOK NOW

(BUENA VISTA) Producer, Robert Dorfmann; Direction and Screenplay, Gerard Oury; In Panavision and EastmanColor; February release.

CAST

Reginald	Terry-Thomas
Augustin	Bourvil
Stanislas	Luis De Funes
Achbach	Bennio Sterzenbach
Macintosh	Mike Marshall
Peter	Claudio Brook
Sister Marie-Odile	Andrea Parisy
Mother Superior	Marie Marquet
Juliette	Marie Dubois
Germaine	Colette Brosset

TWISTED NERVE

(NATIONAL GENERAL) Producers, George W. George, Frank Granat; Director, Roy Boulting; Screenplay, Leo Marks, Roy Boulting; Photography, Gerry Anstiss; Assistant Director, Doug Hermes; Music, Bernard Herrmann; A Boulting Brothers Production in Technicolor; February release.

CAST

Susan Harper	Hayley Mills
Martin Durnley and Georgie Clifford	Hywel Bennett
Joan Harper	Billie Whitelaw
Enid Durnley	Phyllis Calvert
Gerry Henderson	Barry Foster
Shashi Kumar	Salmaan Peer
Sir John Forrester	Thorley Walters
Philip	Christian Roberts
Superintendent Dakin	Timothy West
Mrs. Clarke	Gretchen Franklin
Inspector Goddard	Clifford Cox
Henry Durnley	Frank Finlay
Taffy Evans	Richard Davies
Det. Sgt. Thompson	Brian Peck
Professor Fuller	Russell Napier
Hospital Attendant	Russell Waters
Mac	Michael Cadman
Judy	Mary Land
Nursing Sister	Hazel Bainbridge

Hayley Mills, Hywel Bennet. Below: Hayley Mills, Billie Whitelaw

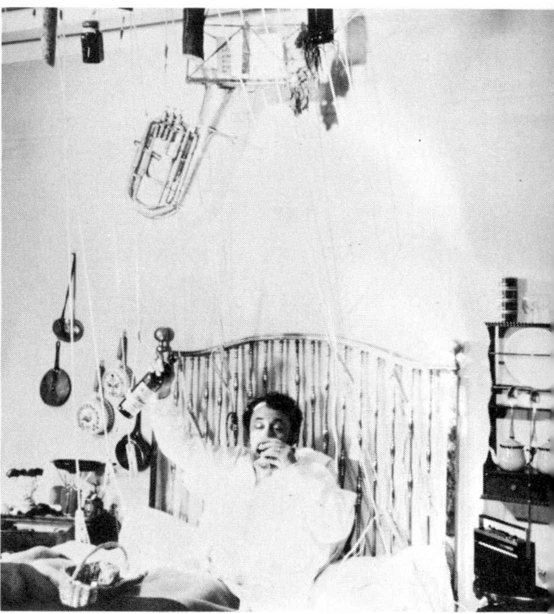

ALEXANDER

(CINEMA V) Producers, Daniele Delorme, Yves Roberts; Director, Yves Robert; Executive Producer, Leon Carre; Screenplay and Adaptation, Yves Robert, Pierre Levy-Corti; Story, Yves Robert; Photography, Rene Mathelin; Music, Vladimir Cosma; English titles, Noelle Gillmor; In Eastmancolour; February release.

CAST

Alexander	Philippe Noiret
La Grande	Francoise Brion
Agathe	Marlene Jobert
Angele Sanguin	Antoinette Moya
Sanguin	Paul Le Person
Colibert	Pierre Richard
La Fringale	Jean Carmet

Philippe Noiret, Marlene Jobert
Above: Philippe Noiret

BEFORE WINTER COMES

(COLUMBIA) Producer, Robert Emmett Ginna; Director, J. Lee Thompson; Screenplay, Andrew Sinclair; Story, Frederick L. Keefe; Photography, Gil Taylor; Assistant Director, Jake Wright; A Windward Film Production in Color; March release.

CAST

Major Burnside	David Niven
Janovic	Topol
Maria	Anna Karina
Lt. Pilkington	John Hurt
Brigadier Bewley	Anthony Quayle
Kamenev	Ori Levy
Sgt. Woody	John Collin
Bill	George Innes
Joe	Hugh Futcher
Ted	Tony Selby
Alf	Colin Spaull
Johnny	Christopher Sandford
Al	Larry Dann
Count Kerassy	Karel Stepanek
Kovacs	Guy Deghy
Komenski	Mark Malicz
Russian Major	Gertan Klauber
Beata	Hana-Maria Pravda
Captain Roots	Jeffry Wickham
Russian Corporal	Constantine de Goguel

John Hurt, Jeffry Wickham, Anthony Quayle, David Niven. Above: David Niven, John Hurt, Topol

Anna Karina, Topol, John Hurt. Above: Anna Karina, David Niven. Top: David Niven, Topol

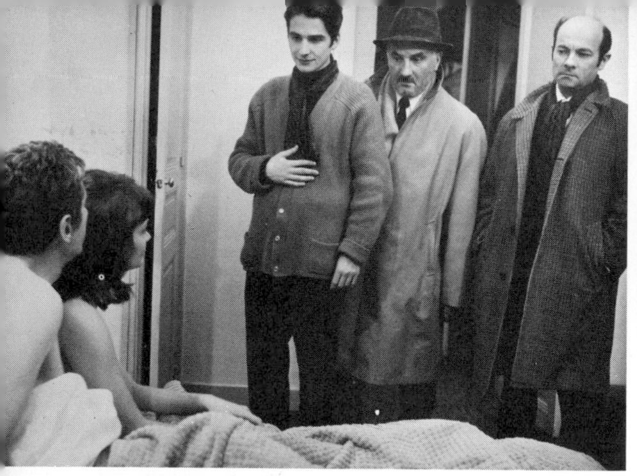

Jean-Pierre Leaud, Claude Jade. Above: Harry Max, Jean-Pierre Leaud. Top: (C) Jean-Pierre Leaud, Harry Max

STOLEN KISSES

(LOPERT) Director, Francois Truffaut; Screenplay, Francois Truffaut, Claude de Givray, Bernard Revon; Photography, Denys Clerval; Music, Antoine Duhamel; Assistant Directors, Jean-Jose Richer, Alain Deschamps; Produced by Les Films du Carrosse in DeLuxe Color; March release.

CAST

Antoine Doinel	Jean-Pierre Leaud
Madame Tabard	Delphine Seyrig
Monsieur Tabard	Michael Lonsdale
Christine Darbon	Claude Jade
Monsieur Henri	Harry Max
Monsieur Darbon	Daniel Ceccaldi
Madame Darbon	Claire Duhamel
Catherine	Catherine Lutz
Monsieur Piddy	Andre Falcon

Top: Jean-Pierre Leaud
Below: Delphine Seyrig

Claude Jade, Claire Duhamel, Daniel Ceccaldi, Jean-Pierre Leaud. Above: Claude Jade, Jean-Pierre Leaud

Jean-Pierre Leaud, Claude Jade

THE PRIME OF MISS JEAN BRODIE

(20th CENTURY-FOX) Producer, Robert Fryer; Co-Producer, James Cresson; Director, Ronald Neame; Screenplay, Jay Presson Allen; Based on her play from Muriel Sparks' novel; Photography, Ted Moore; Music, Rod McKuen; Assistant Director, Ted Sturgis; In DeLuxe Color; March release.

CAST

Jean Brodie	Maggie Smith
Teddy Lloyd	Robert Stephens
Sandy	Pamela Franklin
Gordon Lowther	Gordon Jackson
Miss MacKay	Celia Johnson
Mary McGregor	Jane Carr
Jenny	Diane Grayson
Monica	Shirley Steedman
Miss Campbell	Margo Cunningham
Miss Gaunt	Ann Way
Miss MacKenzie	Isla Cameron
Miss Kerr	Helena Gloag
Miss Allison Kerr	Molly Weir
Emily Carstairs	Lavinia Lang
Miss Lockhart	Rona Anderson

Diane Grayson, Pamela Franklin, Maggie Smith, Shirley Steedman, Jane Carr. Above: Gordon Jackson, Maggie Smith, Celia Johnson

Robert Stephens, Maggie Smith
Above: Maggie Smith
(For this performance she received the 1969 Academy Award)

OTLEY

(COLUMBIA) Producer, Bruce Cohn Curtis; Director, Dick Clement; Executive Producer, Carl Foreman; Screenplay, Ian La Frenais, Dick Clement; Based on novel by Martin Waddell; Music, Stanley Myers; Lyrics, Don Partridge; Photography, Austin Dempster; Assistant Director, Dominic Fulford; In Color by Perfect Pathe; March release.

CAST

Gerald Arthur Otley	Tom Courtenay
Imogen	Romy Schneider
Hadrian	Alan Badel
Hendrickson	James Villiers
Johnston	Leonard Rossiter
Albert	James Bolam
Lin	Fiona Lewis
Proudfoot	Freddie Jones
Jeffcock	James Cossins
Rollo	James Maxwell
Lambert	Edward Hardwicke
Curtis	Ronald Lacey
Jean	Phyllida Law
Hewett	Geoffrey Bayldon
Bruce	Frank Middlemas
Miles	Damian Harris
Paul	Robert Brownjohn
Landlady	Maureen Toal
Larry	Barry Fantoni
Tony	Bernard Sharpe
Constable	Paul Angelis
Ground Steward	David Kernan
Ground Stewardess	Sheila Steafel
Newsagent	Katherine Parr
Dietician	Kathleen Helm
Businessmen	Norman Shelley, John Savident, Ken Parry
Young Man at Party	Jonathan Cecil
Young Girl at Party	Georgina Simpson

and Ron Owen, Stella Tanner, Robin Askwith, Kevin Bennett, Kenneth Cranham, Robert Gillespie, Donald McKillop, The Herd, Jimmy Young, Pete Murray

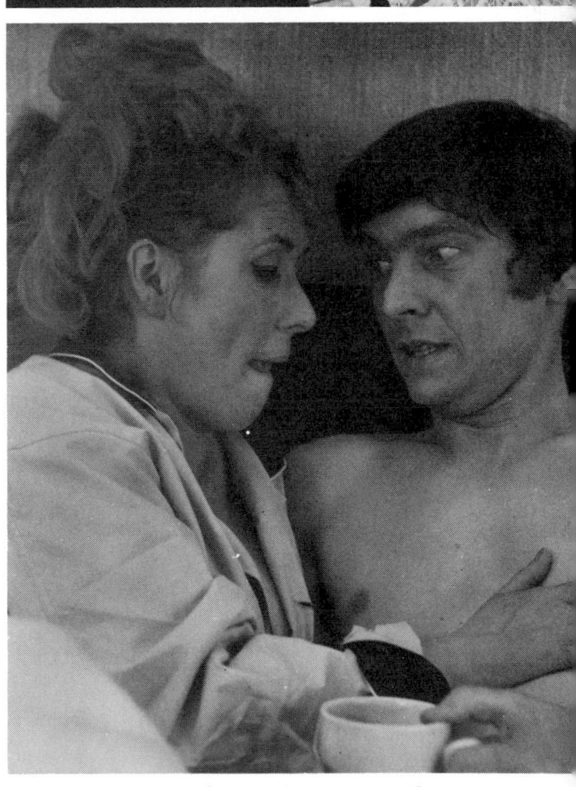

Maureen Toal, Tom Courtenay. Above: Courtenay, Fiona Lewis. Top: Robert Brownjohn, Courtenay. Left: Courtenay, Romy Schneider

"The Paul Street Boys" await "The Red Shirts"
Top: Anthony Kemp

THE BOYS OF PAUL STREET

(20th CENTURY-FOX) Executive Producer, Bud Groskopf; Producer, Endre Bohem; Director, Zoltan Fabri; Screenplay, Zoltan Fabri, Endre Bohem; Based on novel by Ferenc Molnar; Photography, Gyorgy Illes; Music, Emil Petrovics; Costumes, Judit Schaffer; In DeLuxe Color; March release.

CAST

Nemecsek .... Anthony Kemp
Boka .... William Burleigh
Gereb .... John Moulder-Brown
Csonakos .... Robert Efford
Csele .... Mark Colleano
Weisz .... Gary O'Brien
Kolnay .... Martin Beaumont
Barabas .... Paul Bartlett
Leszik .... Earl Younger
Richter .... Gyorgy Vizi
Feriats .... Julien Holdaway
Older Pasztor .... Peter Delmar
Younger Pasztor .... Miklos Jancso
Wendaver .... Attila Nemethy
Szebenits .... Imre Ebergenyi
Torok .... Sandor Kentner
Szabo .... Andras Avar
Younger Szabo .... Janos Pach
Bespectacled Boy .... Istvan Seri
Girl with Diabolo .... Orsolya Zeitler
Nemecsek's Mother .... Mari Torocsik
Professor Racz .... Sandor Pecsi
Jano .... Laszlo Zokak
Nemecsek's Father .... Laszlo Paal
Doctor .... Arpad Teri

CAN HEIRONYMUS MERKIN EVER FORGET MERCY HUMPPE AND FIND TRUE HAPPINESS?

(REGIONAL) Producer-Director, Anthony Newley; Associate Producer, George Fowler; Assistant Director, Ray Frift; Screenplay, Anthony Newley; Photography, Otto Heller; Costumes, Loudon Sainthill; Music, Anthony Newley; Lyrics, Herbert Kretzmer; Choreographer, Johnny Greenland; In Technicolor; March release.

CAST

Heironymus Merkin ---------- Anthony Newley
Polyester Poontang ---------- Joan Collins
Goodtime Eddie Filth ---------- Milton Berle
The Presence ---------- George Jessel
Fat Writer ---------- Stubby Kaye
Uncle Limelight ---------- Bruce Forsyth
Grandma ---------- Patricia Hayes
Sharpnose ---------- Victor Spinetti
Producer Ron ---------- Tom Stern
Mercy Humppe ---------- Connie Kreski
Filigree Fondle ---------- Judy Cornwell
Fran ---------- Berri Cornish
The Mask ---------- Roy Desmond
Automation Bunny ---------- Sally Douglas
Philip Bluster ---------- Desmond Walter Ellis
Maidenhead Fern ---------- Gilly Grant
Marge ---------- Isabel Hurll
Penelope ---------- Rosalind Knight
Harriet ---------- Aleta Morrison
Producer Peter ---------- Louis Negin
Thumbelina ---------- Tara Newley
Thaxted ---------- Alexander Newley
Little Assistance ---------- Margaret Nolan
Red Cardinal ---------- Julian Orchard
Bentley ---------- Ronald Radd
Skinny Writer ---------- Ronald Rubin
Miss Hope Climax ---------- Margo Segrave
Miss Quiche Lorraine ---------- Sue Shepherd
Icicle Ike ---------- Bernard Stone
Trampolena Whambang ---------- Yolanda

Right: Anthony Newley, Bruce Forsyth. Top: Anthony Newley, Joan Collins, Milton Berle, Tara and Sasha Newley. Below: Margaret Nolan, Anthony Newley, Milton Berle

Veronica Carlson, Christopher Lee

DRACULA HAS RISEN FROM THE GRAVE

(WARNER BROS.-7 ARTS) Producer, Aida Young; Director, Freddie Francis; Assistant Director, Dennis Robertson; Screenplay, John Elder; Photography, Arthur Grant; Music, James Bernard; A Hammer Film Production in Technicolor; March release.

CAST

Count Dracula ---------- Christopher Lee
Monsignor ---------- Rupert Davies
Maria ---------- Veronica Carlson
Zena ---------- Barbara Ewing
Paul ---------- Barry Andrews
Priest ---------- Ewan Hooper
Max ---------- Michael Ripper
Landlord ---------- George A. Cooper
Anna ---------- Marion Mathie

IF

(PARAMOUNT) Producers, Michael Medwin, Lindsay Anderson; Director, Lindsay Anderson; Screenplay, David Sherwin; From "The Crusaders" by David Sherwin, John Howlett; Photography, Miroslav Ondricek; Music, Marc Wilkinson; Assistant Director, John Stoneman; In EastmanColor; March release.

CAST

Mick	Malcolm McDowell
Johnny	David Wood
Wallace	Richard Warwick
The Girl	Christine Noonan
Rowntree	Robert Swann
Denson	Hugh Thomas
Stephans	Guy Ross
Headmaster	Peter Jeffrey
Matron	Mona Washbourne
Housemaster	Arthur Lowe
History Master	Graham Crowden
Chaplain	Geoffrey Chater
Housemaster's Wife	Mary MacLeod
Undermaster	Ben Aris
General Denson	Anthony Nicholls

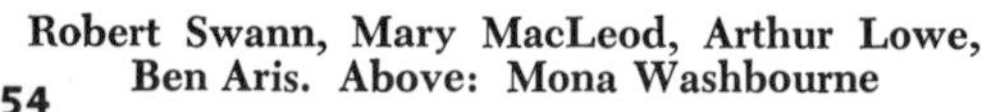

Robert Swann, Mary MacLeod, Arthur Lowe, Ben Aris. Above: Mona Washbourne

Geoffrey Chatter (L)
Above: Robert Swann (C)

Christine Noonan, Malcolm McDowell
Top: Robert Swann

Malcolm McDowell, Robert Swann
Above: Peter Jeffrey (C)

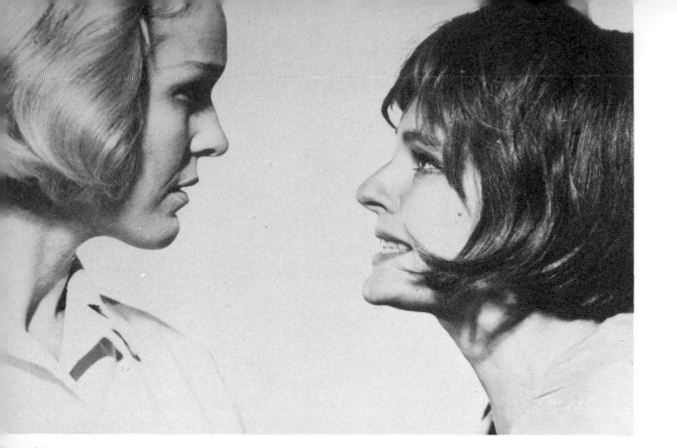

THE CATS

(NATIONAL SHOWMANSHIP) Producer, Lorens Marmstedt; Director, Henning Carlsen; Photography, Mac Ahlberg; Music, Krzystzof Komeda; Based on play by Valentin Chorelle; Screenplay, Sigyn Sahlin; English Titles, Rose Sokol; March release.

CAST

Marta	Eva Dahlbeck
Rike	Gio Petre
Mirka	Monica Nielsen
Ragni	Lena Granhagen
Anna	Hjordis Petterson
Tora	Isa Quensel
Xenia	Ruth Kasdan
Klara	Inga Gill
Sally	Lena Hansson
Johnny	Per Myrberg

Top Left: Eva Dahlbeck, Gio Petre

LA PRISONNIERE

Producer, Robert Dorfmann; Direction and Screenplay, Henri-Georges Clouzot; Photography, Andreas Winding; Assistant Director, Serge Witta; Story and Adaptation, Henri-Georges Clouzot; Presented by Joseph E. Levine; March release.

CAST

Stanislas Hassler	Laurent Terzieff
Gilbert Moreau	Bernard Fresson
Jose	Elisabeth Wiener
Maguy	Dany Carrel
Sala	Dario Moreno
Maurice	Daniel Riviere

Left: Laurent Terzieff, Elisabeth Wiener

Linda Hayden, Derek Lamden

BABY LOVE

(AVCO EMBASSY) Executive Producer, Michael Klinger; Producer, Guido Coen; Director, Alastair Reid; Screenplay, Alastair Reid, Guido Coen, Michael Klinger; Based on novel by Tina Chad Christian; Photography, Desmond Dickinson; Assistant Director, Ray Corbett; Costumes, Harry Haynes; Presented by Joseph E. Levine; A Klinger-Shipman Production; In Color; March release.

CAST

Amy	Ann Lynn
Robert	Keith Barron
Luci	Linda Hayden
Nick	Derek Lamden
Liz	Diana Dors
Mrs. Carmichael	Patience Collier
Harry Pearson	Dick Emery
Tessa Pearson	Sheila Steafel
Margo Pearson	Sally Stephens
Jeremy	Timothy Carlton
Jonathan	Christopher Witty

SEVEN GOLDEN MEN

(WARNER BROS.-7 ARTS) Director, Marco Vicario; Story and Screenplay, Marco Vicario; English Adaptation written and directed by Noelle Gillmor; Photography, Ennio Guarnieri; Music, Armando Trovajoli; Costumes, Gala Romanini; Assistant Directors, F. Massaro, F. Ariza; In Technicolor; April release.

CAST

Giorgia	Rossana Podesta
Albert	Philippe Leroy
Adolf	Gastone Moschin
August	Giampiero Albertino
Anthony	Dario De Grassi
Alfonso	Manuel Zarzo
Alfred	Maurice Poli
Police Chief	Ennio Balbo
Radio Ham	Alberto Bonucci
Bank Manager	Jose Suarez

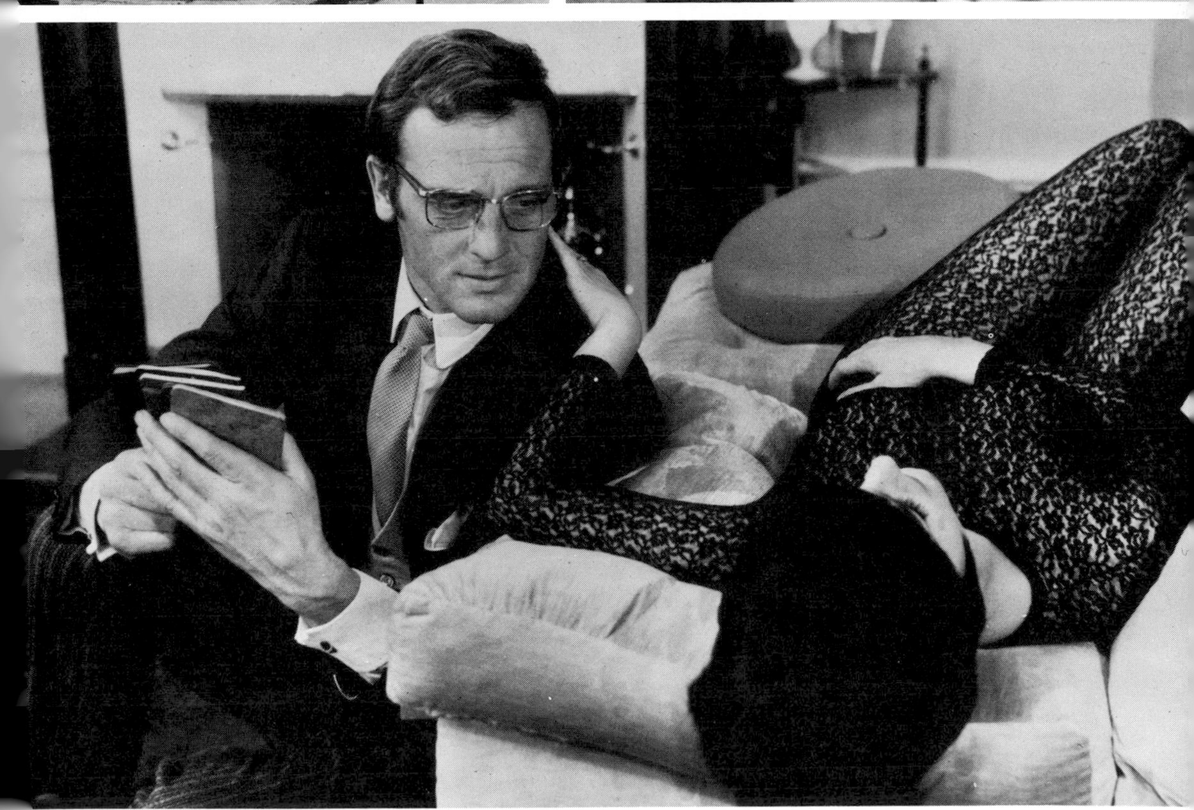

Philippe Leroy, Rossana Podesta. Above Left: Gastone Moschin, Giampiero Albertini, Gabriele Tinti, Maurice Poli, Manuel Zarzo, Dario De Grassi. Top Right: Jose Suarez, Rossana Podesta

THE LOVES OF ISADORA

(UNIVERSAL) Producers, Robert and Raymond Hakim; Director, Karel Reisz; Screenplay, Melvyn Bragg, Clive Exton; Based on "My Life" by Isadora Duncan and "Isadora Duncan" by Sewell Stokes; Music, Maurice Jarre; Photography, Dennis Lewiston; Assistant Director, Claude Watson; Choreographer, Litz Pisk; In Technicolor; April release; Original Title "Isadora."

CAST

Isadora .... Vanessa Redgrave
Gordon Craig .... James Fox
Paris Singer .... Jason Robards
Sergei Essenin .... Ivan Tchenko
Roger .... John Fraser
Mrs. Duncan .... Bessie Love
Mary Desti .... Cynthia Harris
Elizabeth Duncan .... Libby Glenn
Raymond Duncan .... Tony Vogel
Archer .... Wallace Eaton
Pim .... John Quentin
Bedford .... Nicholas Pennell
Miss Chase .... Ronnie Gilbert
Armand .... Christian Duvalex
Raucous Woman .... Margaret Courtnay
Hearty Husband .... Arthur White
Alicia .... Iza Teller
Bugatti .... Vladimir Leskovar
Mr. Stirling .... John Warner
Tour Manager .... Alan Gifford
Russian Teacher .... Ina De La Haye
Góspel Billy .... John Brandon
Deirdre .... Lucinda Chambers
Patrick .... Simon Lutton Davies

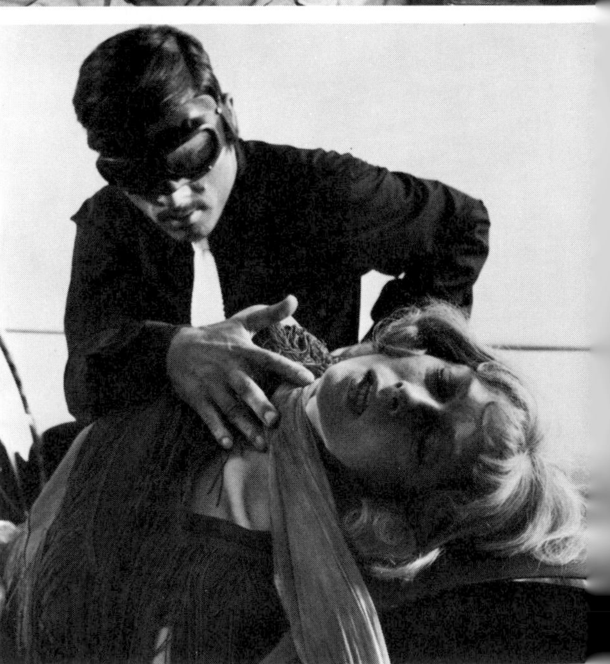

Vladimir Leskovar, Vanessa Redgrave. Above: Ivan Tchenko, Vanessa Redgrave
Top: James Fox, Vanessa Redgrave

Top: Vanessa Redgrave with Bessie Love, and below with Jason Robards

HANNIBAL BROOKS

(UNITED ARTISTS) Producer-Director, Michael Winner; Screenplay, Dick Clement, Ian La Frenais; Story, Michael Winner, Tom Wright; Photography, Robert Paynter; Music, Francis Lai; Assistant Directors, Michael Dryhurst, Udo Graf Lambsdorff; A Scimitar Films Production in DeLuxe Color, April release.

CAST

Brooks	Oliver Reed
Packy	Michael J. Pollard
Col. Von Haller	Wolfgang Preiss
Willi	Helmut Lohner
Vronia	Karin Baal
Kurt	Peter Karsten
Dr. Mendel	Ralf Wolter
Bernard	John Alderton
Sami	Jurgen Draeger
Anna	Maria Brockerhoff
Kellerman	Ernst Fritz Furbringer
Josef	Fred Haltiner
Stern	Eric Jelde
Von Haller's Sgt.	Til Kiwe
Geordie	John Porter Davison
Twilight	Terence Seward
Padre	James Donald

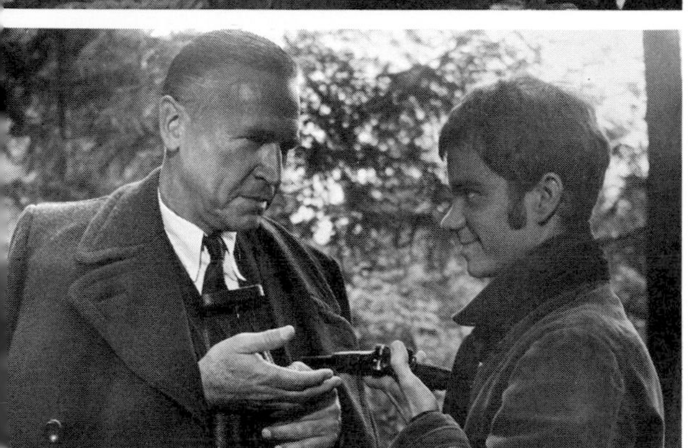

Peter Karsten, Oliver Reed, Karin Baal. Above: Wolfgang Preiss, Michael J. Pollard
Top: Oliver Reed, Michael J. Pollard

Oliver Reed, Maria Brockerhoff, Ralf Wolter
Above: Oliver Reed, Michael J. Pollard, Karin Baal

WHERE EAGLES DARE

(MGM) Producer, Elliott Kastner; Director, Brian G. Hutton; Story and Screenplay, Alistair MacLean; Photography, Arthur Ibbetson; Music, Ron Goodwin; Associate Producer, Denis Holt; Assistant Director, Colin Brewer; A Jerry Gershwin-Elliott Kastner Picture in Panavision and Metrocolor; April release.

CAST

John Smith	Richard Burton
Lt. Morris Schaffer	Clint Eastwood
Mary Ellison	Mary Ure
Vice-Admiral Rolland	Michael Hordern
Col. Wyatt-Turner	Patrick Wymark
Cartwright-Jones	Robert Beatty
Col. Kramer	Anton Diffring
Olaf Christiansen	Donald Houston
Reichmarshal Rosemeyer	Ferdy Mayne
Torrance-Smythe	Neil McCarthy
Edward Carraciola	Peter Barkworth
Lee Thomas	William Squire
Sergeant Harrod	Brook Williams
Col. Weissner	Victor Beaumont
Heidi	Ingrid Pitt
Capt. Von Haagen	Derren Nesbitt
Telephone Orderly	Richard Beale
German Officer	Ivor Dean
German Woman	Lyn Kennington
Young German Soldier	Nigel Lambert
Radio Operator	Michael Rooney
Airport Control Officer	Ernst Walder

Derren Nesbitt, Ingrid Pitt, Mary Ure. Above: William Squire, Neil McCarthy, Richard Burton, Clint Eastwood, Peter Barkworth, Donald Houston

Richard Burton, Clint Eastwood. Above: Robert Beatty, Ferdy Mayne, Anton Diffring, Olga Lowe. Top Left: Eastwood, Pitt, Ure, Burton

Capucine, Suzy Kendall. Top Right: Kenneth More (C), Suzy Kendall

FRAULEIN DOKTOR

Producer, Dino DeLaurentiis; Director, Alberto Lattuada; Screenplay, Duilio Coletti, Stanley Mann, H. C. Craig, Alberto Lattuada; Photography, Luigi Kuveilder; Costumes, Maria de Matteis; Assistant Directors, Marcello Aliprandi, Dusko Dimitrijevic; A Yugoslav-Italian Co-Production in Technicolor; May release.

CAST

Fraulein Doctor	Suzy Kendall
Colonel Foreman	Kenneth More
Dr. Saforet	Capucine
Meyer	James Booth
General Peronne	Alexander Knox
Mathesius	Nigel Green
Hans Schell	Roberto Bisacco
Cartwright	Malcolm Ingram
Lt. Hans Ruppert	Giancarlo Giannini
Sgt. Otto Latemar	Mario Novelli
Lt. Ernst Wiechert	Kenneth Poitevin
Lt. Wilhelm von Oberdorff	Bernhard de Vries
Lean Agent	Ralph Nossek
Tom	Michael Elphick
Marchioness de Haro	Olivera
Dona Elena de Rivas	Adreina Paul
Margarita	Silvia Monti
Dona Julia	Virginia Bell
General Metzler	Colin Tapley
Capt. Munster	Gerard Herter
General von Hindenburg	Walter Williams
Major Rops	John Atkinson
Sergeant	Neale Stainton
First Agent	John Webb
Landlady	Joan Geary
Chemist	Aca Stojkovic
Chaplain	Mavid Popovic
Colonel Delveaux	Dusan Bulajic
Blondel	Miki Micovic

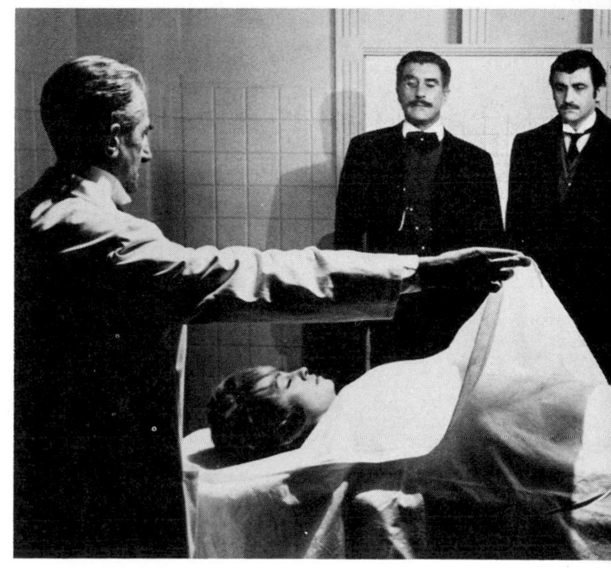

Suzy Kendall, Nigel Green, James Booth
Above: Kenneth More (L), (R) Roberto Bisacco, James Booth

WHERE'S JACK?

(**PARAMOUNT**) Producer, Stanley Baker; Director, James Clavell; Screenplay, Rafe and David Newhouse; Executive Producer, Michael Deeley; Associate Producer, Robert Porter; Photography, John Wilcox; Choreographer, Malcolm Goddard; An Oakhurst Production in EastmanColor; May release.

CAST

Jack Sheppard	Tommy Steele
Jonathan Wild	Stanley Baker
Edgworth Bess	Fiona Lewis
Lord Chancellor	Alan Badel
Blueskin	Dudley Foster
Leatherchest	Noel Purcell
Tom Sheppard	William Marlowe
Lady Darlington	Sue Lloyd
King	Harold Kasket
Lord Mayor	Cardew Robinson
Ballad Singer	Esmond Knight
Rev. Wagstaff	Eddie Byrne
Captain	John Hallam
Deeley	Leon Lissek
Lady Clarissa	Yole Marinelli
Mistress Barrow	Carolyn Montagu
Emma	Carla Challoner
Mr. Woods	Jack Woolgar
Mr. Hind	Roy Evans
Hogarth	Michael Elphick
Mme. Vendonne	Caroline Munro
Countess Bethune	Rona Newton-John

and Bernadette Brady, Daffyd Havard, Roc Brynner, Skip Martin, Vernon Hayden, Norman Smythe, Cecil Nash, Howard Goorney, George Woodbridge, Clare Mullen, Ivan Dixon, Danny Cummins, Fred Johnson, Loretta Clarke, Danny Holland, Michael Douglas, Terry Plummer, Liam Sweeney, John Kelly, Mary Willoughby, John Morley, Paschal Perry

Tommy Steele (also top left). Above: Stanley Baker, Tommy Steele. Top: Fiona Lewis, Tommy Steele

THOSE DARING YOUNG MEN IN THEIR JAUNTY JALOPIES

(PARAMOUNT) Producer-Director, Ken Annakin; Associate Producer, Basil Keys; Screenplay, Ken Annakin, Jack Davies; Photography, Gabor Pogany; Costumes, John Furniss; In Panavision and Color; May release.

CAST

Chester Schofield	Tony Curtis
Betty	Susan Hampshire
Sir Cuthert Ware-Armitage	Terry-Thomas
Perkins	Eric Sykes
Schickel	Gert Frobe
Otto	Peer Schmidt
Maj. Digby Dawlish	Peter Cook
Lt. Kit Barrington	Dudley Moore
Angelo Pincelli	Walter Chiari
Marcello Agosti	Lando Buzzanca
Marie-Claude	Mireille Darc
Pasquale	Marie Dubois
Dominique	Nicoletta Machiavelli
M. Vendredi	Bourvil
Motorcycle Gendarme	Jacques Duby
Lady Journalist	Hattie Jacques
Waleska	Derren Nesbitt
Golfer	Nicholas Phipps
John O'Groats Official	William Rushton
German Rally Official	Michael Trubshawe
Golf Club Secretary	Richard Wattis
German Customs Official	Walter Williams
Driving Team	Joe Wadham, Roy Scammel, Dinny Powell, Frank Henson, Mark Boyle, Jeff Silk

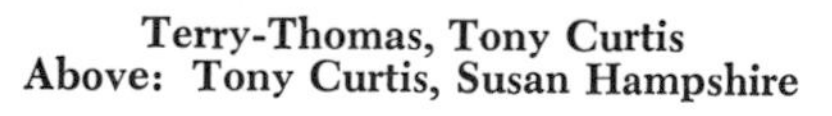

Terry-Thomas, Tony Curtis
Above: Tony Curtis, Susan Hampshire

Bourvil, Susan Hampshire
Top: Susan Hampshire

KRAKATOA, EAST OF JAVA

(CINERAMA) Producer, William R. Forman; Co-Producer, Lester A. Sansom; Director, Bernard L. Kowalski; Screenplay, Clifford Gould, Bernard Gordon; Photography, Manuel Berenguer; Costumes, Laure de Zarate; Assistant Directors, Frank Kowalski, Jose Maria Ochoa; An American Broadcasting Companies Presentation in Technicolor; Music, DeVol; Songs, Mack David; May release.

CAST

Hanson .... Maximilian Schell
Laura .... Diane Baker
Connerly .... Brian Keith
Charley .... Barbara Werle
Rigby .... John Leyton
Giovanni .... Rossano Brazzi
Leoncavallo .... Sal Mineo
Danzig .... J. D. Cannon
Toshi .... Jacqui Chan
Jacobs .... Mark Lawrence
Bazooki Man .... Geoffrey Holder
Henley .... Niall MacGinnis
Jan .... Alan Hoskins
Guard .... Robert Hall
Japanese Divers .... Sumi Hari, Victoria Young, Medori Arimoto

Top Right: Maximilian Schell, Diane Baker, Peter Kowalski. Below: (C) Peter Kowalski, Maximilian Schell

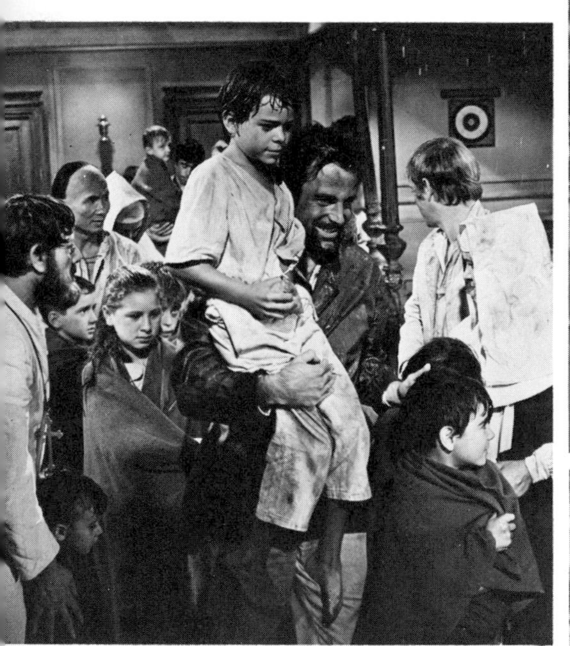

GOD FORGIVES—I DON'T!

(AMERICAN INTERNATIONAL) Producer, Enzo D'Ambrosio; Direction, Story and Screenplay, Giuseppe Colizzi; Photography, Alfio Contini; Music, Angel Oliver Pina; Assistant Director, Silvana Mangini Colizzi; In Berkey Pathe Color; May release.

CAST

Cat .... Terence Hill
Bill San Antonio .... Frank Wolff
Earp .... Bud Spencer
Rose .... Gina Rovere
Bud .... Jose Manuel Martin

Frank Wolff. Above: Terence Hill

ONCE UPON A TIME . . . IN THE WEST

(PARAMOUNT) Executive Producer, Fulvio Morsella; Associate Producer, Bino Cicogna; Director, Sergio Leone; Screenplay, Sergio Leone, Sergio Donati; Story, Dario Argento, Bernardo Bertolucci, Sergio Leone; Assistant Director, Giancarlo Santi; Photography, Tonino Delli Colli; Music, Ennio Morricone; A Rafran-San Marco Production in Widescreen and Technicolor; May release.

CAST

Frank .... Henry Fonda
Jill .... Claudia Cardinale
Cheyenne .... Jason Robards
The Man .... Charles Bronson
McBain .... Frank Wolff
Morton .... Gabriele Ferzetti
Sheriff .... Keenan Wynn
Sam .... Paolo Stoppa
Wobbles .... Marco Zuanelli
Barman .... Lionel Stander
Knuckles .... Jack Elam
Member of Frank's gang .... John Frederick
Stony .... Woody Strode
Timmy .... Enzo Santianello

Henry Fonda, Charles Bronson. Left Center: Claudia Cardinale, Jason Robards

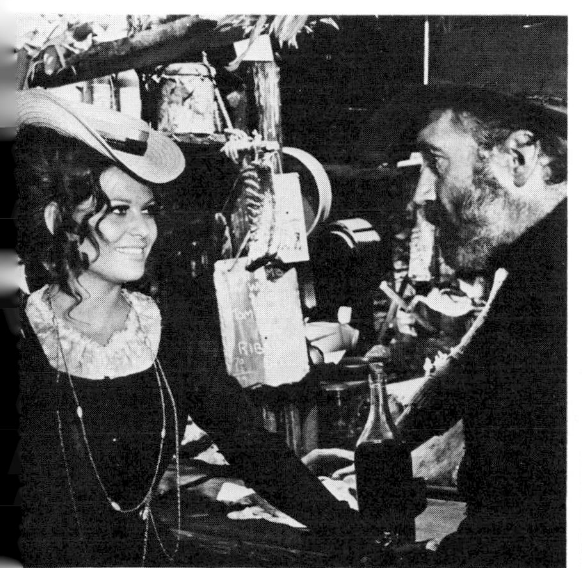

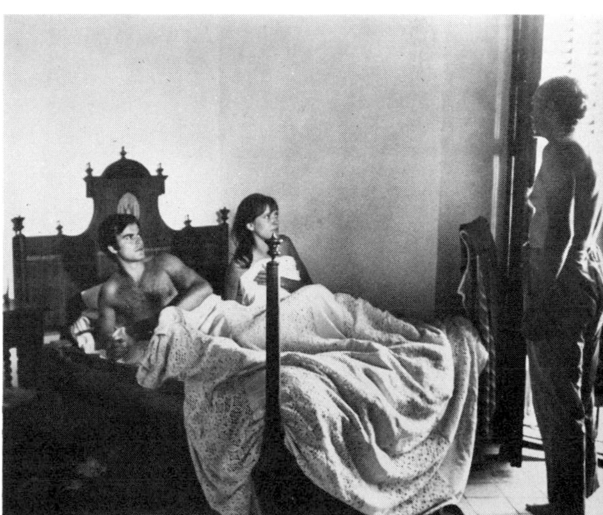

LAUGHTER IN THE DARK

(LOPERT) Producer, Neil Hartley; Director, Tony Richardson; Screenplay, Edward Bond; Adapted from novel by Vladimir Nabokov; Photography, Dick Bush; Assistant Directors, Andrew Grieve, Gerry Harrison, Terry Hodgkinson, Graham Cottle; A Woodfall Films Production in Widescreen and DeLuxe Color; May release.

CAST

Sir Edward More .... Nicol Williamson
Margot .... Anna Karina
Herve Tourace .... Jean-Claude Drouot
Paul .... Peter Bowles
Lady Pamela More .... Sian Phillips
Brian .... Sebastian Breaks
Amelia More .... Kate O'Toole
Chauffeur .... Edward Gardener
Maid .... Helen Booth
Miss Porly .... Sheila Burrell
Colonel .... Willoughby Goddard
Woman at gallery .... Mavis Villiers
Girl at gallery .... Allison Blair
Girls at party .... Diana Harris, Celia Brook
Art Dealers .... Basil Dignam, John Atkinson, Donald Bissett, John Golightly

Nicol Williamson, Anna Karina. Above: Jean-Claude Drouot, Anna Karina, Nicol Williamson

Richard Jaeckel, Robert Horton, Luciana Paluzzi. Below: Jaeckel, Horton

THE GREEN SLIME

(MGM) Producers, Ivan Reiner, Walter H. Manley; Director, Kinji Fukasaku; Screenplay, Charles Sinclair, William Finger, Tom Rowe; Music, Toshiaki Tsushima; Photography, Yoshikazu Yamasawa; Assistant Producers, Kaname Ogisawa, Kohji Ohta; Associate Producer, William Ross; Assistant Director, Kazuhiko Yamaguchi; Costumes, Mami; In Metrocolor; May release.

CAST

Jack Rankin .... Robert Horton
Vince Elliott .... Richard Jaeckel
Lisa Benson .... Luciana Paluzzi
Jonathan Thompson .... Bud Widom
Dr. Halvorsen .... Ted Gunther
Capt. Martin .... Robert Dunham
Lt. Curtis .... David Yorston
Ferguson .... William Ross
Cordier .... Gary Randolf
Michael .... Richard Hylland
Doctor .... Strong Ilimaiti
Barnett .... Arthur Stark
Secretary .... Lynne Frederickson
Sargent .... Tom Conrad
Officer .... David Sentman
Patient .... Clarence Howard
Soldiers .... Hans Jorgseeberger, Bob Morris
Rocket Pilots .... Jack Morris, Carl Bengs, Tom Scott
Technicians .... Don Plante, Enver Altenbay, Gunther Greve, Eugene Vince, George Uruf
Nurses .... Linda Hardisty, Kathy Horan, Ann Ault, Susan Skersick, Helen Kirkpatrick, Linda Miller, Patricia Elliot, Linda Malson

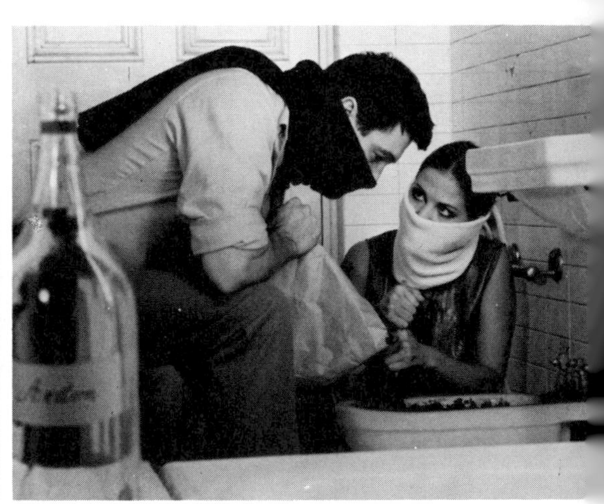

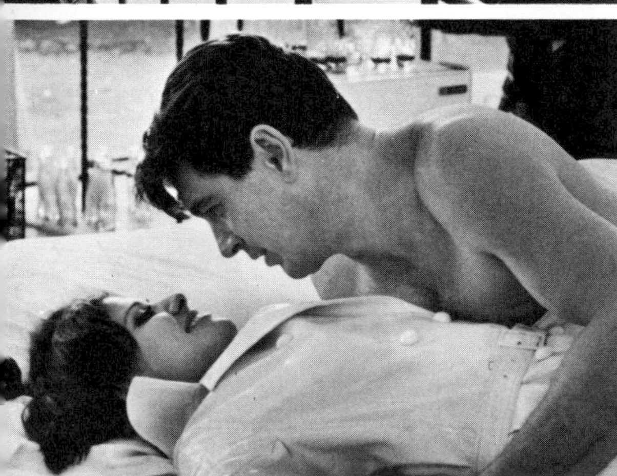

Claudia Cardinale, Rock Hudson (also right center)

A FINE PAIR

(NATIONAL GENERAL) Executive Producer, Franco Cristaldi; Producer, Leo L. Fuchs; Director, Francesco Maselli; Story, Luisa Montagnana; Screenplay, Francesco Maselli, Luisa Montagnana, Larry Gelbart, Virgil C. Leone; Photography, Alfio Contini; Music, Ennio Morricone; Costumes, Enrico Sabbatini; A Vides Film in Technicolor; May release.

CAST

Capt. Mike Harmon .... Rock Hudson
Esmeralda .... Claudia Cardinale
Roger .... Tomas Milian
Chief Wellman .... Leon Askin
Mrs. Walker .... Ellen Corby
Franz .... Walter Giller
Uncle Camillo .... Guido Alberti
Albert .... Peter Dane

RING OF BRIGHT WATER

(CINERAMA) Executive Producer, Edgar J. Scherick; Producer, Joseph Strick; Director, Jack Couffer; Screenplay, Jack Couffer, Bill Travers; Based on novel by Gavin Maxwell; Assistant Producer, Betty Botley; Music, Frank Cordell; Assistant Directors, Ernie Lewis, Brian Lawrence; A Brightwater Film Production and Palomar Presentation in Technicolor; June release.

CAST

Graham Merrill	Bill Travers
Mary MacKenzie	Virginia McKenna
Colin Wilcox	Peter Jeffrey
Storekeeper	Jameson Clark
Flora	Helena Gloag
Lighthouse Keeper	W. D. Joss
Bus Driver	Roddy McMillan
Sarah	Jean Taylor-Smith

and Christopher Benjamin, Kevin Collins, Archie Duncan, June Ellis, Philippa Gail, Tommy Godfrey, Walter Hall, Bill Horsley, Phil McCall, Philip Morant, Michael O'Halloran, John Young.

Left: Virginia McKenna, Bill Travers
Below: Bill Travers, Mijbil

Sally Geeson, Christopher Lee. Right Center: Hilary Dwyer, Vincent Price

THE OBLONG BOX

(AMERICAN INTERNATIONAL) Producer-Director, Gordon Hessler; Executive Producer, Louis M. Heyward; Screenplay, Lawrence Huntingdon; Based on story by Edgar Allen Poe; Photography, John Coquillon; Music, Harry Robinson; In Color by Berkey Pathe; June release.

CAST

Julian	Vincent Price
Dr. Neuhartt	Christopher Lee
Sir Edward Markham	Alastair Williamson
Elizabeth	Hilary Dwyer
Samuel Trench	Peter Arne
N'Galo	Harry Baird
Mark Norton	Carl Rigg
Tom Hackett	Maxwell Shaw
Ruddock	Michael Balfour
Weller	Godfrey James
Joshua Kemp	Rupert Davies
Sally Baxter	Sally Geeson
Hawthorne	Ivor Dean

RUN WILD, RUN FREE

(COLUMBIA) Executive Producer, Andrew Donally; Producer, John Danischewsky; Director, Richard C. Sarafian; Screenplay, David Rook from his novel "The White Colt"; Photography, Wilkie Cooper; Assistant Director, Bill Graf, Jr.; Music, David Whitaker; An Irving Allen Production in Technicolor; June release.

CAST

The Moorman	John Mills
Philip Ransome	Mark Lester
Ellen Ransome	Sylvia Syms
James Ransome	Gordon Jackson
Reg	Bernard Miles
Diana	Fiona Fullerton

Right: John Mills, Mark Lester, Fiona Fullerton

Sylvia Syms, Mark Lester, Gordon Jackson
Above: Mark Lester

John Mills. Above: John Mills, Sylvia Syms

WISE GUYS

(UNIVERSAL) Producer, Michel Ardan; Screenplay, Robert Enrico, Jose Giovanni; From novel "Le Haut-Fer"; Photography, Jean Boffety; Music, Francois de Roubaix; Assistant Directors, Jean-Philippe Merand, Lionel De Souza; In Techniscope and Technicolor; June release.

CAST

Hector	Bourvil
Laurent	Lino Ventura
Jackie	Marie Dubois
Mick	Jean-Claude Rolland
Nenesse	Jess Hahn
Therraz	Nick Stephanini
Pelissier	Paul Crauchet
Capester	Roger Jacquet
Christiane	Henia Suchar
Yvonne	Reine Courtois
Fanfan	Pierre Frag
L'Educateur	Marc Eyraud
Skida	Constantin

Top: Bourvil, Lino Ventura
Top Right: Marie Dubois, Lino Ventura

Jean-Claude Rolland, Lino Ventura. Above: Jess Hahn, Marie Dubois, Lino Ventura, Bourvil, Jean-Claude Rolland

Jean Rochefort, Maria Schell, Yves Montand, Madeleine Renaud. Above: Montand, Clotilde Joano. Top: Jean-Pierre Marielle, Tanya Lopert

THE DEVIL BY THE TAIL

(LOPERT) Director, Philippe de Broca; Screenplay, Daniel Boulanger; Photography, Jean Penzer; Assistant Directors, Georges Pellegrin, Christian Fuin; Music, Georges Delerue; Costumes, Jacques Fonteray; A Franco-Italian Co-Production in DeLuxe Color; June release.

CAST

Cesar Maricorne	Yves Montand
Diane	Maria Schell
Georges	Jean Rochefort
Leroy-Martin	Jean-Pierre Marielle
Monsieur Patin	Claude Pieplu
Charlie	Xavier Gelin
Cookie	Tanya Lopert
Amelie	Marthe Keller
La Marquise	Madeleine Renaud
Balaze	Jacques Balutin
Schwartz	Pierre Tornade
Madame Passereau	Janine Berdin
Monsieur Passereau	Eddy Roos

Top: Clotilde Joano, Madeleine Renaud, Yves Montand, Maria Schell, Marthe Keller
Below: Marthe Keller, Xavier Gelin

THREE INTO TWO WON'T GO

(UNIVERSAL) Producer, Julian Blaustein; Director, Peter Hall; Screenplay, Edna O'Brien; From the novel by Andrea Newman; Photography, Walter Lassally; Assistant Director, Christopher Dryhurst; In Color; June release.

CAST

Steve Howard	Rod Steiger
Frances	Claire Bloom
Ella Patterson	Judy Geeson
Belle	Peggy Ashcroft
Jack	Paul Rogers
Janet	Lynn Farleigh
Marcia	Elizabeth Spriggs
Beth	Sheila Allen

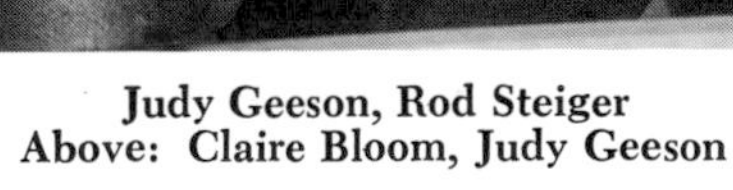

Judy Geeson, Rod Steiger
Above: Claire Bloom, Judy Geeson

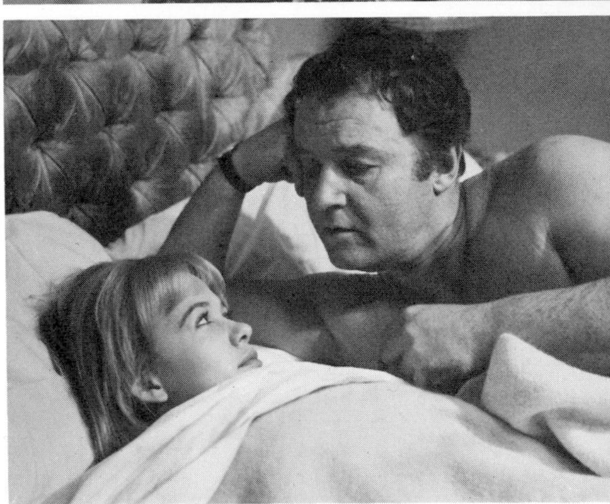

Judy Geeson, Rod Steiger
Above: Claire Bloom, Rod Steiger
Top: Geeson, Steiger, Bloom

YOU ONLY LOVE ONCE

(SIGMA III) Executive Producers, Rene Thevenet, Louis Duchesne; Director, Dirk Sanders; Screenplay, Dirk Sanders; Photography, Roger Duculot; Music, Jacques Loussier; In Color; June release.

CAST

Clara	Karen Blanguernon
Julie	Leslie Bedos
Patrice	Frederic de Pasquale
Roger	Jean Moussy
Rene	Victor Lanoux
Charles	Rene Goliard

Leslie Bedos, Karen Blanguernon. Top Right: Frederic de Pasquale

THAT COLD DAY IN THE PARK

(COMMONWEALTH UNITED) Producers, Donald Factor, Leon Mirell; Director, Robert Altman; Screenplay, Gillian Freeman; Based on novel by Richard Miles; Music, Johnny Mandel; Photography, Laslo Kovacs; Associate Producer, Robert Eggenweiler; In Eastman Color; June release.

CAST

Frances Austen	Sandy Dennis
The Boy	Michael Burns
Nina	Susanne Benton
Nick	John Garfield, Jr.
The Girl	Luana Anders

Sandy Dennis, Michael Burns
Above: Michael Burns

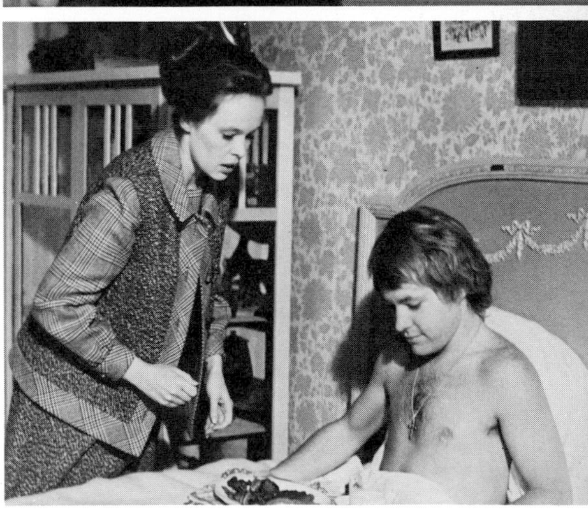

Sandy Dennis, Michael Burns. Above: Sandy Dennis. Top: Michael Burns, Susanne Benton, John Garfield, Jr.

SECRET WORLD

(20th CENTURY-FOX) Producer, Jacques Strauss; Director, Robert Freeman; Screenplay, Gerard Brach, Jackie Glass; Music, Antoine Duhamel; Photography, Peter Biziou; Associate Director, Alain Franchet; In DeLuxe Color; July release.

CAST

Wendy .... Jacqueline Bisset
Florence .... Giselle Pascal
Philippe .... Pierre Zimmer
Olivier .... Marc Porel
Francois .... Jean-Francois Maurin

Left: Jean-Francois Maurin, Jacqueline Bisset

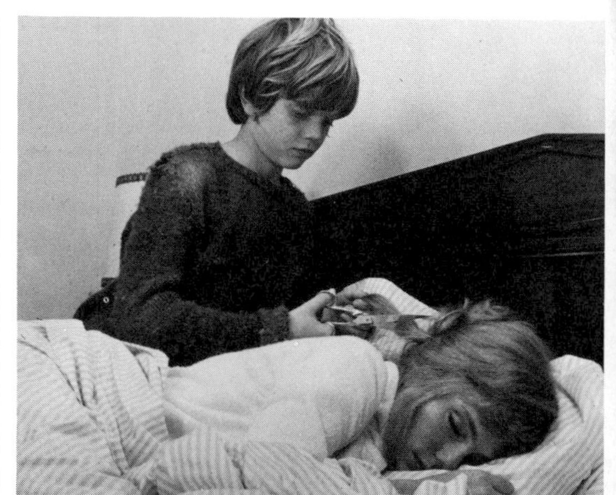

Jacqueline Bisset, Jean-Francois Maurin, Marc Porel (also above)

THE BEST HOUSE IN LONDON

(MGM) Producers, Philip Breen, Kurt Unger; Director, Philip Saville; Screenplay, Denis Norden; Music, Mischa Spoliansky; Photography, Alex Thomson; Assistant Director, David Tringham; Associate Producer, Clifford Parkes; Costumes, Yvonne Blake; A Carlo Ponti Production in Eastmancolor; July release.

CAST

Walter Leybourne and Benjamin Oakes	David Hemmings
Josephine Pacefoot	Joanna Pettet
Sir Francis Leybourne	George Sanders
Babette	Dany Robin
Count Pandolfo	Warren Mitchell
Home Secretary	John Bird
Sylvester Wall	William Rushton
Inspector MacPherson	Bill Fraser
Editor of "Times"	Maurice Denham
Chinese Trade Attache	Wolfe Morris
Headmistress	Martita Hunt
Charles Dickens	Arnold Diamond
Lord Tennyson	Hugh Burden
Oscar Wilde	John DeMarco
Lady Dilke	Jan Holden
Algernon Charles Swinburne	Mike Lennox
Mr. Fortnum	Arthur Howard
Mr. Mason	Clement Freud
Dr. Livingstone	Neal Arden
Mr. Barrett	Walter Brown
Miss Elizabeth Barrett	Suzanne Hunt
Flora	Carol Friday
Phoebe	Marie Rogers
Singer	Tessie O'Shea
Flora's Mother	Avril Angers
Felicity	Betty Marsden

Top: Joanna Pettet (C)
Below: Dany Robin, George Sanders

David Hemmings, Joanna Pettet, also above with Warren Mitchell. Top: David Hemmings, Joanna Pettet(R)

MARRY ME! MARRY ME!

(ALLIED ARTISTS) Produced, Directed and Written by Claude Berri; Photography, Ghislain Cloquet; Assistant Directors, Pierre Grunstein, Claude Confortez; Music, Emile Stern; Costumes, Paola Pilla; In DeLuxe Color; Original Soundtrack Album on RCA Records; July release.

CAST

Isabelle	Elisabeth Wiener
Marthe	Regine
Mme. Schmoll	Luisa Colpeyn
M. Schmoll	Gregoire Aslan
Helen	Prudence Harrington
Second English Teacher	Betsy Blair
Claude	Claude Berri
M. Avram	Gabriel Jabbour
Mme. Avram	Estera Galion

Right: Claude Berri, Elisabeth Wiener
Below: Regine

Rupert Davies, George Roubicek, James Caan
Above: Diana Beevers, David Sumner

SUBMARINE X-1

(UNITED ARTISTS) Producer, John C. Champion; Director, William Graham; Executive Producer, Irving Temaner; Screenplay, Donald S. Sanford, Guy Elmes; Photography, Paul Beeson; Associate Producer, Ted Lloyd; Assistant Director, Anthony Waye; A Mirisch Film in DeLuxe Color; August release.

CAST

Commander Bolton	James Caan
Vice Admiral Redmayne	Rupert Davies
Lt. Davies	David Sumner
Lt. Gogan	William Dysart
Sub Lt. Pennington	Norman Bowler
CPO Barquist	Brian Grellis
Leading Seaman Quentin	Paul Young
Sub Lt. Willis	John Kelland
CPO Knowles	Kenneth Farrington
Sub Lt. X-3	Keith Alexander
CPO Kennedy	Carl Rigg
Redmayne's Flag Officer	George Roubicek
Leading Seaman X-2	Steve Kirby
Leading Seaman X-1	Nicholas Tate
Sub Lt. X-1	Dennis Mayers
WREN Officer	Diana Beevers
Cmdr. Steiner	Paul Hansard
German Lieutenant	Hans De Vries
Captain R. N.	Richard Steele
Naval Doctor	Desmond Jordan
Captain Erlich	George Pravda

THANK YOU ALL VERY MUCH

(COLUMBIA) Producers, Max Rosenberg, Milton Subotsky; Executive Producer, Edgar J. Scherick; Director, Waris Hussein; Screenplay, Margaret Drabble; Based on her novel "The Millstone"; Photography, Peter Suchitzky; In Technicolor; August release.

CAST

Rosamund	Sandy Dennis
George	Ian McKellen
Lydia	Eleanor Bron
Roger	John Standing
Joe	Michael Coles
Sister Harvey	Rachel Kempson
Mrs. Stacey	Peggy Thorpe-Bates
Mr. Stacey	Kenneth Benda
Octavia	Sarah Whalley
Miss Guernsey	Shelagh Fraser
Beatrice	Deborah Stanford
Sister Bennett	Margaret Tyzack

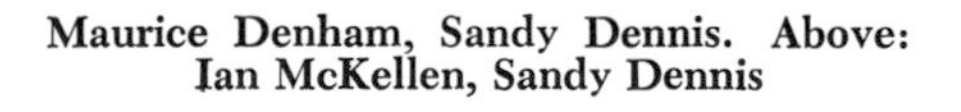

Maurice Denham, Sandy Dennis. Above: Ian McKellen, Sandy Dennis

Sandy Dennis (also above and top)

JUSTINE

(20th CENTURY-FOX) Producer, Pandro S. Berman; Director, George Cukor; Associate Producer, Kathryn Hereford; Screenplay, Lawrence B. Marcus; Based on "The Alexandria Quartet" by Lawrence Durell; Music, Jerry Goldsmith; Costumes, Irene Sharaff; Choreography, Gemze de Lappe; Photography, Leon Shamroy; Assistant Director, Maurice Vaccarino; In Panavision and DeLuxe Color; August release.

CAST

Justine	Anouk Aimee
Pursewarden	Dirk Bogarde
Narouz	Robert Forster
Melissa	Anna Karina
Pombal	Philippe Noiret
Darley	Michael York
Nessim	John Vernon
Cohen	Jack Albertson
Toto	Cliff Gorman
Mountolive	George Baker
Liza	Elaine Church
Memlik Pasha	Michael Constantine
French Consul General	Marcel Dalio
Mnemjian	Michael Dunn
Maskelyne	Barry Morse
Balthazar	Severn Darden
Mrs. Serapamoun	Amapola Del Vando
Proprietor	Abraham Sofaer
Kawwass	Peter Mamkos
Serapamoun	Stanley Waxman
Woman at ball	DeAnn Mears
Prisoner	Tutte Lemkow

Cliff Gorman, Dirk Bogarde, John Vernon, Anouk Aimee, Michael York. Above: Bogarde, Aimee. Top: Vernon, Aimee, Robert Forster

Michael York, Jack Albertson
Above: Michael York, Anouk Aimee

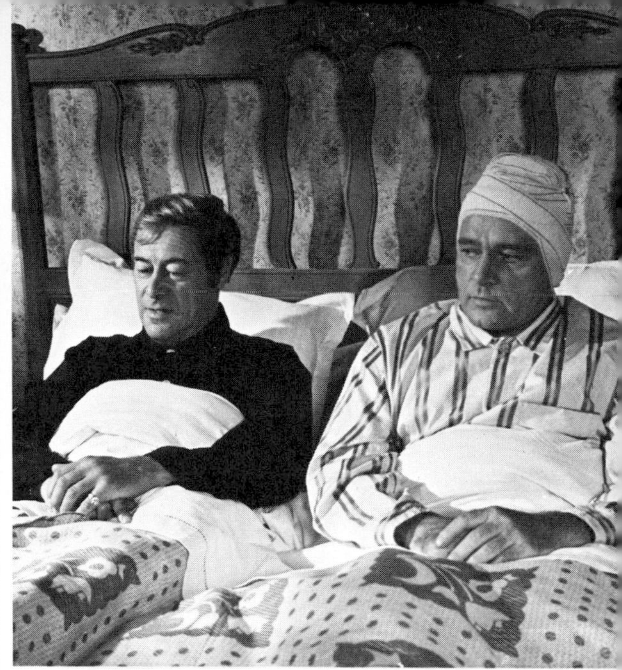

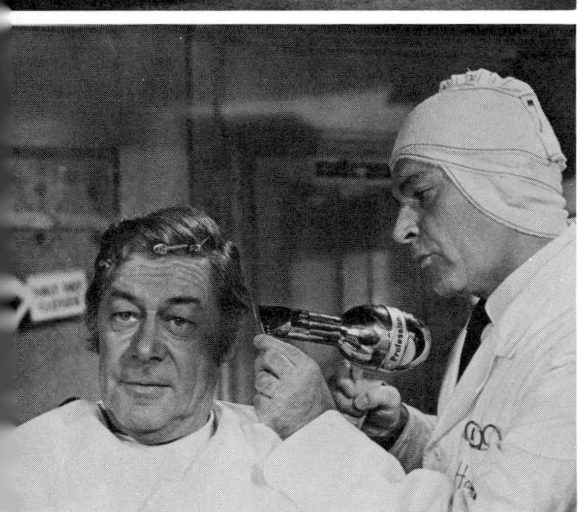

STAIRCASE

(20th CENTURY-FOX) Producer-Director, Stanley Donen; Screenplay, Charles Dyer; From his play; Music, Dudley Moore; Photography, Christopher Challis; Assistant Directors, Marc Grunebaum, Pierre Roubaud; In Panavision and DeLuxe Color; August release.

CAST

Harry	Richard Burton
Charlie	Rex Harrison
Harry's Mother	Cathleen Nesbitt
Charlie's Mother	Beatrix Lehmann
Jack	Stephen Lewis
Policeman	Neil Wilson
Postman	Gordon Heath
Miss Ricard	Avril Angers
Cub Mistress	Shelagh Fraser
Matron	Gwen Nelson
Nurse	Pat Heywood
Gravedigger	Dermot Kelly
Choirboy	Jake Kavanagh
Opening Song	Rogers and Starr

Richard Burton, Cathleen Nesbitt. Above and Top: Rex Harrison, Richard Burton

ON MY WAY TO THE CRUSADES, I MET A GIRL WHO . . .

(WARNER BROS.-7 ARTS) Producer, Francesco Mazzei; Director, Pasquale Festa Campanile; Screenplay, Luigi Magni, Larry Gelbart; Photography, Carlo di Palma; Costumes, Danilo Donati; Music, Riz Ortolani; Assistant Directors, Elvira D'Amico, Carlo Cotti; In Technicolor; September release.

CAST

Guerrando da Montone	Tony Curtis
Boccadoro	Monica Vitti
Sultan of Bari	Hugh Griffith
Drogone	John Richardson
Duke of Padolfo	Ivo Garrani
Marculfo	Nino Castelnuovo
Bertuccio	Franco Sportelli
Hermit	Lauro Gazzolo

Top Left: Tony Curtis, Monica Vitti

DE SADE

(AMERICAN INTERNATIONAL) Producers, Samuel Z. Arkoff, James H. Nicholson; Executive Producers, Arthur Brauner, Louis M. Heyward; Director, Cy Enfield; Screenplay, Richard Matheson; Photography, Heinz Pehlke; Music, Billy Strange; Assistant Director, Alex von Richthofen; Costumes, Vangie Harrison; Color by Berkey Pathe; September release.

CAST

Marquis de Sade	Keir Dullea
Anne Montreuil	Senta Berger
Mme. de Montreuil	Lilli Palmer
Renee de Montreuil	Anna Massey
La Beauvoisin	Sonja Ziemann
Rose Keller	Uta Levka
M. de Montreuil	Herbert Weissbach
Marquis' Mistress	Christiane Kruger
de Sade as a boy	Max Kiebach
The Abbe	John Huston

Left: Anna Massey, Keir Dullea

Susan George, Victor Henry

ALL NEAT IN BLACK STOCKINGS

(NATIONAL GENERAL) Producer, Leon Clore; Director, Christopher Morahan; Co-Producer, John Arnold; Screenplay, Jane Gaskell, Hugh Whitemore; Based on novel by Jane Gaskell; Photography, Larry Pizer; Assistant Directors, Ted Morley, Ewan Pearson, Philip Livingstone; An Anglo Amalgamated-National General Production in Technicolor; September release.

CAST

Ginger	Victor Henry
Jill	Susan George
Dwyer	Jack Shepherd
Carole	Vanessa Forsyth
Old Gunge	Terence De Marney
Sis	Anna Cropper
Issur	Harry Towb
Babette	Jasmina Hamzavi
New Bird	Deirdre Costello
Jocasta	Nita Lorraine
First Bird	Rosalind Elliott
Mother	Clare Kelly
Hospital Sister	Anna Welsh
First Orderly	Geoffrey Reed
Second Orderly	Michael McKevitt
New Bird	Tanya Trude
Businessman	Eric Longworth
Pakistani	Shivendra Sinha
Suburban Housewife	Gwendolyn Watts
Young Bloke	Graham Jones
Toddler	Marc Bregman

TWO GENTLEMEN SHARING

(AMERICAN INTERNATIONAL) Producer, J. Barry Kulick; Director, Ted Kotcheff; Screenplay, Evan Jones; From novel by David Stuart Leslie; Associate Producer, Douglas Pierce; Photography, Billy Williams; Music, Stanley Myers; Assistant Director, Scott Wodehouse; Costumes, Gabriella Falk; Presented by Samuel Z. Arkoff and James H. Nicholson; In Movielab Color Prints; September release.

CAST

Roddy	Robin Phillips
Jane	Judy Geeson
Andrew	Hal Frederick
Caroline	Esther Anderson
Phil	Norman Rossington
Ethne	Hilary Dwyer
Mrs. Ashby-Kydd	Rachel Kempson
Amanda	Daisy Mae Williams
Marcus	Ram John Holder
Charles	Earl Cameron
Helen	Shelagh Fraser
Mr. Pater	David Markham
Mrs. Pater	Avice Landon
Mr. Burrows	Philip Stone
Mrs. Burrows	Elspeth March
Mutt	Thomas Baptiste
Jeff	Linbert Spencer
Bizerte	Willy Payne
Eugene Valentine	Thors Piers
Chicomo	Nathan Dambuza
O'Reilly	Robert Burnell
Dickson Senior	Hamilton Dyce
Dickson Junior	John Humphrey
Young Man	Harold Lang
Bill	Lionel Ngakane

Esther Anderson, Robin Phillips. Above: Hilary Dwyer, Phillips. Top: Anderson, Hal Frederick, Judy Geeson

Judy Geeson, Philip Stone
Above: Robin Phillips, Judy Geeson

ADALEN 31

(PARAMOUNT) Direction and Screenplay, Bo Widerberg; Photography, Jorgen Persson; Produced by AB Svensk Filmindustri in Techniscope and Technicolor; October release.

CAST

Kjell	Peter Schildt
His Mother	Kerstin Tidelius
His Father	Roland Hedlund
His brother Ake	Stefan Feierbach
His brother Martin	Martin Widerberg
Anna	Marie DeGeer
Her Mother	Anita Bjork
Her Father	Olof Bergstrom
Strikebreaker	Olle Bjorling
Nisse	Jonas Bergstrom
Foreman	Pierre Lindstedt

Marie DeGeer, also left, and top with Peter Schildt

LOCK UP YOUR DAUGHTERS!

(COLUMBIA) Producer, David Deutsch; Director, Peter Coe; Associate Producer, Anthony Nelson Keys; Photography, Peter Suschitzky; Based on Lionel Bart-Laurie Johnson musical that was based on Henry Fielding's "Rape Upon Rape," and Sir John Vanbrugh's "The Relapse"; Assistant Director, Bert Batt; Costumes, Alan Barrett; In Color; October release.

CAST

Lord Foppington .... Christopher Plummer
Hilaret .... Susannah York
Mrs. Squeezum .... Glynis Johns
Ramble .... Ian Bannen
Shaftoe .... Tom Bell
Cloris .... Elaine Taylor
Lusty .... Jim Dale
Lady Clumsey .... Kathleen Harrison
Sir Tunbelly Clumsey .... Roy Kinnear
Nell .... Georgia Brown
Hoyden .... Vanessa Howard
Gossip .... Roy Dotrice
Lady Eager .... Fenella Fielding
Lord Eager .... Paul Dawkins
Mr. Justice Squeezum .... Peter Bayliss
Coupler .... Richard Wordsworth
Bull .... Peter Bull
Staff .... Wallas Eaton
Quill .... Trevor Ray
Faithful .... Blake Butler
Night Watchman .... Arthur Mullard
Mr. Justice Worthy .... Edward Atienza
La Verole .... Michael Darbyshire
Nurse .... Patricia Routledge
Bottle .... Roy Pember
Earl of Ware .... Fred Emney
Nobleman .... John Morley
Boswell .... Clive Morton
Johnsonian Figure .... Roger Hammond
Clerk of the Court .... Tony Sumpson
Constables .... Martin Crosbie, Cecil Sheehan, Tom Irwin, Danny O'Connor, Vernon Hayden, Derry Power

Peter Bayliss, Susannah York
Top Right: Ian Bannen, Jim Dale, Tom Bell

Georgia Brown, Christopher Plummer
Above: Christopher Plummer (C)

Francoise Brion, Jacques Doniol-Valcroze (also above)

L'IMMORTELLE

(GROVE) Executive Producers, Michel Fano, Samy Halfon; Directed and Written by Alain Robbe-Grillet; Photography, Maurice Barry; Music, Georges Delerue, Tashin Kavalcioglu; Produced by Tamara Films, Como Films, and Dino de Laurentiis; October release.

CAST

She .... Francoise Brion
He .... Jacques Doniol-Valcroze and Guido Celano

THE BATTLE OF BRITAIN

(UNITED ARTISTS) Producers, Harry Saltzman, S. Benjamin Fisz; Director, Guy Hamilton; Screenplay, James Kennaway, Wilfred Greatorex; Photography, Freddy Young, Bob Huke, Skeets Kelly, John Jordan; Associate Producer, John Palmer; Assistant Director, Derek Cracknell; In Panavision and Technicolor; October release.

CAST

Senior Civil Servant ---------- Harry Andrews
Sqn. Ldr. Canfield ---------- Michael Caine
Air Vice Marshall Keith Park -- Trevor Howard
Baron von Richter ---------- Curt Jurgens
Sgt. Pilot Andy ---------- Ian McShane
Group Captain Baker ---------- Kenneth More
Air Chief Marshal Sir Hugh Dowding ---------- Laurence Olivier
Group Captain Hope ---------- Nigel Patrick
Flt. Lt.-Sqn. Ldr. Harvey ---------- Christopher Plummer
Air Vice Marshal Evill ---------- Michael Redgrave
British Minister in Switzerland ---------- Ralph Richardson
Sqn. Ldr. Skipper ---------- Robert Shaw
Air Vice Marshal Trafford Leigh-Mallory ---------- Patrick Wymark
Section Officer Harvey ---------- Susannah York
Warrant Officer Warrick ---------- Michael Bates
Andy's Wife ---------- Isla Blair
Farmer ---------- John Bascomb
Asst. Controller ---------- Tom Chatto
Jamie ---------- James Cosmo.
Wing Cmdr. Willoughby ---------- Robert Flemyng
Sqn. Ldr. Evans ---------- W. G. Foxley
Sgt. Pilot Chris ---------- David Griffin
Senior Air Staff Officer ---------- Jack Gwillim
Peter ---------- Myles Hoyle
Flt. Sgt. Arthur ---------- Duncan Lamont
Skipper's Wife ---------- Sarah Lawson
Pasco ---------- Mark Malicz
French NCO ---------- Andre Maranne
A Minister ---------- Anthony Nicholls
Simon ---------- Nicholas Pennell
Ox ---------- Andrzey Scibor
Jean Jacques ---------- Jean Wladon
Kesselring ---------- Peter Hager
Goering ---------- Hein Reiss
Hitler ---------- Rolf Stiefel

Michael Caine. Top Right: Michael Redgrave, Laurence Olivier

Robert Shaw. Above: Christopher Plummer, Susannah York

ALFRED THE GREAT

(MGM) Producer, Bernard Smith; Director, Clive Donner; Screenplay, Ken Taylor, James R. Webb; Story, James R. Webb; From novel by Elenor Shipley Duckett; Photography, Alex Thomson; Music, Raymond Leppard; Costumes, Jocelyn Rickards; Assistant Director, Peter Price; In Panavision and Metrocolor; October release.

CAST

Alfred	David Hemmings
Guthrum	Michael York
Aelhswith	Prunella Ransome
Asher	Colin Blakely
Athelstan	Julian Glover
Rober	Ian McKellen
Ethelred	Alan Dobie
Buhrud	Peter Vaughan
Ivar	Julian Chagrin
Wulfstan	Barry Jackson
Freda	Vivien Merchant
Cerdic	Christopher Timothy
Cuthbert	John Rees
Edwin	Andrew Bradford
Offa	Michael Billington
Bishop	Ralph Nossek
Olaf	David Glaisyer
Brother Thomas	Eric Brooks
Hadric	Keith Buckley
Sigurd	Trevor Jones
Eafa	Peter Plythe

David Hemmings, Prunella Ransome, Michael York. Above: Colin Blakely (L), David Hemmings, Prunella Ransome

Vivien Merchant. Above: Michael York, Prunella Ransome. Top: Michael York (C)

Robert Shaw, Christopher Plummer (also above). Top: Leonard Whiting, Robert Shaw

THE ROYAL HUNT OF THE SUN

(NATIONAL GENERAL) Producers, Eugene Frenke, Philip Yordan; Director, Irving Lerner; Screenplay, Philip Yordan; Based on play by Peter Shaffer; Photography, Peter Barlow; Assistant Director, Jose Maria Ochoa; Costumes, Anthony Powell; In Technicolor; October release.

CAST

Pizarro .... Robert Shaw
Atahuallpa .... Christopher Plummer
DeSoto .... Nigel Davenport
Estete .... Michael Craig
Young Martin .... Leonard Whiting
Valverde .... Andrew Keir
King Carlos V .... James Donald
Candia .... William Marlowe
Diego .... Percy Herbert
DeNizza .... Alexander Davion
Felipillo .... Sam Krauss

Top: Christopher Plummer
Below: Nigel Davenport, Robert Shaw

OH! WHAT A LOVELY WAR

(PARAMOUNT) Producers, Brian Duffy, Richard Attenborough; Director, Richard Attenborough; Associate Producer, R. L. M. Davidson; Assistant Director, Claude Watson; Photography, Gerry Turpin; Choreographer, Eleanor Fazan; Costumes, Anthony Mendleson; In Technicolor; October release.

CAST

Grandpa Smith .... John Rae
Mother Smith .... Mary Wimbush
Bertie Smith .... Corin Redgrave
George Smith .... Maurice Roeves
Jack Smith .... Paul Shelley
Freddie Smith .... Malcolm McFee
Harry Smith .... Colin Farrell
Betty Smith .... Angela Thorne
Flo Smith .... Wendy Allnutt
Dickie Smith .... Kim Smith
Emma Smith as a baby .... Kathleen Wileman
Emma Smith as a girl .. Charlotte Attenborough
Sir John French .... Laurence Olivier
Count Leopold von Berchtold .... John Gielgud
Sir Edward Grey .... Ralph Richardson
Sir Henry Wilson .... Michael Redgrave
Von Moltke .... John Clements
Sir Douglas Haig .... John Mills
Sylvia Pankhurst .... Vanessa Redgrave
Stephen .... Dirk Bogarde
Eleanor .... Susannah York
Music Hall Star .... Maggie Smith
Emperor Franz Josef .... Jack Hawkins
Kaiser Wilhelm II .... Kenneth More
Poincare .... Ian Holm
Tsar Nicholas .... Paul Daneman
French Colonel .... Jean Pierre Cassel
French Singer .... Pia Colombo
Fritz .... Christian Doermer
Poppyman .... Joe Melia
Rich Man .... Cecil Parker
Staff Major .... Robert Flemyng
Nurses .... Nanette Newman, Juliet Mills and David Lodge (Sgt.), Wensley Pithey (Archduke Ferdinand), Frank Forsyth (Woodrow Wilson), John Gabriel (Lenin), Anthony Morton (Italian Attache), Steve Plytas (Turkish Attache), Meriel Forbes (Lady Grey), Pamela Abbott (Tsarina), Stella Courtney (Mme. Poincare), Elizabeth Craven (Kaiserin), Ruth Gower (Von Moltke's Lady), Kathleen Helme (Berchtold's Lady), Ruth Kettlewell (Archduchess), Phyllis Calvert (Lady Haig), Natasha Parry (Barbara), Isobel Dean (Fanny), Thorley Walters (Carlton), Guy Middleton (Robertson), Vincent Ball (Australian Soldier), Edward Fox (First Aide), Derek Newark (Dodds), Norman Bird (Training Sgt.), Gerald Sim (Chaplain)

Michael Redgrave, Laurence Olivier
Above: Vanessa Redgrave (C)

Susannah York, Dirk Bogarde
Top Left: The Smith Family

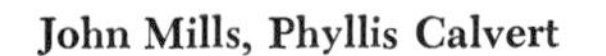
John Mills, Phyllis Calvert

Ralph Richardson, Kenneth More, Frank Forsyth, Ian Holm, John Gabriel

Top: Stella Courtney, Ian Holm, Paul Daneman, Pamela Abbott, Ruth Kettlewell, Wensley Pithey, Kenneth More, Elizabeth Craven, John Clements, Ruth Gower, John Gielgud

THE FILE OF THE GOLDEN GOOSE

(UNITED ARTISTS) Producer, David E. Rose; Director, Sam Wanamaker; Screenplay, John C. Higgins, James B. Gordon; Associate Producer, George Fowler; Photography, Ken Hodges; Assistant Director, Ray Frift; A Caralan-Dador Production in DeLuxe Color; October release.

CAST

Novak	Yul Brynner
Owl	Charles Gray
Thompson	Edward Woodward
Sloane	John Barrie
Tina	Adrienne Corri
Collins	Bernard Archard
Firenzo	Anthony Jacobs
Mueller	Karel Stepanek
Leeds	Walter Gotell
Smythe	Graham Crowden
Martin	Geoffrey Reed
Stroud	Ken Jones
Debbie	Janet Rossini
Grodie	Joe Cornelius
Vance	Denis Shaw
Croupier	Ray Marioni
Bongo Player	Illario Pedro
Laboratory Technician	Philip Anthony

Right: Edward Woodward, John Barrie, Yul Brynner. Above: Charles Gray, Yul Brynner

Nicol Williamson, Rachel Roberts
Above: Ann Bell, Nicol Williamson

THE RECKONING

(COLUMBIA) Producer, Ronald Shedlo; Director, Jack Gold; Screenplay, John McGrath; Based on novel "The Harp That Once" by Patrick Hall; Music, Malcolm Arnold; Photography, Geoffrey Unsworth; Assistant Director, Douglas Hermes; In Technicolor; October release.

CAST

Michael Marler	Nicol Williamson
Rosemary Marler	Ann Bell
Maria	Lilita De Barros
Brunzy	Tom Kempinski
Davidson	Kenneth Hendel
Moyle	Douglas Wilmer
Joan	Barbara Ewing
Hilda Greening	Zena Walker
John Hazlitt	Paul Rogers
Marler's Mother	Gwen Nelson
Kath	Christine Hargreaves
Dad (John Joe)	Ernest Jennings
Joyce Eglington	Rachel Roberts
Dr. Carolan	Godfrey Quigley
Father Madden	Desmond Perry
Singer	Patricia Gratton
Pop Group	The Spectrum
Cocky Burke	J. G. Devlin
Drunk	Joe Gladwin
Mitchell	Edward Hardwicke
Benham	John Normington
Mrs. Reynolds	Joan Henley
Sir Miles Bishton	John Hussey
Garner	Donald Douglas
Mrs. Garner	Sheila Gish
Mrs. Davies	Clare Kelly
Bottomly	Joby Blanshard
Aunt Tess	Catherine Finn
Aunt Nellie	Jean Campbell
Aunt Christina	Marjorie Hogan
Jones	Christian Rodska
Philip	John Malcolm

THE BRAIN

(PARAMOUNT) Producer, Alain Poire; Director, Gerard Oury; Screenplay, Adaptation, and Dialogue, Gerard Oury, Marcel Julian, Daniele Thompson; Music, Georges Delerue; Assistant Director, Marc Monnet; Costumes, Tanine Autre; A Gaumont International Production in Franscope and Eastmancolor; October release.

CAST

The Brain .... David Niven
Arthur .... Jean-Paul Belmondo
Anatole .... Bourvil
Scannapieco .... Eli Wallach
Sofia .... Silvia Monti
Bruno .... Fernand Valois
Le Commanissaire .... Raymond Gerome
Pochet .... Jacques Balutin
Duboeuf .... Jacques Ciron
Mazurel .... Fernand Guiot
Man from fifth floor .... Jean Le Poulain
Belgian with cold .... Robert Dalban
Belgians .... Raoul Del Frosse, Pierre Torrade, Paul Mercey
Chief Guard .... Henri Genes
Guards .... Yves Bersacq, Dominique Zardi
Superintendent Cummings .... Tommy Duggan
Brain's First Accomplice .... Guy Delorme
Second Accomplice .... Michel Garland

Right: Bourvil, Eli Wallach, David Niven
Above: Jean-Paul Belmondo, Bourvil

Eli Wallach. Right: Terence Hill, Eli Wallach, Brock Peters, Bud Spencer

ACE HIGH

(PARAMOUNT) Director, Giuseppe Colizzi; Produced by Chrono Cinematografica and Dinanziaria; In Techniscope and Technicolor; October release.

CAST

Cacopoulos .... Eli Wallach
Cat Stevens .... Terence Hill
Hutch .... Bud Spencer
Thomas .... Brock Peters
Drake .... Kevin McCarthy
Harold .... Steffen Zacharias
Paco Rosa .... Livio Lorenzon
Thomas' Wife .... Tiffany Hoyveld
Cangaceiro .... Remo Capitani

GOODBYE, MR. CHIPS

(MGM) Director, Herbert Ross; Associate Producer, Mort Abrahams; Screenplay, Terence Rattigan; Based on novel by James Hilton; Music and Lyrics, Leslie Bricusse; Photography, Oswald Morris; Costumes, Julie Harris; Assistant Director, Dominic Fulford; Produced by APJAC Productions in Panavision and Technicolor; November release.

CAST

Arthur Chipping	Peter O'Toole
Katherine	Petula Clark
Headmaster	Michael Redgrave
Lord Sutterwick	George Baker
Ursula Mossbank	Sian Phillips
Max Staefel	Michael Bryant
William Baxter	Jack Hedley
Headmaster's Wife	Alison Leggatt
Bill Calbury	Clinton Greyn
Mrs. Paunceforth	Barbara Couper
Johnny Longbridge	Michael Culver
Lady Sutterwick	Elspet Gray
General Paunceforth	Clive Morton
Algie	Ronnie Stevens
Sutterwick, Jr.	John Gugolka
David	Michael Ridgway
Farley	Tom Owen
Pompeii Guide	Mario Maranzana
Tilly	Sheila Steafel
Johnson	Jeremy Lloyd
Mrs. Summersthwaite	Elspeth March
New Boy	Craig Marriott
Price	Jack May
Elder Master	Leo Britt
Policeman	Boyston Tickner
Miss Honeybun	Patricia Hayes

and the boys of Sherborne School

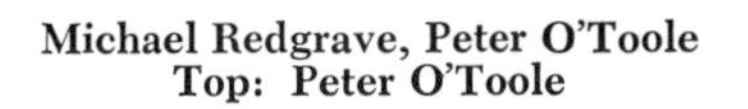

Michael Redgrave, Peter O'Toole
Top: Peter O'Toole

Petula Clark

Peter O'Toole, Petula Clark
(also above and top)

Peter O'Toole, Michael Bryant. Above: Peter
O'Toole. Top: Petula Clark, Peter O'Toole

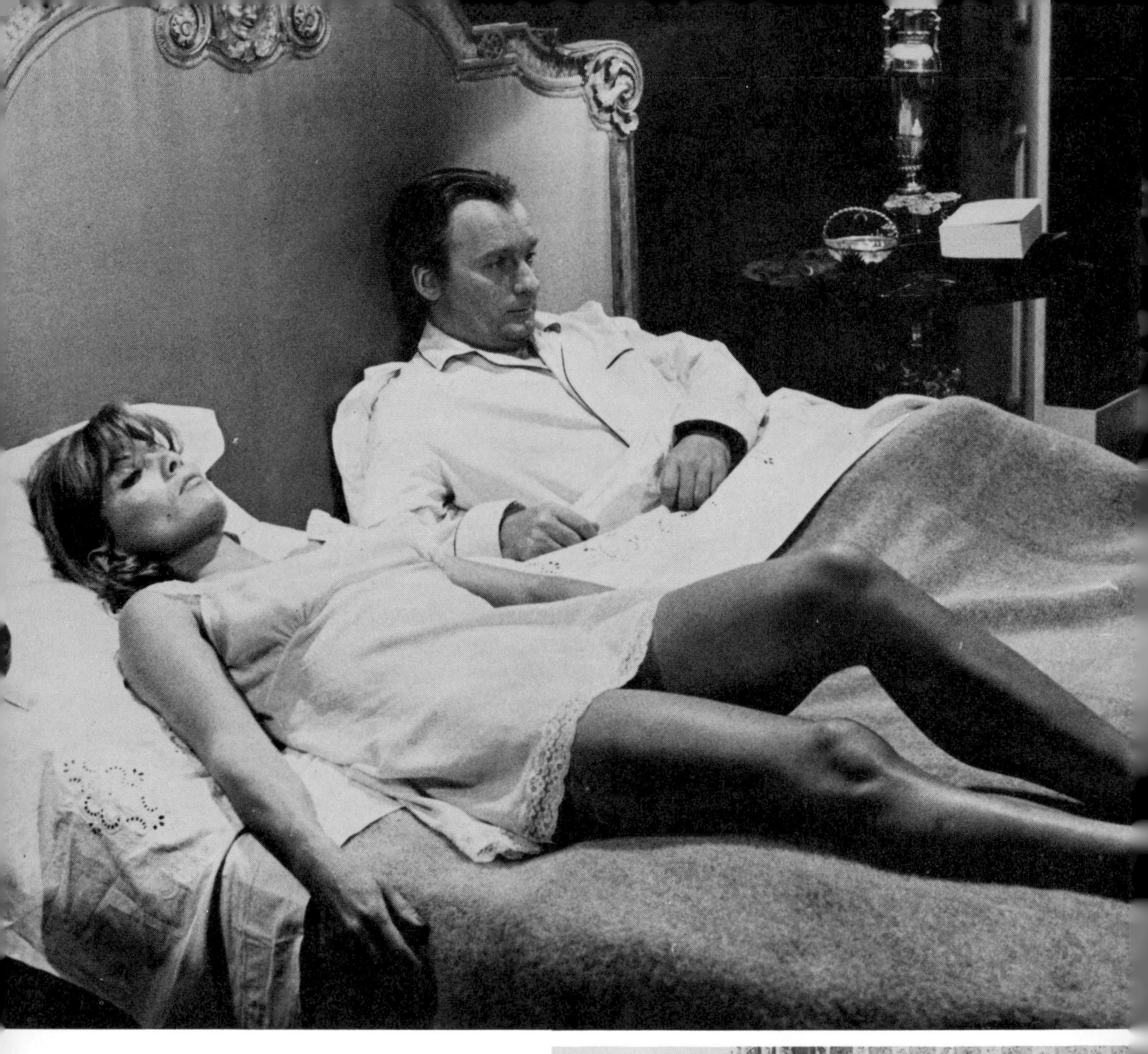

LA FEMME INFIDELE

(ALLIED ARTISTS) Producer, Andre Genoves; Direction and Screenplay, Claude Chabrol; Photography, Jean Rabier; In Eastman Color; November release.

CAST

Helene	Stephane Audran
Charles	Michel Bouquet
Victor	Maurice Ronet
Michel	Stephen Di Napolo
Inspector	Michel Duchaussoy
Police Detective	Guy Marly
Private Detective	Serge Bento

Stephane Audran,
also above with Michel Bouquet

Terry Whitmore, also above

TERRY WHITMORE, FOR EXAMPLE

(GROVE) Producer, Hasse Seiden; Director, Bill Brodie; Screenplay, Bill Brodie, Hasse Seiden; Photography, Hasse Seiden; November rëlease.

CAST

Terry Whitmore

THE DAMNED

(WARNER BROS.-7 ARTS) Producers, Alfredo Levy, Ever Haggiag; Director, Luchino Visconti; Executive Producer, Pietro Notarianni; Screenplay, Nicola Badalucco, Enrico Medioli, Luchino Visconti; Photography, Armando Nannuzzi, Pasquale de Santis; Music, Maurice Jarre; Costumes, Piero Tosi; Assistant Director, Albino Cocco; A Pegaso-Praesidens Film in Technicolor; December release.

CAST

Friederich Bruckmann .... Dirk Bogarde
Baroness Sophie von Essenbeck .. Ingrid Thulin
Aschenbach .... Helmut Griem
Martin von Essenbeck .... Helmut Berger
Elisabeth Thallman .... Charlotte Rampling
Olga .... Florinda Bolkan
Baron Konstantin
von Essenbeck .... Rene Kolldehoff
Herbert Thallman .... Umberto Orsini
Baron Joachim
von Essenbeck .... Albrecht Shoenhals
Guenther von Essenbeck .... Renaud Verley
Governess .... Nora Ricci
Lisa Keller .... Irina Wanka
Thilde (at 11) .... Valentina Ricci
Erika (at 8) .... Karin Mittendorf

Helmut Griem, Renaud Verley, Rene Kolldehoff, Ingrid Thulin, Helmut Berger, Charlotte Rampling. Top Left: Ingrid Thulin, Dirk Bogarde

Dirk Bogarde, Helmut Berger, Ingrid Thulin
Top: (R) Ingrid Thulin, Dirk Bogarde

HAMLET

(**COLUMBIA**) Producer, Neil Hartley; Director, Tony Richardson; Screenplay, William Shakespeare; Photography, Gerry Fisher; Music, Patrick Gowers; Executive Producers, Martin Ransohoff, Leslie Linder; A Woodfall Films Production in Technicolor; December release.

CAST

Hamlet	Nicol Williamson
Horatio	Gordon Jackson
Claudius	Anthony Hopkins
Gertrude	Judy Parfitt
Polonius	Mark Dignam
Laertes	Michael Pennington
Ophelia	Marianne Faithfull
Rosencrantz	Ben Aris
Guildenstern	Clive Graham
Osric	Peter Gale
Player King	John Carney
Player Queen	Richard Everett
Lucianus/Gravedigger	Roger Livesey
Francisco	Robin Chadwick
Priest	Ian Collier
Captain	Michael Elphick
Messenger	Mark Griffith
Court Lady	Anjelica Huston
Courtier	Bill Jarvis
Reynaldo	Roger Lloyd-Pack
First Sailor	John Railton
Barnardo	John Trenaman
Court Lady	Jennifer Tudor

Marianne Faithfull, Michael Pennington
Above: Mark Dignam, Anthony Hopkins, Judy Parfitt

Judy Parfitt, Nicol Williamson. Above: Marianne Faithfull, Nicol Williamson
Top: Nicol Williamson

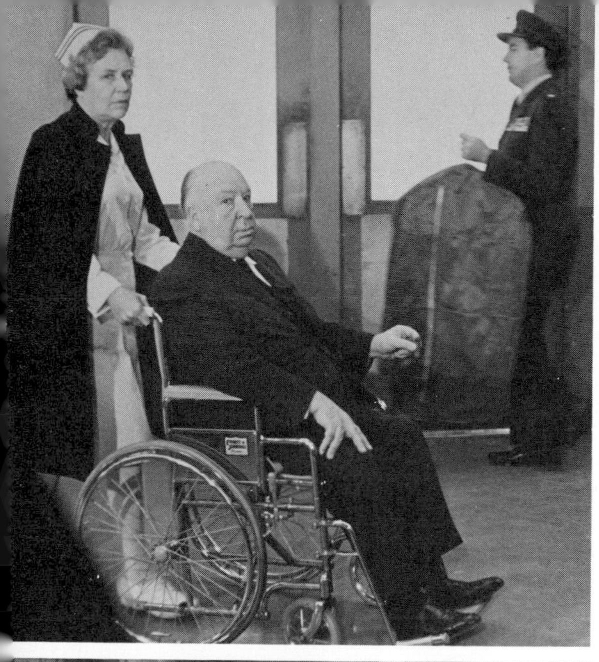

TOPAZ

(UNIVERSAL) Director, Alfred Hitchcock; Associate Producer, Herbert Coleman; Screenplay, Samuel Taylor; Based on novel by Leon Uris; Photography, Jack Hildyard; Music, Maurice Jarre; Costumes, Edith Head; Assistant Directors, Douglas Green, James Westman; In Technicolor; December release.

CAST

Michael Nordstrom	John Forsythe
Andre Devereaux	Frederick Stafford
Nicole Devereaux	Dany Robin
Rico Parra	John Vernon
Juanita de Cordoba	Karin Dor
Jacques Granville	Michel Piccoli
Henri Jarre	Philippe Noiret
Michele Picard	Claude Jade
Francois Picard	Michel Subor
Philippe Dubois	Roscoe Lee Browne
Boris Kusenov	Per-Axel Arosenius

Top: Alfred Hitchcock. Below: Claude Jade, Michel Subor, Dany Robin, Frederick Stafford

Tina Hedstrom, John Forsythe. Above: John Roper, Frederick Stafford
Top: Karin Dor, John Vernon

"Z"

(CINEMA V) Producers, Jacques Perrin, Hamed Rachedi; Director, Costa-Gavras; Screenplay, Jorge Semprun, Costa-Gavras; Dialogue, Jorge Semprun; From novel by Vassili Vassilikos; Music, Mikis Theodorakis; Photography, Raoul Coutard; In Eastmancolor; December release.

CAST

The Deputy .... Yves Montand
Helene .... Irene Papas
The Investigating Judge .... Jean-Louis Trintignant
Manuel .... Charles Denner
Nick .... Georges Geret
The Journalist .... Jacques Perrin
The Public Prosecutor .... Francois Perier
Matt .... Bernard Fresson
The General .... Pierre Dux
The Colonel .... Julien Guiomar
Vago .... Marcel Bozzufi
Sister of the witness .... Magali Noel
Yago .... Renato Salvatori
Pirou .... Jean Bouise

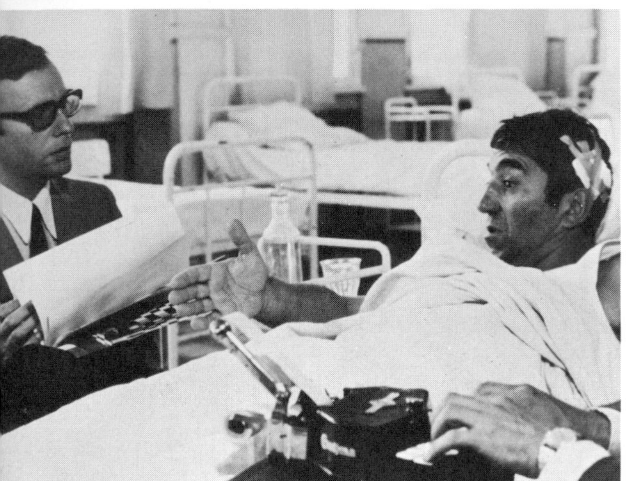

Marcel Bozzufi, Jacques Perrin. Above: Jean-Louis Trintignant, Georges Geret
Top: Charles Denner, Yves Montand

Irene Papas, Bernard Fresson

Irene Papas, Yves Montand. Top: (L) Jacques Perrin, (R) Yves Montand
(Winner of 1969 Academy Award for best foreign language film)

WHAT'S GOOD FOR THE GOOSE

(NATIONAL SHOWMANSHIP) Producer, Tony Tenser; Associate Producer; Norman Wisdom; Direction and Story and Screenplay, Menahem Golan; Dialogue, Christopher Gilmore; Music, Reg Tilsley; Title Song, Reg Tilsley, Howard Blaikley; Sung by Norman Wisdom; Other Songs, The Pretty Things; In Color; December release.

CAST

Timothy Bartlett	Norman Wisdom
Nikki	Sally Geeson
Frisby	Terence Alexander
Meg	Sarah Atkinson
Margaret	Sally Bazely
Harrington	Derek Francis
Porter	David Lodge
Clark	Paul Whitsun-Jones

Top Right: Norman Wisdom, Sally Geeson (also left center below)

Barbara Ferris, Bill Hinnant. Right Center: Harry Andrews, Barbara Ferris

A NICE GIRL LIKE ME

(AVCO EMBASSY) Executive Producer, Leanard Lightstone; Producer, Roy Millichip; Director, Desmond Davis; Screenplay, Anne Piper, Desmond Davis; Based on novel "Marry at Leisure" by Anne Piper; Assistant Director, Ronnie Appleton; Photography, Gil Taylor; Presented by Joseph E. Levine; A Partisan Production in EastmanColor; December release.

CAST

Candida	Barbara Ferris
Savage	Harry Andrews
Aunt Mary	Gladys Cooper
Ed	Bill Hinnant
Freddie	James Villiers
Aunt Celia	Joyce Carey
Pierre	Christopher Guinee
Miss Grimsby	Fabia Drake
Madame Dupont	Irene Prador
Vicar	Eric Chitty
Miss Charter	Totti Truman Taylor
Museum Attendant	John Serret
Dover Customs Man	John Clive
Miss Garland	Ann Lancaster
Labor Ward Sister	Shelagh Wilcox
Labor Ward Nurse	Sue Whitman
Post Natal Clinic Doctor	Douglas Wilmer
Marie	Carol Gilles
Pensione "Mama"	Madge Brindley
Customs Officer	John Gurnsey

ON HER MAJESTY'S SECRET SERVICE

(UNITED ARTISTS) Producers, Albert R. Broccoli, Harry Saltzman; Director, Peter Hunt; Screenplay, Richard Maibaum; Based on novel by Ian Fleming; Associate Producer, Stanley Sopel; Assistant Director, Frank Ernst; Photography, Michael Reed; Costumes, Marjorie Cornelius; In Panavision and Technicolor; December release.

CAST

James Bond	George Lazenby
Tracy	Diana Rigg
Blofeld	Telly Savalas
Irma Bunt	Ilse Steppat
Draco	Gabriele Ferzetti
Grunther	Yuri Borienko
Campbell	Bernard Horsfall
Sir Hilary Bray	George Baker
"M"	Bernard Lee
Miss Moneypenny	Lois Maxwell
"Q"	Desmond Llewelyn
Ruby	Angela Scoular
Nancy	Catherina Von Schell
Casino Guest	Bessie Love
Toussaint	Geoffrey Cheshire
Che Che	Irvin Allen
Raphael	Terry Mountain
Klett	Bill Morgan
Felsen	Les Crawford
Braun	George Cooper
Gumpold	James Bree
Olympe	Virginia North
Manuel	Brian Worth

and the Piz Gloria Girls: Dani Sheridan (American), Julie Ege (Scandinavian), Joanna Lumley (English), Mona Chong (Chinese), Anoushka Hempel (Australian), Ingrit Back (German), Jenny Hanley (Italian), Zara (Indian), Sylvana Henriques (Jamaican), Helena Ronee (Israeli).

Right: George Lazenby, Diana Rigg
Top: George Lazenby, Lois Maxwell

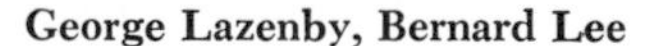

George Lazenby, Bernard Lee

Telly Savalas, George Lazenby

ANNE OF THE THOUSAND DAYS

(UNIVERSAL) Producer, Hal B. Wallis; Associate Producer, Richard McWhorter; Director, Charles Jarrott; Screenplay, Bridget Boland, John Hale; Based on play by Maxwell Anderson; Photography, Arthur Ibbetson; Music, Georges Delerue; Costumes, Margaret Furse; Assistant Director, Simon Relph; Choreography, Mary Skeaping; In Panavision and Technicolor; December release.

CAST

King Henry VIII .... Richard Burton
Anne Boleyn .... Genevieve Bujold
Queen Katherine .... Irene Papas
Wolsey .... Anthony Quayle
Cromwell .... John Colicos
Thomas Boleyn .... Michael Hordern
Elizabeth Boleyn .... Katharine Blake
Norfolk .... Peter Jeffrey
Fisher .... Joseph O'Conor
Thomas More .... William Squire
Mary Boleyn .... Valerie Gearon
Mendoza .... Vernon Dobtcheff
Smeaton .... Gary Bond
Lord Percy .... Terence Wilton
Weston .... Denis Quilley
Kingston .... Esmond Knight
Norris .... T. P. McKenna
George Boleyn .... Michael Johnson
Campeggio .... Marne Maitland
Lady Kingston .... Nora Swinburne
Bess .... June Ellis
Prior Houghton .... Cyril Luckham
Brereton .... Brook Williams
Jane Seymour .... Lesley Paterson
Willoughby .... Kynaston Reeves
Baby Elizabeth .... Amanda Jane Smythe
Princess Mary .... Nicola Pagett

Genevieve Bujold, Richard Burton
Above: Richard Burton, John Colicos

Genevieve Bujold

Genevieve Bujold, Richard Burton
Top: Richard Burton, Anthony Quayle

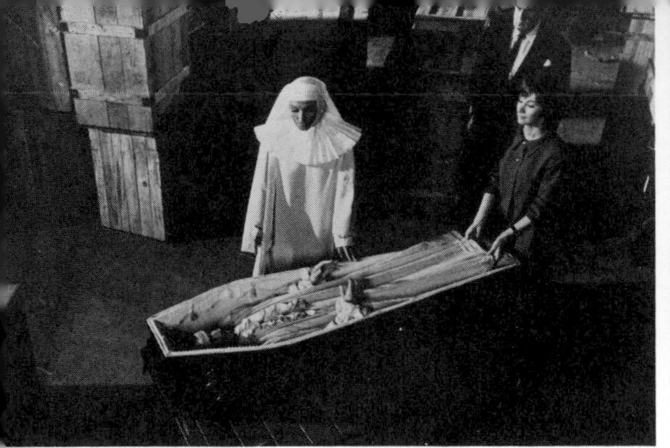

Brigitte Horney, Robert Morley, Susan Hampshire in "The Trygon Factor"

John Gielgud, Patrick O'Neal in "Assignment to Kill"

BLACK GIRL (New Yorker) Producers, Les Actualites Francaises, Films Domirev; Written and Directed by Ousmane Sembene; Based on novel by Ousmane Sembene; Photography, Christian Lacoste; January release. CAST: Mbissine Therese Diop (The maid), Anne-Marie Jelinck (Madame), Momar Nar Sene (Young man), Robert Fontaine (Master), Ibrahima (Boy with mask), Bernard Delbard, Nicole Donati, Raymond Lemery, Suzanne Lemery (Guests).

BOROM SARRET (New Yorker) Written and Directed by Ousmane Sembene; Assistant Director, Ibrahima Barro; Photography, Christian Lacoste; January release. CAST: Ly Abdoulaye (Cartman), Albourah (The Horse).

PICKPOCKET (New Yorker) Producer, Agnes Delahaye; Written and Directed by Robert Bresson; Music, J. B. Lulli; Photography, L. H. Burel; January release. CAST: Martin LaSalle (Michel), Marika Green (Jeanne), Jean Pelegri (Chief Detective), Dolly Scal (Mother), Pierre Leymarie (Jacques), Kassagi, Pierre Etaix (Accomplices), Cesar Gattegno (Detective).

BAD COMPANY (New Yorker) Written and Directed by Jean Eustache; Photography, Philippe Theaudiere; Music, Cesar Gattegno; Assistant Director, Jeanne Delos; January release. CAST: Aristide, Daniel Bart, Dominique Jayr.

THE THREE SISTERS (Brandon) Directed and Screenplay Adapted by Samson Samsonov; From play by Anton Chekhov; Photography, F. Dobronravov; A Mosfilm Studios Production; January release. CAST: Lyubov (Olga), Margarita Volodina (Masha), Tatyana Malchenko (Irina), Leonid Gubanov (Andrei), Alla Larionova (Natalya), Lev Inanov (Vershinin), Leonid Gallis (Kuligan), Konstantin Sorokin (Chubutykin), Oleg Strizhenov (Tusenbach), Vladimir Druzhnikov (Solyony).

THE TRYGON FACTOR (Warner Bros.-7 Arts) Producer, Brian Taylor; Director, Cyril Frankel; Screenplay, Derry Quinn, Stanley Munro; Photography, Harry Waxman; Music, Peter Thomas; A Rialto Film, Preben Philipsen Production in Technicolor; January release. CAST: Stewart Granger (Cooper-Smith), Susan Hampshire (Trudy), Robert Morley (Hubert), Cathleen Nesbitt (Livia), Brigitte Horney (Sister General), Sophie Hardy (Sophie), Diane Clare (Sister Clare), James Culliford (Luke), James Robertson Justice (Sir John).

ASSIGNMENT TO KILL (Warner Bros.-7 Arts) Executive Producer, William Conrad; Written and Directed by Sheldon Reynolds; Photography, Harold Lipstein, Enzo Barboni; Assistant Director, Gil Kissel; Music, William Lava; In Panavision and Technicolor; January release. CAST: Patrick O'Neal (Richard Cutting), Joan Hackett (Dominique), Herbert Lom (Matt Wilson), Eric Portman (Notary), Peter Van Eyck (Walter Green), Oscar Homolka (Inspector), Leon Greene (Big Man), Kent Smith (Eversley), Philip Ober (Bohlen), Fifi D'Orsay (Mrs. Hennie), Eve Soreny (Landlady), John Gielgud (Valayan).

FORTUNA (Trans American) Producer-Director, Menahem Golan; Screenplay, Volodja Semitjov, Alexander Ramati, Joseph Gross; Based on story by Menahem Talmi; Music, Dov Seltzer; Photography, Itzhak Mimish Herbst; Executive Producer, Yoram Globus; A Noah Films Tel Aviv Production; January release. CAST: Pierre Brasseur (Busaglo), Gila Almagor (Margot), Ahuva Goren (Fortuna), Saro Urzi (Simon), Mike Marshall (Pierre), Joseph Banai (Yoseph), Shmuel Oz (Haim), Abraham Mor (Moshe), Avner Hizkyahu (Leon), Miriam Bernstein Cohen (Leon's mother), Isaac Shilo (Davidov).

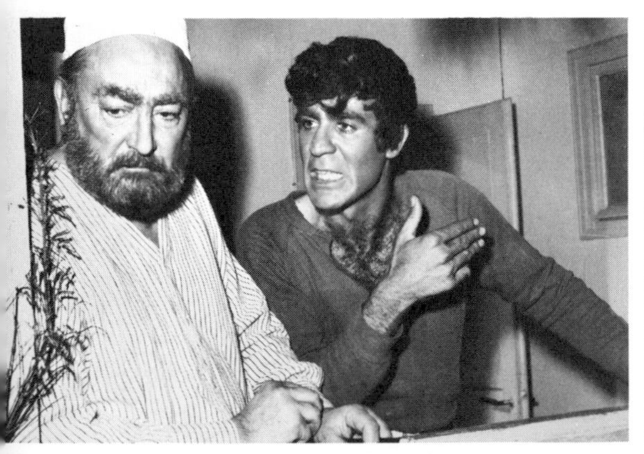

Pierre Brasseur, Shmuel Oz in "Fortuna"

Anna Karina, Jean Paul Belmondo in "Pierrot Le Fou"

Vittorio Gassman, Sophia Loren in "Ghosts—Italian Style"

Petr Kopriva, Marta Kubisova in "Martyrs Of Love"

GHOSTS—ITALIAN STYLE (MGM) Producer, Carlo Ponti; Director, Renato Castellani; Screenplay, Renato Castellani from play by Eduardo De Filippo; English Dialogue, Ernest Pintoff; Photography, Tonino Delli Colli; Music, Luis Enriquez Bacalov; Assistant Director, Maria Teresa Girosi; In Technicolor; January release. CAST: Sophia Loren (Maria), Vittorio Gassman (Pasquale), Mario Adorf (Alfredo), Margaret Lee (Sayonara), Aldo Giuffre (Raffaele), Francesco Tensi (Santanna).

PIERROT LE FOU (Pathe Contemporary) Producer, Georges de Beauregard; Directed and Written by Jean-Luc Godard; Based on novel by Lionel White; In Techniscope and EastmanColor; January release. CAST: Jean Paul Belmondo (Ferdinand), Anna Karina (Marianne), Dirk Sanders ("Brother"), Graziella Galvani (Maria).

NAKED WORLD (Times) Producers, Film Columbus-Mida Film; Director, Francesco DeFeo; Screenplay, Giuseppe Marotta, Giancarlo Fusco; Music, Theo Usuelli; Based on diary of Giuseppe Marotta; In EastmanColor; January release.

DARING GAME (Paramount) Executive Producer, Ivan Tors; Producer, Gene Levitt; Director, Laslo Benedek; Screenplay, Andy White; Based on story by Art Arthur and Andy White; In Color; January release. CAST: Lloyd Bridges (Vic), Nico Minardos (Ricardo), Michael Ansara (Pres. Delgado), Joan Blackman (Kathryn), Shepperd Strudwick (Dr. Carlyle), Alex Montoya (Gen. Tovrea), Irene Dailey (Mrs. Carlyle), Brock Peters (Jonah).

SANTA CLAUS HAS BLUE EYES (New Yorker) Written and Directed by Jean Eustache; Co-Producer, Jean-Luc Godard; Photography, Philippe Theaudiere; Music, Rene Coll, Cesar Gattegno; January release. CAST: Jean-Pierre Leaud, Gerard Zimmerman, Henri Martinez, Rene Gilson, Michel Maynard.

THE MIRACLE OF LOVE (Times) Executive Producer, Karin Wecker-Jacobsen; Director, F. J. Gottlieb; Produced and Written by Oswalt Kolle; Photography, Werner M. Lenz; Title Song by Curtis Lewis; Sung by Marge Dodson; January release. CAST: Biggi Freyer, Katarina Haertel, Ortrud Gross, Regis Vallee, Wilfred Gossler, Manfred Tummler, Matthis Grimm.

IDENTIFICATION MARKS: NONE (New Yorker) Written and Directed by Jerzy Skolimowski; Photography, Witold Mickiewicz; Music, Krzysztof Sadowski; A Film Polski Production; February release. CAST: Jerzy Skolimowski (Draft Dodger), Elzbieta Czysewska (His girl), Tadeusz Mins, Jacek Szczek, Andrzej Zarnecki.

LES CREATURES (New Yorker) Written and Directed by Agnes Varda; Photography, Willy Kurant; Music, Pierre Barbaud; Producer, Mag Bodard; Co-Produced by Parc Film, Madeleine Films, and Sandrew Ateljeerna; In Cinemascope and Color; February release. CAST: Catherine Deneuve (Wife), Michel Piccoli (Writer), Eva Dahlbeck (Hotel Owner), Jacques Charrier (Young Man), Nino Castelnuovo (Electrician), Ursula Kubler (Vamp).

MARTYRS OF LOVE (New Line) Produced and Directed, and Written by Jan Nemec; February release. CAST: Petr Kopriva (Junior Clerk), Marta Kubisova (Girl), Hana Kuberova (Anastasia), Karel Gott (Singer), Jan Klusak (Captain), Vladimir Pleclik (Tramp), Joseph Konicek (Orphan Rudolph), Denisa Dvorakova (Girl).

SIMON OF THE DESERT (Altura) Producer, Gustavo Alatriste; Direction and Story, Luis Bunuel; Screenplay, Luis Bunuel, Julio Alejandro; February release. CAST: Claudio Brook (Simon), Silvia Pinal (The Devil).

Brock Peters, Nico Minardos, Lloyd Bridges in "Daring Game"

Silvia Pinal, Claudio Brook in "Simon of The Desert"

Norman Ashley in "The Immortal Story"

Jim Murphy, Annita Koutsouveli in "The Song And The Silence"

THREE BY JEAN-MARIE STRAUB (New Yorker); NOT RECONCILED: Screenplay, Daniele Huillet-Straub, Jean-Marie Straub; Based on novel by Heinrich Boll; Director, Jean-Marie Straub; Music, Bach, Bartok; Photography, Wendelin Sachtler, Gerhard Ries, Christian Schwarzwald, Jean-Marie Straub; February release. CAST: Henning Harmssen (Faehmel), Ulrich Hopmann (Faehmel at 18), Ernst Kutzinski (Schrella), Ulrich von Thuena (Schrella 20 years later), Heiner Braun (Nettlinger), Heinrich Hargesheimer (Father), Carlheinz Hargesheimer (Father as young man), Daniele Straub (Johanna), Martha Staendner (Old Woman). **MACHORKA-MUFF:** Director, Jean-Marie Straub; Screenplay, Jean-Marie Straub, Daniele Huillet-Straub; Based on story by Heinrich Boll; Photography, Wendelin Sachtler. CAST: Renate Lang, Erich Kuby, Johannes Eckardt, Rolf Thiede, Gunther Strupp, Heiner Braun. **THE BRIDEGROOM, THE COMEDIENNE, AND THE PIMP:** Written and Directed by Jean-Marie Straub; Photography, Klaus Schilling, Hub Hagen. CAST: James Powell (James), Lilith Ungerer (Marie and Lilith), Rainer Werner Fassbinder (Freder and pimp), Peer Raben (Alt and Willi), Irm Hermann (Desiree), Kristin Peterson (Irene), Hanna Schygulla (Lucy), Rudolf Waldemar Brem (Petrell).

THEY CAME TO ROB LOS VEGAS (Warner Bros.-7 Arts) Executive Producer, Nat Wachsberger; Director, Antonio Isasi; Screenplay, A. Isasi, J. Eisinger, L. Comeron, J. Ella; Photography, Juan Gelpi; Music, Georges Garvarentz; In Technicolor and Techniscope; February release. CAST: Gary Lockwood (Tony), Elke Sommer (Anne), Lee J. Cobb (Skorsky), Jack Palance (Douglas), George Geret (Leroy), Gustavo Re (Salvatore), Daniel Martin (Merino), Jean Servais (Gino), Roger Hanin (Boss).

THE SONG AND THE SILENCE (Cloverhouse) Produced, Directed and Written by Nathan Cohen; February release. CAST: Annita Koutsouveli (Rivkeh), Harry Rubin (Rabbi), Jim Murphy (Fievel), Nana Austin (Mrs. Shlomo), Mary Antoianette (Channaleh), Jonathan Scott (David), Harry Leshner (Principal), Felix Fiebich (Matchmaker).

ADELAIDE (Sigma III) Director, Jean-Daniel Simon; Screenplay, Jean-Pierre Petrolacci; A Films Number One Production in Color; February release. CAST: Ingrid Thulin (Elizabeth), Jean Sorel (Frederic), Sylvie Fennec (Adelaide), Faith Brook (Dickson), Jacques Portet (Portier), Jean-Pierre Bernard (Christian), Joelle Bernard (Janine).

DAREDEVIL IN THE CASTLE (Frank Lee) Director, Hiroshi Inagaki; Screenplay, Hiroshi Inagaki, Takeshi Kimura; Based on story by Genzo Murakami; A Toho Production in EastmanColor; February release. CAST: Toshiro Mifune (Mohel), Kyoko Kagawa (Ai), Isuzo Yamada (Yodogimi), Yuriko Hoshi (Senhime), Yoshiko Kuga (Kobue), Akihoko Hirata (Hayato).

THE IMMORTAL STORY (Altura) Producer, Micheline Rozan; Directed and Written by Orson Welles; Based on story by Isak Dinesen; In EastmanColor; February release. CAST: Orson Welles (Clay), Jeanne Moreau (Virginie Ducrot), Roger Coggio (Elishama), Norman Ashley (Paul).

"2" (Chevron) Sequel to **"I, A Woman"**; no credits available; In Color; February release. CAST: Gio Petre (Siv), Lars Lunde (Hans), Hjordis Petterson (Mrs. Holm), Bertel Lauring (Svendsen), Klaus Pagh (Leo).

TO INGRID MY LOVE, LISA (Cannon) Producer, Donald C. Dennis; Director, Joseph Sarno; Photography, Ake Dahlquist; Music, Ken Lauber; March release. CAST: Gun Falck (Lisa), Gunilla Iwanson (Ingrid), Heinz Hopf (Nils).

Elke Sommer, Gary Lockwood in "They Came To Rob Las Vegas"

Gio Petre, Lars Lunde in "2"

Nigel Davenport, John Hurt, Robert Morley in "Sinful Davey"

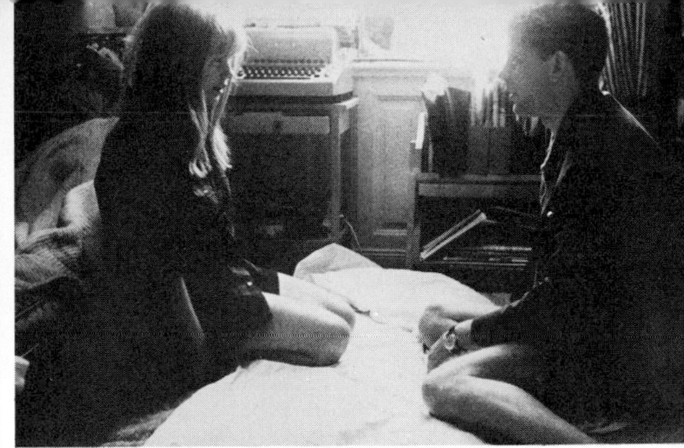

Lena Nyman, Borje Ahlstedt in "I Am Curious (Yellow)"

SINFUL DAVEY (United Artists) Producer, William N. Graf; Director, John Huston; Executive Producer, Walter Mirisch; Screenplay, James R. Webb; Associate Producer, William Kirby; Photography, Freddie Young, Edward Scaife; Music, Ken Thorne; Title Song sung by Esther Ofarim; Costumes, Margaret Furse; Assistant Directors, Tom Pevsner, John O'Connor; Choreography, Alice Dalgarno; A Mirisch-Webb Production in DeLuxe Color; March release. CAST: John Hurt (Davey), Pamela Franklin (Annie), Nigel Davenport (Constable), Ronald Fraser (MacNab), Robert Morley (Duke of Argyll), Fidelma Murphy (Jean), Maxine Audley (Duchess of Argyll), Fionnuala Flanagan (Penelope), Donal McCann (Sir James), Allan Cuthbertson (Capt. Douglas), Eddie Byrne (Bill), Niall MacGinnis (Boots), Noel Purcell (Jock), Judith Furse (Mary), Francis de Wolff (Andrew), Paul Farrell (Bailiff), Geoffrey Golden (Warden), Leon Collins (Dr. Gresham), Mickser Reid (Billy the Goat), Derek Young (Bobby), John Franklyn (George), Eileen Murphy (Mary Kidd).

THE CASTLE (Continental) Producer, Maximilian Schell; Direction and Screenplay, Rudolf Noelte; Photography, Wolfgang Treu; Costumes, Barbara Bilabel; Assistant Directors, Ilona Perl, Peter Pauker; Based on Franz Kafka's "The Castle"; In Color; March release. CAST: Maximilian Schell (K), Cordula Trantow (Frieda), Trudik Daniel (Innkeeper's Wife), Helmut Qualtinger (Burgel), Franz Misar (Arthur), Johann Misar (Jeremiah), Hanns Ernst Jager (Landlord), Friedrich Maurer (Mayor), Else Ehser (Mizzi), Iva Janzurova (Olga), Martha Wallner (Amalia), Georg Lehn (Barnabas), Karl Hellmer (Schoolmaster), Ilse Kunkele (Schoolmistress), Benno Hoffmann (Uniformed Man), E. O. Fuhrmann (Momus), Leo Mally (Gerstaecker), Hans Possnebacher (Innkeeper), Armand Ozory (Erlanger).

I AM CURIOUS (YELLOW) (Grove Press) Executive Producer, Lena Malmsjo; Producer, Goran Lindgren; Direction and Story, Vilgot Sjoman; Photography, Peter Wester; Music, Bengt Ernryd; A Sandrews Production; An Evergreen Film; March release. CAST: Lena Nyman (Lena), Borje Ahlstedt (Borje), Peter Lindgren (Rune), Magnus Nilsson (Magnus), Chris Wahlstrom (Chris), Marie Goranzon (Marie), Ulla Lyttkens (Ulla), Holger Lowenadler (King).

THE SWEET BODY OF DEBORAH (Warner Bros.-7 Arts) Executive Producer, Sergio Martino; Director, Romolo Guerrieri; Producers, Mino Loy, Luciano Martino; Screenplay, Ernesto Gastaldi; Photography, Marcello Masciocchi; Music, Nora Orlandi; Assistant Director, Roberto Pariante; In Cromoscope and Technicolor; March release. CAST: Carroll Baker (Deborah), Jean Sorel (Marcel), Evelyn Stewart (Susan), Luigi Pistilli (Philip), Michel Bardinet (Police Commissioner), Renato Montalbano (Telephone Man), Mirelia Panfili (Telephone Clerk), Domenico Ravenna (Maitre d'), George Hilton (Robert).

TROPICI (New Yorker) Producer, Gianni Barcelloni; Director, Gianni Amico; Screenplay, Gianni Amico, Francesco Tullio Altan; Photography, Giorgio Pelloni; Music, Mozart; March release. CAST: Joel Barcelos (Miguel), Janira Santiago (Maria), Graciele Campos (Graciele), Batista Campos (Batista), Antonio Pitanga (Black Man), Roque Aranjo (Julio), Maria Euridice (Herself), Giorgio Poppi (Doctor).

LE SOCRATE (New Yorker) Producer, Claude Nedjar; Direction and Screenplay, Robert Lapoujade; Photography, Jean-Jacques Renon; Music, Bernard Parmegiani; In Color; March release. CAST: Pierre Luzan (Le Socrate), R. J. Chauffard (Lemay), Martine Brochard (Sylvie), Stephane Fay (Pierre), Jean-Pierre Sentier (Adam).

Maximilian Schell, Cordula Trantow in "The Castle"

Carroll Baker, Jean Sorel in "The Sweet Body Of Deborah"

Clint Eastwood, Silvana Mangano in "The Witches"

Oliver Reed, Diana Rigg in "The Assassination Bureau"

THE WITCHES (Lopert) "The Witch Burned Alive" Directed by Luchino Visconti; Story and Screenplay, Giuseppe Patroni Griffi; with Silvana Mangano, Annie Girardot, Francisco Rabal, Massimo Girotti, Elsa Albani, Helmut Steinberger. "Civic Sense" Directed by Mauro Bolognini; Story and Screenplay, Age and Scarpelli, Bernardino Zapponi; with Silvano Mangano, Alberto Sordi. "The Earth as Seen From The Moon" Directed and Written by Pier Paolo Pasolini; with Silvana Mangano, Toto, Ninetto Davoli. "The Girl from Sicily" Directed by Franco Rossi; Screenplay, Franco Rossi, Luigi Mani; with Silvana Mangano, Pietro Tordi; "A Night Like Any Other" Directed by Vittorio De Sica; Screenplay, Cesare Zavattini, Fabio Carpi, Enzio Muzii; March release; with Silvana Mangano, Clint Eastwood, Armando Bottin, Gianni Gori, Paolo Gozlino, Angelo Santi, Piero Torrisi, Valentino Macchi.

THE ASSASSINATION BUREAU (Paramount) Producer, Michael Relph; Director, Basil Dearden; Screenplay, Michael Relph; From an idea by Jack London and Robert Fish; Photography, Geoffrey Unsworth; Assistant Director, John Peverall; Costumes, Beatrice Dawson; In EastmanColor; March release. CAST: Oliver Reed (Ivan), Diana Rigg (Sonya), Telly Savalas (Lord Bostwick), Curt Jurgens (Gen. Von Pinck), Warren Mitchell (Herr Weiss), Philippe Noiret (Lucoville), Kenneth Griffith (Popescu), Clive Revill (Sgt. Spado), Vernon Dobtcheff (Muntzov), Beryl Reid (Madame Otero), Annabella Incontrera (Eleanora).

QUEEN OF BLOOD (American International) Producer, George Edwards; Directed and Written by Curtis Harrington; Music, Leonard Morand; In Color; March release. CAST: John Saxon (Allan), Basil Rathbone (Dr. Farraday), Dennis Hopper (Paul), Judi Meredith (Judi), Florence Marly (Green Woman), Robert Boon, Don Eitner, Virgil Frye, Robert Porter, Terry Lee, Forrest Ackerman.

THE FIRE WITHIN (New Yorker) Direction and Screenplay, Louis Malle; Based on novel by Drieu La Rochelle; Music, Erik Satie; Collaborating Director, Volker Schloendorff; Photography, Ghislain Cloquet; March release. CAST: Maurice Ronet (Alain), Lena Skerla (Lydia), Yvonne Clech (Mlle. Farnoux), Hubert Deschamps (d'Averseau), Jean-Paul Moulinot (Doctor), Mona Dol (Mrs. Barbinais), Jeanne Moreau (Jeanne), Pierre Moncorbier (Moraire), Rene Dupuy (Charlie), Bernard Tiphaine (Milou), Bernard Noel (Dubourg), Ursula Kubler (Fanny).

THE BIG CUBE (Warner Bros.-7 Arts) Producer Lindsley Parsons; Director, Tito Davison; Screenplay, William Douglas Lansford; Story, Tito Davison, Edmundo Baez; Photography, Gabriel Figueroa; Music, Val Johns; Assistant Director, Winfield Sanchez; A Francisco Diez Barroso Production in Technicolor; March release. CAST: Lana Turner (Adriana), George Chakiris (Johnny), Richard Egan (Frederick), Daniel O'Herlihy (Charles), Karin Mossberg (Lisa), Pamela Rodgers (Bibi), Carlos East (Lalo), Augusto Benedico (Doctor), Victor Junco (Delacroix), Norma Herrera (Stella), Pedro Galvan (Dean), The Finks (Themselves), Regina Torne (Queen Bee).

THE MAN OUTSIDE (Allied Artists) Producer, William Gell; Direction and Screenplay, Samuel Gallu; Photography, Gil Taylor; A Trio Films and Group W Production in Techniscope and Technicolor; March release. CAST: Van Heflin (Bill), Heidelinde Weis (Kay), Pinkas Braun (Rafe), Peter Vaughan (Nikolai), Charles Gray (Charles), Paul Maxwell (Judson), Ronnie Baker (George), Linda Marlowe (Dorothy), Gary Cockrell (Brune), Bill Nagy (Morehouse), Larry Cross (Austen), Archie Duncan (Det. Barnes), Willoughby Gray (Det. Inspector), Christopher Denham (Det. Sgt.), Rita Webb (Landlady), Carole Ann Ford (Cindy), Carmel MacSharry (Olga).

Basil Rathbone (L), John Saxon (R) in "Queen Of Blood"

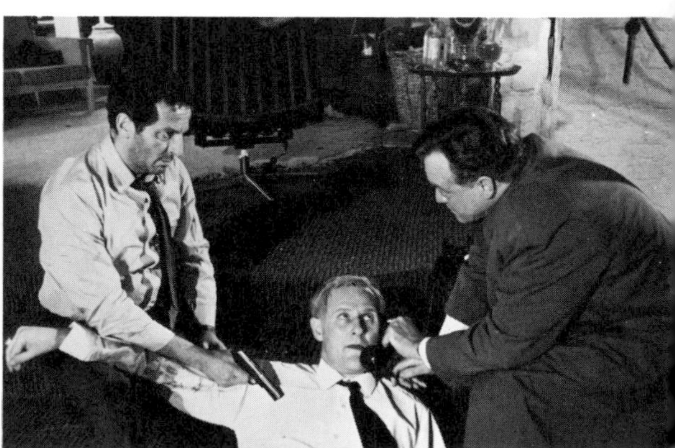

Pinkus Braun, Peter Vaughan, Van Heflin in "The Man Outside"

Karin Mossberg, Lana Turner, George Chakiris in "The Big Cube"

Galina Vishnevskaya (R) in "Katerina Izmailova"

THE RED AND THE WHITE (Brandon) Co-Producers, Mafilm Studio IV and Mosfilm Studio; Director, Miklos Jancso; Screenplay, Georgi Mdivan, Gyula Hernadi, Miklos Jancso; March release. CAST: Tatyana Konyukova (Yelizaveta), Krystyna Mikolaiewska (Olga), Mikhail Kozakov (Nestor), Viktor Avdyushko (Sailor), Bolot Beisenalyev (Chingiz), Sergei Nikonenko (Cossack), Anatoli Yabbarov (Chelpanov), Jozsef Madaras (Commander).

NOT MINE TO LOVE (Edward Meadow) Producer, Amatsia Hiuni; Director, Uri Zohar; Screenplay, Uri Zohar; Based on Story by A. B. Yehoshua; March release. CAST: Odded Kotler (Eli), Shuy Osherov (Shuy), Judith Soleh (Noa), Misha Asherov (Shuy's father), Illy Gorlitzky (Zvi), Germaine Unikovsky (Yael), Stella Avni (Neighbor), Baruch David (Her husband), Shoshana Duer (Yael's mother), Nissan Yatif (Yael's father).

THE SISTERS (Joseph Brenner) No credits; Greek with English titles; March release. CAST: Petros Fissoun (Constantis), Elli Fotiou (Thalia), Nicos Rizos (Yorghis), Despo Diamantidou (The Lady), Vangelis Kazan (Yorghis' mother), Niki Shellby (English Bar Girl).

MORIRE GRATIS (New Yorker) Producer, Enzo Giulioli; Directed and Written by Sandra Franchina; March release. CAST: Franco Angeli (Sculptor), Karen Blanguernon (Michele), Mario Pisu, Gerard Herter, Isabel D'Avila, Adrano Amedel Migliano, Madeleine Santoro, Sandro Brunori.

THE LAST ADVENTURE (Universal) Director, Robert Enrico; Screenplay, Jose Giovanni, Robert Enrico, Pierre Pelegri; A Societe Nouvelle de Cinematographic Production in Color; March release. CAST: Alain Delon (Younger man), Lino Ventura (Older man), Joanna Shimkus (Girl), Serge Regianni (Pilot).

CHRONICLE OF ANNA MAGDALENA BACH (New Yorker) Producer, Gian Vittorio Baldi; Director, Jean-Marie Straub; Screenplay, Jean-Marie Straub, Daniele Huillet; Photography, Ugo Piccone; Music, Bach; Hanover Boys Choir; April release. CAST: Gustav Leonhardt (J. S. Bach), Christiane Lang (Anna Magdalena Bach).

WALKOVER (New Yorker) Producer, Syrena Films; Direction and Screenplay, Jerzy Skolimowski; Photography, Antoni Nurszynski; Music, Andrzej Trzaskowski; April release. CAST: Jerzy Skolimowski (Andrzej Leszczyz), Alexandra Zawjeruszanka (Teresa).

THE SMUGGLERS (New Yorker) Produced, Directed, and Written by Luc Moullet; Photography, Philippe Theaudiere; April release. CAST: Francoise Vatel (Brigitte), Monique Thiriet (Francesca), Johnny Monteilhet (Customs Officer), Albert Juross (Poacher), Paul Martin (Official), Bernard Cazassus (Nomad).

KATERINA IZMAILOVA (Artkino) Director, Mikhail Shapiro; Libretto, Dmitri Shostakovich; After novel by Nikolai Leskov; Photography, R. Davidov, V. Ponomaryov; A Lenfilm Production in Color; April release. CAST: Galina Vishnevskaya (Katerina), A. Inotemtsev (Sergei, sung by V. Tretyak), N. Boyarsky (Zinovy, sung by V. Radziyevsky), A. Sokolov (Boris, sung by A. Vedernikov), R. Tkachuk (Seedy Lout, sung by S. Strezhnev), T. Gavrilova (Sonetka, sung by V. Reka), Chorus and Orchestra of Shevchenko Opera and Ballet Theatre, Kiev, conducted by Konstantin Simeonov.

THE BLIND BEAST (Daiei) Director, Yasuzo Masumura; Screenplay, Yoshio Shirasaka; Story, Ranpo Edogawa; Photography, Setsuo Kobayashi; In Daiei Color-Scope; April release. CAST: Eiji Funakoshi (Michio), Mako Midori (Aki), Noriko Sengoku (Shino).

Alain Delon, Joanna Shimkus, Lino Ventura in "The Last Adventure"

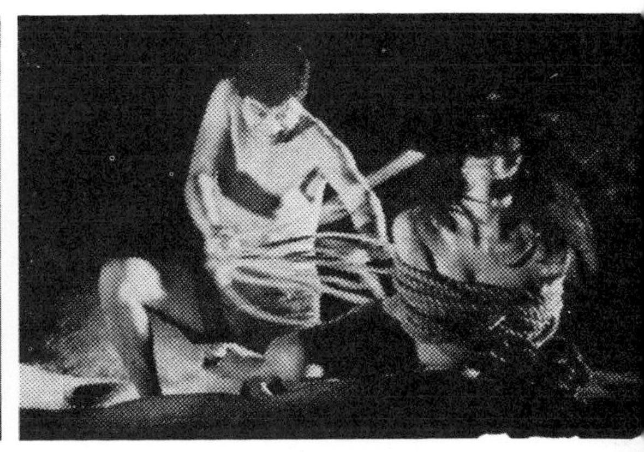

"The Blind Beast"

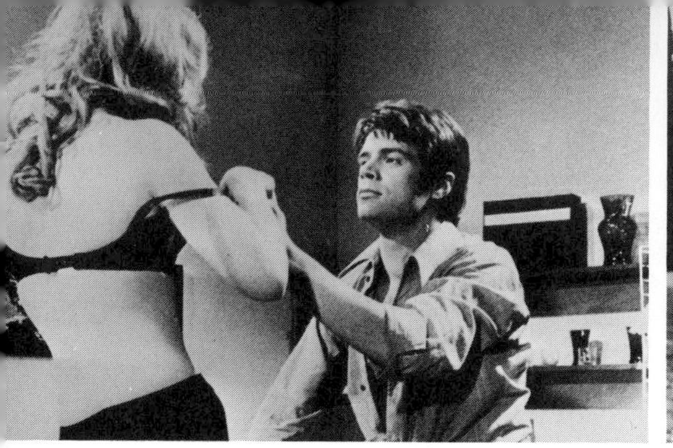

"Michael & Helga"

Terence Stamp, Silvana Mangano in "Teorema"

MICHAEL AND HELGA (American International) Producer, Dr. Roland Cammerer; Director, Erich F. Bender; Screenplay, Erich F. Bender, Roland Cammerer; Photography, Fritz Baader, Erdmann Beyer; Music, Karl Barthel; In Pathe Color; April release. CAST: Ruth Gassmann (Helga), Felix Franchy (Michael), Elfi Reuter, Hildegard Linden, Sonja Lindorf, Claus Hoeft.

SUCCUBUS (Trans American) Producer, Adrian Hoven; Director, Jess Franco; Screenplay, Pier A. Caminneci; A Color Film Production of Aquila Film Enterprises; April release. CAST: Janine Reynaud (Lorna), Jack Taylor (Bill), Nathalie Nord (Bella), Eva Brauner (Olga), Pier A. Caminneci (Hermann), Adrian Hoven (Psychiatrist).

LOLA MONTES (Brandon) Director, Max Ophuls; Screenplay, Max Ophuls, Annette Wademant, Franz Geiger; Based on novel by Cecil St. Laurent; A Gamma Films-Florida and Oska Films Co-Production in CinemaScope and EastmanColor; April release. CAST: Martine Carole (Lola), Peter Ustinov (Circus Master), Anton Walbrook (King of Bavaria), Ivan Desny (James), Will Quadflieg (Liszt), Oskar Werner (Student), Lise Delamare (Mrs. Craigie), Henri Guisol (Maurice), Willy Eichberger (Doctor), Paulette Dubost (Josephine).

DOCTOR GLAS (20th Century-Fox) Executive Producer, Mogens Skot-Hansen; Producers, Joseph Hardy, Benni Korzen; Associate Producer, Charles K. Weiss; Director, Mai Zetterling; Screenplay, Mai Zetterling, David Hughes; Photography, Rune Ericsson; April release. CAST: Per Oscarsson (Dr. Glas), Ulf Palme (Pastor Gregorius), Lone Hertz (Helga), Nils Eklund (Markel), Bente Dessau (Eva), Lars Lunoe (Klas Recke), Bendt Rothe (Birck), Ingolf David (Father), Helle Hertz (Anita), Jonas Bergstrom (Friend).

TEOREMA (Continental) Producers, Franco Rossellini, Manolo Bolognini; Written and Directed by Pier Paolo Pasolini; Photography, Giuseppe Ruzzolini; Costumes, Marcella De Marchis; Music, Ennio Morricone; Color by Movielab; April release. CAST: Terence Stamp (Visitor), Silvano Mangano (Wife), Massimo Girotti (Husband), Anne Wiazemsky (Daughter), Laura Betti (Maid), Andres Jose Cruz Soublette (Son).

PEOPLE MEET AND SWEET MUSIC FILLS THE HEART (Trans-Lux) Executive Producer, Bertil Ohlsson; Producers, Henning Carlsen, Goran Lindgren; Director, Henning Carlsen; Screenplay, Henning Carlsen, Poul Borum; From Novel by Jesn August Schade; Photography, Henning Kristiansen; Music, Krzyszztof Komeda; Costumes, Ull-Britt Soderlund; May release. CAST: Harriet Andersson (Sofia), Preben Neergaard (Sjalof), rik Wedersoe (Hans), Eva Dahlbeck (Mrs. Sorensen), Lone Rode (Mrs. Hansen), Georg Rydeberg (Impresario).

LES GAULOISES BLEUES (Lopert) Producers, Alexandre Mnouchkine, Georges Danciger, Claude Lelouch; Directed and Written by Michel Cournot; Photography, Alain Levent; In DeLuxe Color; May release. CAST: Annie Girardot (Mother), Jean-Pierre Kalfon (Ivan at 30), Nella Bielski (Jeanne), Bruno Cremer (Father), Henri Garcin (Hunter), Jean Lescot (Hunter), Georges Demestre (Ivan at 6).

THE LIBERTINE (Audubon) Producer, Silvio Clementelli; Director, Pasquale Festa, Campanile; Screenplay, Nicolo Ferrari, Ottavio Jemma; In EastmanColor; May release. CAST: Catherine Spaak (Mimi), Jean-Louis Trintignant (De Marchi), Luigi Proietti (Maldini), Luigi Pistilli (Architect), Rezo Montagnani (Fabrizio), Nora Ricci (Mimi's mother), Fabienne Dali (Claudia), Paolo Stoppa (Doctor).

Lone Hertz, Per Oscarsson in "Doctor Glas"

Jack Taylor, Janine Reynaud in "Succubus"

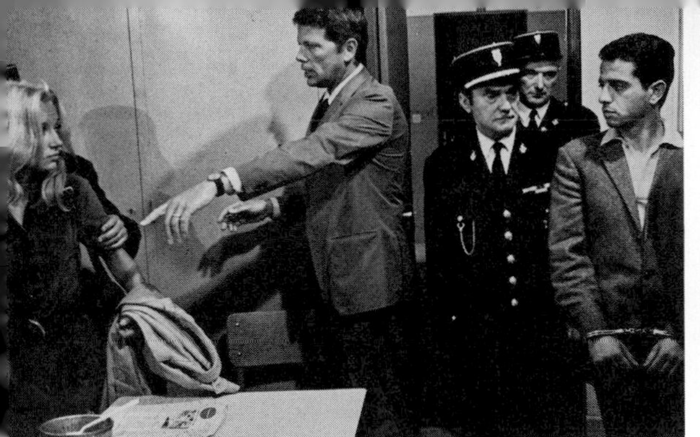

Caroline Cellier, Pierre Zimmer, Amidou (R) in "Life Love Death"

William Dysart, Hugh Marlowe, Patricia Haines in "The Last Shot You Hear"

LIFE LOVE DEATH (Lopert) Producers, Alexandre Mnouchkine, Georges Dancigers; Director, Claude Lelouch; Screenplay, Pierre Uytterhoeven, Claude Lelouch; Music, Francis Lai; Photography, Jean Collomb; Assistant Directors, Claude Pinoteau, Albert Rajau; In DeLuxe Color; May release. CAST: Amidou (Francois Toledo), Caroline Cellier (Caroline), Janine Magnan (Jeanne), Marcel Bozzoffi (Inspector), Pierre Zimmer (Police Officer), Catherine Samie (Julie), Lisette Bersy (Helene), Albert Naud (Defense Lawyer), Jean Pierre Sloan (Partie Civil), Nathalie Durrand (Sophie), Sylvia Saurel (1st Murder), Denyse Roland (3rd Murder), Claudia Morin, Rita Maiden, Pierre Collet, Albert Rajau, Jacques Henry, Jean-Marc Allegre, Colette Taconnat, Jean Collomb, El Cordobes.

A MATTER OF DAYS (Royal) Producer-Direcrector, Yves Ciampi; Story and Screenplay, Yves Ciampi, Rodolphe M. Arlaud, Vladimir Kalina, Alena Vostra; In Color; May release. CAST: Thalle Fruges (Francoise), Vit Olmer (Pavel), Philippe Baronnet (Jean Louis), Milan Mach (Father), Michel Ducrocq (Philippe), Josef Cap (Stasek), Valerie Vienne (Maite).

THE SOUTHERN STAR (Columbia) Producer, Roger Duchet; Director, Sidney Hayers; Screenplay, David Pursall, Jack Seddon; Based on novel by Jules Verne; Photography, Raoul Coutard; Assistant Director, Jack Bourdon; Costumes, Berman Limited; Music, George Garvarentz; Title Song Sung by Matt Monro; Lyrics, Don Black; In Techniscope and Technicolor; May release. CAST: George Segal (Dan), Ursula Andress (Erica), Orson Welles (Plankett), Ian Hendry (Karl), Johnny Sekka (Matakit), Michel Constantin (Jose), George Geret (Andre), Sylvain (Louis), Charles Lamb (Todd), Guy Delorme (Michael), Harry Andrews (Kramer).

THE LAST SHOT YOU HEAR (20th Century-Fox) Executive Producer, Robert Lippert; Producer, Jack Parsons; Director, Gordon Hessler; Screenplay, Tim Shields; From play "The Sound of Murder" by William Fairchild; Music, Bert Shefter; Assistant Directors, Ray Frift, Michael Higgins; A Lippert Films Production; May release. CAST: Hugh Marlowe (Charles), Zena Walker (Eileen), Patricia Haines (Anne), William Dysart (Peter), Thorley Walters (Gen. Jowett), Joan Young (Mrs. Jowett), Lionel Murton (Rubens), Helen Horton (Dodie Rubens), John Nettleton (Nash), John Wentworth (Chambers), Alistair Williamson (CID Officer), Daphne Barker (Reporter), Lynley Laurence (Girl), Julian Holloway (Young Man), James Mellor (Reporter), Ian Hamilton (Reporter), Shaun Curry (Diver), Stephen Moore (Peter's Colleague), Job Stewart (Policeman), Janet Kelly (Receptionist).

THE ROUND UP (Altura) Director, Miklos Jancso; Screenplay, Gyula Hernadi; Presented by Clem Perry/Fleetwood Productions; May release. CAST: Janos Gorbe (Gaidor), Tibor Molnar (Kabai, Sr.), Andras Kozak (Kabai, Jr.), Gabor Agardy (Torma), Zoltan Latinovitz (Veszelka).

99 WOMEN (Commonwealth) Producer, Harry Alan Towers; Director, Jess Franco; Screenplay, Peter Welbeck; A Towers of London Production in Color; May release. CAST: Maria Schell (Leonie), Luciana Paluzzi (Natalie), Mercedes McCambridge (Thelma), Herbert Lom (Governor).

Ursula Andress, George Segal in "The Southern Star"

Maria Schell, Mercedes McCambridge in "99 Women"

Gene Barry, Richard Todd in "Subterfuge"

"Destroy All Monsters"

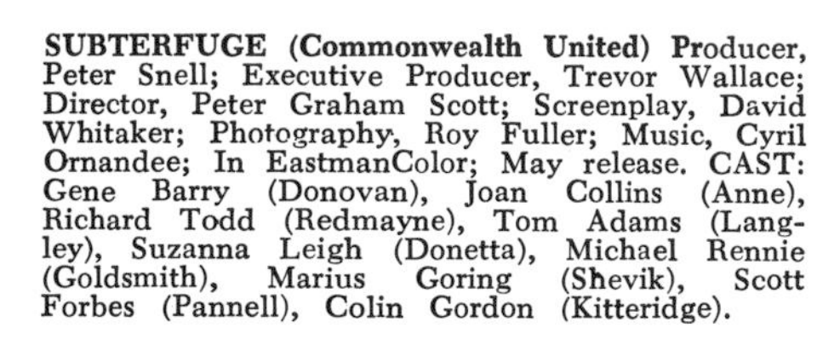

SUBTERFUGE (Commonwealth United) Producer, Peter Snell; Executive Producer, Trevor Wallace; Director, Peter Graham Scott; Screenplay, David Whitaker; Photography, Roy Fuller; Music, Cyril Ornandee; In EastmanColor; May release. CAST: Gene Barry (Donovan), Joan Collins (Anne), Richard Todd (Redmayne), Tom Adams (Langley), Suzanna Leigh (Donetta), Michael Rennie (Goldsmith), Marius Goring (Shevik), Scott Forbes (Pannell), Colin Gordon (Kitteridge).

LISTEN, LET'S MAKE LOVE (Lopert) Producer, Alberto Grimaldi; Director, Vittorio Caprioli; Screenplay, Vittorio Caprioli, Enrico Medioli, Franca Valeri; Music, Ennio Morricone; Assistant Director, Franco Cirino; Photography, Pasquale DeSantis; Costumes, Ferdinando Scarfiotti; In DeLuxe Color; June release. CAST: Pierre Clementi (Lallo), Beba Loncar (Aunt Lidia), Carlo Caprioli (Uncle Carlo), Edwige Feuillere (Giuditta), Juliette Mayniel (Gilberta), Tanya Lopert (Flavia), Claudine Auger (Ida), Roberto Gatto (Ida's husband), Mario Meniconi (Bruener), Anna Maria Covacci (Mrs. Bruener), Valentian Cortese (Lall's mother), Franca Valeri (Diraghi), Martine Malle (Sveva), Massimo Girotti (Tassi), Fabian Fabre (Puccio), Antonietta Fiorito (Guardarobiera), Ivan Giovanni Scratuglia (Lallo's friend), Ornella Polito Santoliquido (Amparo), Americo Tot (Baron).

THE CONCUBINES (Boxoffice International) Director, Kohji Takamatsu; Screenplay, Jiku Yamatoya; Photography, Hideo Itoh; Music, Masao Yaki; A Unicorn Production in EastmanColor;. June release. CAST: Tomoko Mayama (Pan Chin Lein), Shikyoku Takashima (Wu-Sung), Juuzo Itami (Hsi-Men-Ching), Ruriko Asari (Li-Ping-Brh), Riko Yurenai (Chun-Mei), Hatsuo Yamatani (Wu-Ta), Ko-hei Tsusaki (Ying), Yuzo Tachikawa (Hau Yung).

DESTROY ALL MONSTERS (American International) Executive Producer, Tomoyuki; Director, Ishiro Honda; Screenplay, Kaoru Mabuchi; Music, Akira Ifukube; Photography, Taiichi Kankura; In Color by Berkey Pathe; June release. CAST: Akira Kubo, Jun Tazaki, Yoshio Tsuchiya, Kyoko Ai, Yukiko Kobayashi, Kenji Sahara, Andrew Hughs, Rodan, Mothra, Manda, Godzilla.

CARRY ON CAMPING (RANK) Producer, Peter Rogers; Director, Gerald Thomas; Screenplay, Talbot Rothwell; Photography, Ernest Steward; Music, Eric Rogers; Assistant Director, Jack Causey; In Color; June release. CAST: Sidney James (Sid), Kenneth Williams (Dr. Soaper), Charles Hawtrey (Charlie), Joan Sims (Joan), Terry Scott (Peter), Hattie Jacques (Miss Haggerd), Barbara Windsor (Babs), Bernard Bresslaw (Bernie), Peter Butterworth (Joshua), Betty Marsden (Harriet), Dilys Laye (Anthea), Sandra Caron (Fanny), Trisha Noble (Sally).

BARREN LIVES (Pathe Contemporary) Producers, Luiz Carlos Barreto, Herbert Richers, Darulo Trellers; Directed and Written by Nelson Pereira dos Santos; Based on novel "Vidas Secas" by Gracilliano Ramos; June release. CAST: Athila Iorio (Father), Maria Riberio (Mother), Jofre Soares (Policeman).

SPOILS OF THE NIGHT (William Mishkin) Director, Shinji Murayama; Screenplay, Masashige Narusawa; A Toei Company Production; June release. CAST: Tatsuo Unemiya (Toru), Mako Midori (Kazuko) Reiko Ohara (Hatsue).

MISSION STARDUST (Times) Director, Primo Zeglio; Music, Marcello Giombini; Photography, Riccardo Pallottini; In Techniscope and Technicolor; July release. CAST: Essy Persson (Thora), Lang Jeffries (Maj. Perry Roan), John Karelsen (Kress), Pinkas Braun (Rotkin), Luis Davila (Capt. Bull).

Claudine Auger, Pierre Clementi in "Listen, Let's Make Love"

"Barren Lives"

Catherine Deneuve, Michel Piccoli in "La Chamade"

John Phillip Law, Lee Van Cleef in "Death Rides A Horse"

LA CHAMADE ("Heartbeat") (Lopert) Director, Pierre Laurent; Adaptation and Dialogue, Francoise Sagan, Alain Cavalier; Based on Novel by Francoise Sagan; Photography, Pierre L'Homme; Assistant Director, Florence Malraux; Miss Deneuve's Wardrobe, Yves St. Laurent; In DeLuxe Color; July release. CAST: Catherine Deneuve (Lucile), Michel Piccoli (Charles), Roger Van Hool (Antoine), Irene Tunc (Diane), Jacques Sereys (Johnny), Philippine Pascal (Claire).

SPIRITS OF THE DEAD (American International) In Color by Berkey Pathe; July release. CAST: "Spirits of the Dead" (Song by Ray Charles) Brigitte Bardot (Giuseppina), Alain Delon (William Wilson), Jane Fonda (Countess Frederica), Terence Stamp (Toby Dammit), Peter Fonda (Baron Wilhelm); "Metzengerstein" (Director, Roger Vadim; Photography, Claude Renoir; Music, Jean Prodromides; Costumes, Jacques Fonteray): Jane Fonda (Countess Frederica), Peter Fonda (Baron Wilhelm), Carla Marlier (Claude), Francoise Prevost (Friend of Frederica), James Robertson Justice (Frederica's Adviser), Annie Duperrey (First Guest), Philippe Lemaire (Philippe), Serge Marquand (Hugues), Andreas Voutsinas (Second Guest), Audoin de Bardot (Page), Douking (du Lissier); "William Wilson" (Direction and Screenplay, Louis Malle; Photography, Tonino Delli Colli; Music, Diego Masson): Brigitte Bardot (Giuseppina), Alain Delon (Wilson), Katia Cristina (Young Girl), Umberto D'Orsi (Hans), Daniele Vargas (Professor), Renzo Palmer (Priest); "Never Bet The Devil Your Head" (Director, Federico Fellini; Screenplay, Federico Fellini, Bernardino Zapponi; Photography, Giuseppe Rotunno; Music, Nino Rota): Terence Stamp (Toby Dammit), Salvo Randone (Priest), Ernesto Colli (Second Director), Fabrizio Angeli (First Director), Marina Yaru (Child), Anna Tonietti (Television Commentator), Aleardo Ward (First Interviewer), Paul Cooper (Second Interviewer).

DEATH RIDES A HORSE (United Artists) Producers, Alfonso Sansone, Enrico Chroscicki; Director, Giulio Petroni; Screenplay, Luciano Vincenzoni; Assistant Directors, Giancarlo Santi, Mario Molli; Photography, Carlo Carlini; Costumes, Enzo Bulgarelli; In Techniscope and Technicolor; July release. CAST: John Phillip Law (Bill), Lee Van Cleef (Ryan), Luigi Pistilli (Wolcott), Anthony Dawson (Manina), Jose Torres (Pedro), Carla Cassola (Betsy), Archie Savage (Vigro), Mario Brega (One-Eye), Guglielmo Spoletini (Manuel).

WAITING FOR CAROLINE (Lopert) Executive Producer, Robert Allen; Producer, Walford Hewitson; Director, Ron Kelly; Screenplay, George C. Robertson, Ron Kelly; Music, Eldon Rathburn; Party Music, The Jaybees; Photography, Denis Gillson, Paul Leach; Assistant Directors, Frank Phillips, Michael Scott; In DeLuxe Color; July release. CAST: Alexandra Stewart (Caroline), Francoise Tasse (Marc), Robert Howay (Peter), Sharon Acker (Emily), William Needles (Stephen), Aileen Seaton (Lally), Paul Guevremont (Simard), Daniel Gadouas (Jean-Pierre), Lucie Poitras (Mme. Simard), Monique Mercure (Yvette), Reg McReynolds (Hagan), Paul Buissonneau (Louis).

CAMILLE 2000 (Audubon) Producer-Director, Radley Metzger; Screenplay, Michael DeForrest; Based on "The Lady of the Camellias" by Alexandre Dumas fils; Photography, Ennio Guarnieri; Music, Piero Piccioni; Assistant Director, Francesco Cinieri; A Spear Production in Panavision and Technicolor; July release. CAST: Daniele Gaubert (Marguerite), Nino Castelnuovo (Armand), Eleanora Rossi-Drago (Prudence), Philippe Forquet (Duke), Roberto Bisacco (Gaston), Massimo Serato (Armand's father), Silvana Venturelli (Olympe), Zachary Adams (Gody).

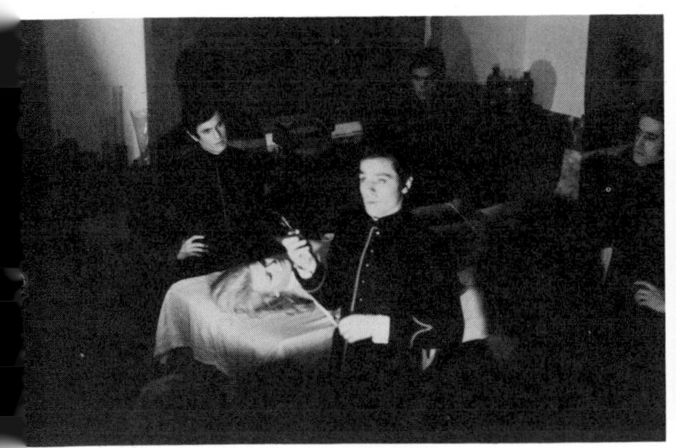

Brigitte Bardot, Alain Delon in 'Spirits Of The Dead"

Alexandra Stewart, Francois Tasse in "Waiting For Caroline"

Carroll Baker, Lou Castel, Collette Descombes in "Paranoia"

Marcello Mastroianni, Faye Dunaway in "A Place For Lovers"

DETOUR (Brandon) Producer, Bulgarian State Films; Directors, Grisha Ostrovski, Todor Stoyanov; Screenplay, Blaga Dimitrova from his story; July release. CAST: Nevena Kokanova (Neda), Ivan Andonov (Boyan).

MORE (Cinema V) Producer-Director, Barbet Schroeder; Screenplay and Dialogue, Paul Gegauff, Barbet Schroeder; Story, Barbet Schroeder; Photography, Nestor Almendros; Music, The Pink Floyd; August release. CAST: Mimsy Farmer (Estelle), Klaus Grunberg (Stefan), Heinz Engelmann (Wolf), Michel Chanderli (Charlie), Louise Wink (Cathy), Henry Wolf (Henry).

PARANOIA (Commonwealth United) Producer, Salvatore Alabiso; Director, Umberto Lenzi; A Titanus Film in Eastman Color; August release. CAST: Carroll Baker (Kathryn), Lou Castel (Peter), Collette Descombes (Eva), Tino Carraro (Brian).

THE PEACH THIEF (Brandon) Directed and Written by Vulo Radev; Based on story by Emilian Stanev; August release. CAST: Nevena Kokanova (Lisa), Rade Markovich (Ivo), Mikhail Mikhailov (Colonel).

A BLACK VEIL FOR LISA (Commonwealth United) Producer, Georgio Venturini; Director, Massimo Dallamano; Screenplay, Giuseppe Belli, Vittoriano Patrick, Massimo Dallamano, Audrey Nohra; Story, Giuseppe Belli; Photography, Angelo Lotti; Music, Dick Markowitz; Assistant Director, Monica Felt; In Eastman Color; August release. CAST: John Mills (Bulov), Luciana Paluzzi (Lisa), Robert Hoffmann (Max), Renata Kasche (Marianne), Tullio Altamura (Ostermeyer), Carlo Hintermann (Mansfeld), Enzo Fiermonte (Siegert), Loris Bazzocchi (Kruger), Giuseppe Terranova (Rabbit), Rodolfo Licari (Olaf), Bernardino Solitari (Muller), Vanna Polverosi (Ursula), Robert Van Daalen (Dr. Gross), Carlo Spadoni (Eric).

A PLACE FOR LOVERS (MGM) Producers, Carlo Ponti, Arthur Cohn; Director, Vittorio De Sica; Screenplay, Julian Halevy, Peter Baldwin, Ennio DeConcini, Tonio Guerra, Cesare Zavattini; Photography, Pasquale De Santis; Assistant Director, Peter Baldwin; Costumes, Theodora Van Runkel; In Metrocolor; August release. CAST: Faye Dunaway (Julia), Marcello Mastroianni (Valerio), Caroline Mortimer (Maggie), Karin Engh (Griselda).

SWEDEN—HEAVEN AND HELL (AVCO Embassy) Producer, Mario Bregini; Directed and Written by Luigi Scattini; Narrated by Edmund Purdom; Photography, Claudio Racca; Music, Piero Umiliani; In Widescreen and Eastmancolor; August release. CAST: Real life and re-created segments of Swedish freedom of expression.

LOVING FEELING (U-M) Producer, Bachoo Sen; Director, Norman J. Warren; Screenplay, Robert Hewison, Bachoo Sen; In Color; August release. CAST: Simon Brent (Stevee), Georgina Ward (Suzanne), Paula Patterson (Carol), John Railton (Scott), Francoise Pascal (Model), Heather Kyd (Christine).

THE BED SITTING ROOM (United Artists) Producer-Director, Richard Lester; Executive Producer, Oscar Lewenstein; Associate Producer, Roy Stevens; Screenplay, John Antrobus; Adapted by Charles Wood; From play by Spike Milligan, John Antrobus; Photography, David Watkin; In Eastmancolor; September release. CAST: Rita Tushingham (Penelope), Ralph Richardson (Lord Fortnum), Peter Cook (Inspector) Dudley Moore (Sergeant), Spike Milligan (Mate), Michael Hordern (Bules), Roy Kinnear (Plastic Mac), Richard Warwick (Allan), Arthur Lowe (Father), Mona Washbourne (Mother), Ronald Fraser (Field Marshall Sgt.), Dandy Nichols (Ethyl), Frank Thornton (BBC Man) Ron Moody (Dwarf), Gordon Rollings (Patient).

Robert Hoffman, Luciana Paluzzi in "A Black Veil For Lisa

Richard Warwick, Spike Milligan, Michael Hordern, Rita Tushingham in "The Bed Sitting Room"

Loni Von Friedl, Roy Thinnes in "Journey To The Far Side Of The Sun"

Virna Lisi, Terry-Thomas in "Arabella"

JOURNEY TO THE FAR SIDE OF THE SUN (Universal) Producers, Gerry and Sylvia Anderson; Associate Producer, Ernest Holding; Director, Robert Parrish; Screenplay, Gerry and Sylvia Anderson, Donald James; Story, Gerry and Sylvia Anderson; Photography, John Read; Music, Barry Gray; Assistant Director, John O'Connor; In Technicolor; September release. CAST: Ian Hendry (John), Roy Thinnes (Col. Ross), Patrick Wymark (Jason), Lynn Loring (Sharon), Loni Von Friedl (Lise), Herbert Lom (Dr. Hassler), George Sewell (Mark), Franco Derosa (Paulo), Edward Bishop (David).

THE ADDING MACHINE (Regional) Produced, Directed, and Written by Jerome Epstein; Based on play by Elmer Rice; Photography, Walter Lassally; Music, Mike Leander, Lambert Williamson; Costumes, Gabriella Falk; Assistant Director, Ray Corbett; In Technicolor; September release. CAST: Phyllis Diller (Mrs. Zero), Milo O'Shea (Zero), Billie Whitelaw (Daisy), Sydney Chaplin (Lt. Charles), Julian Glover (Shrdlu), Raymond Huntley (Smithers), Phil Brown (Don), Libby Morris (Ethel), Hugh McDermott (Harry), Paddie O'Neil (Mabel), Carol Cleveland (Judy), Bruce Boa (Detective), John Brandon (First Cell Jailer), Kenny Damon (Joe), Hal Galili (Second Cell Jailer), Tony Caunter (Third Cell Jailer), Bill Hutchinson (Judy's Lover), Helen Elliott (Second Apartment Girl), C. Denier Warren (Jury Foreman), Tommy Duggan (Judee), John Bloomfield, Helena Stevens, Alan Surtees, Christine Pryor, Cal McCord, Shirley Cooklin, Anthony Harwood (Apartment Tenants), Bill Nagy (Lawyer), Nicholas Stuart (District Attorney), Gordon Sterne, Mike Reed (Yard Guards), Lola Lloyd (Coffee Girl), George Margo (Gateman), Janet Brown (Fat & Thin Woman), John Cook (Husband).

ARABELLA (Universal) Producer, Maleno Malenotti; Director, Mauro Bolognini; Screenplay, Adriano Barocco; Associate Producer, Salvatore Argento; Photography, Ennio Guarnieri; Music, Ennio Morricone; Costumes, Piero Tosi; Assistant Director, Roberto Malenotti; A Cram Film in Technicolor; September release. CAST: Virna Lisi (Arabella), James Fox (Giorgio), Margaret Rutherford (Princess Ilaria), Terry-Thomas (Hotel Manager, General, Duke, Insurance Manager), Paola Borboni (Duchess Moretti), Antonio Casagrande (Filberto), Giancarlo Giannini (Saverio), Milena Vukotic (Graziella).

FANNY HILL (Cinemation) Producer, Jore Sjoberg; Directed and Written by Mac Ahlberg; Photography, Jan Lindstrom; Presented by Jerry Gross and Nicholas Demetroules; A Minerva-Europa Production in DeLuxe Color; September release. CAST: Diana Kjaer (Fanny Hill), Hans Ernback (Roger), Keve Hjelm (Leif), Oscar Ljung (Otto), Tina Hedstrom (Monika), Gio Petre (Fru Schoon), Mona Seilitz (Charlotte), Astrid Bye (Hanna), Bo Loof (Will), Gosta Pruzelius (Skeppsredare).

THE ITALIAN JOB (Paramount) Producer, Michael Deeley; Director, Peter Collinson; Screenplay, Troy Kennedy Martin; Music, Quincy Jones; Assistant Director, Scott Wodehouse; An Oakhurst Production in Panavision and Technicolor; September release. CAST: Michael Caine (Charlie Croker), Noel Coward (Bridger), Maggie Blye (Lorna), Benny Hill (Prof. Simon Peach), Tony Beckley (Freddie), Raf Vallone (Altabani), Rossano Brazzi (Beckerman), Lelia Goldoni (Madame Beckerman), George Innes (Bill), Harry Baird (Big William), Robert Powell (Yellow), John Forgeham (Frank), Michael Standing (Arfur), Derek Ware (Rozzer), Frank Jarvis (Roger), Stanley Caine (Coco).

Milo O'Shea, Phyllis Diller in "The Adding Machine"

Michael Caine, Graham Payn, Noel Coward in "The Italian Job"

Marié Du Toit, Gert Von Den Bergh in "Wild Season"

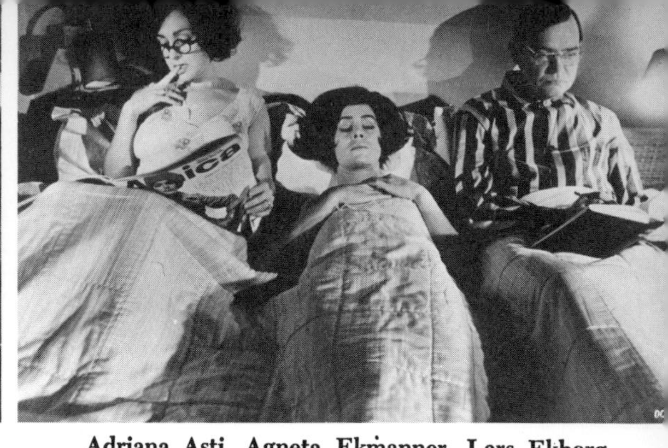

Adriana Asti, Agneta Ekmanner, Lars Ekborg in "Duet For Cannibals"

THE FOUNTAIN OF LOVE (Crown International) Producer, Carl Spiehs; Director, Ernst Hofbauer; Screenplay, Walter Schneider; Photography, Franz Lederle; Music, Claudius Alzner; Assistant Director, Zlata Mehlers; An Intercontinental Production in Pathe Color; September release. CAST: Eddi Arent (Alwin), Han-Jurgen Baumler (Leif), Ann Smyrner (Stina), Sieghardt Rupp (Nils), Hartmuth Hinrichs (Carl), Christa Linder (Britta), Christiane Rucker (Grit), Marianne Schonauer (Mrs. van Weyden), Helga Marlo (Caroline), Werner Abrolat (John), Emely Reuer (Frieda).

THE BABYSITTER (Crown International) Producer, George E. Carey; Director, Don Henderson; Screenplay, James E. McLarty; Story, George E. Carey, Don Henderson; Photography, Stanton R. Fox; Music, Robert O. Ragland; Lyrics, Sid Wayne; Assistant Director, Lord Douglas; September release. CAST: Patricia Wymer (Candy), George E. Carey (George), Ann Bellamy (Edith) Cathy Williams (Julie), Robert Tessier (Laurence), Ken Hooker (Raymond), Ted C. Frank (Kyle), James E. McLarty (Inkie), Sheri Jackson (Joan), Ruth Noonan (Doris), Warren Rose (Ben), Doris Rose (Aggie), Charles Messenger (Frank), Mary Messenger (Lena), Paul Wilmuth (Richard), Devon Blaine (dancer), Kari Longacre (dancer).

NANAMI (Golden Eagle) Director, Susumu Hani; Screenplay, Susumu Hani, Shuji Terayama; Photography, Yuji Okumura; September release. CAST: Akio Takahashi (Shun), Kuniko Ishii (Nanami), Koji Mitsui (Foster Father), Kazuko Fukuda (Foster Mother), Minoru Yuasa (Bearded man), Ischiro Kimura (Gang leader), Haruo Asano (Algebra).

WILD SEASON (Universal) Direction and Screenplay, Emil Hofal; October release. CAST: Gert Von Den Bergh, Marie Du Toit, Joe Stewardson, Janis Reinhardt, Antony Thomas, Johan Du Plooy, Ian Yule.

DUET FOR CANNIBALS (Grove) Producer, Goran Lindgren; Executive Producer, Peter Hald; Direction and Screenplay, Susan Sontag; Photography, Lars Swanberg; A Sandrew Films Production; October release. CAST: Adriana Asti (Francesca), Lars Ekborg (Bauer), Costa Ekman (Tomas), Agneta Ekmanner (Ingrid).

A WALK WITH LOVE AND DEATH (20th Century-Fox) Producer, Carter DeHaven; Director, John Huston; Associate Producer and author of Screenplay, Dale Wasserman; Adaptation, Hans Koningsberger from his novel; Music, Georges Delerue; Photography, Ted Scaife; Assistant Directors, Richard Overstreet, Wolfgang Glattes; Costumes, Leonor Fini; In DeLuxe Color; October release. CAST: Anjelica Huston (Claudia), Assaf Dayan (Heron), Anthony Corlan (Robert), John Hallam (Sir Meles), Robert Lang (Pilgrim Leader), Guy Deghy (Priest), Michael Gough (Mad Monk), George Murcell (Captain), Eileen Murphy (Gypsy), Anthony Nicholls (Father Superior), Joseph O'Connor (St. Jean), John Huston (Robert the Elder), John Franklin (Whoremaster), Francis Heim (Knight), Melvin Hayes, Barry Keegan, Nicholas Smith, Antoinette Reuss, Gilles Segal, Med Hondo, Luis Masson, Eugen Ledebur, Otto Dworak, Max Sulz, John Veenenbos, Dieter Tressler, Paul Hoer, Myra Malik, Michael Baronne Yvan Strogoff.

BLACK ON WHITE (Audubon) Director, Tinto Brass; Music, Freedom; A Lions Film Production in Eastmancolor; October release. CAST: Anita Sanders (Barbara), Nino Segurino (Paolo), Terry Carter (Negro).

FUEGO (Haven International) Produced, Directed, and Written by Armando Bo; Photography, Ricardo Younis; Music, Humberto Ubriaco, Armando Bo; In Eastmancolor; October release. CAST: Isabel Sarli (Laura), Armando Bo (Carlos), Alba Mujica (Andrea), Roberto Airaldi (Zalazar).

Anjelica Huston, Assaf Dayan in "A Walk With Love And Death"

Jona Obermayecova in "The Sign Of The Virgin"

"Deserter USA"

Doris Kuntsmann, Bernard De Vries in "The Sex Of Angels"

DESERTER USA (Kanawha) Producer, Lars Lambert/Sandrews; Executive Producer, Tomas Dyfverman; Directed and Written by Lars Lambert, Olle Sjogren; Photography, Roland Lundin; Music, Grapes of Wrath, Christer Eklund; November release. CAST: Bill Jones, Mark Shapiro, John Ashley, Jim Dotson, Steve Gershater, Warren Hamerman, John Toler, Lennart Schlytern.

INTIMATE LIGHTING (Altura) Director, Ivan Passer; Screenplay, Vaclav Sasek, Jaroslav Papousek, Ivan Passer; A Barrandov Film Studios Production; November release. CAST: Vera Kresadlova (Stepa), Zdenek Bezusek (Peter), Jan Vostrcil (Grandfather), Vlastimila Vlkova (Grandmother), Karel Blazek (Bambas), Jaroslava Stedra (Marie), Karel Uhlik (Pharmacist).

KAYA, I'LL KILL YOU! (Altura) Director, Vatroslav Mimica; Screenplay, Vatroslav Mimica, Kruno Quien; In Color; November release. CAST: Zaim Muzaferija (Kaya), Ugljesa Kojadinovic (Piero), Antun Nalis (Tonko), Jolanda Dacic (Mare), Izet Hajdarhodzic (Ugo), Husein Cokic (Niki).

SIGN OF THE VIRGIN (Brandon) Director, Zbynek Brynych; Screenplay, Milan Uhde, Zbynek Brynych; Based on story by Milan Uhde; November release. CAST: Josef Cap (Stan), Jaroslava Obermaierova (Jana), Vladimir Pucholt (Veleba), Jiri Wimmer (Beiman), Ilja Prachar (Capt. Pazourek), Jiri Adamira (Lt. Brezina), Rudolf Jelinek (Lt. Tonelser).

IN THE YEAR OF THE PIG (Pathe Contemporary) Producer-Director, Emile de Antonio; November release. A documentary giving the history of American intervention in Vietnam.

POPCORN (Sherpix) Producer, Peter Ryan; Director, Peter Clifton; In Color; November release. A documentary featuring popular recording entertainers, including, Mick Jagger, The Rolling Stones, Jimi Hendrix, Otis Redding, Vanilla Fudge, Bee Gees, Jo Cocker, The Groove, Beach Boys, Twiggy, Sebastian Jorgensen, Emperor Rosko.

THE SEX OF ANGELS (Lopert) Producer, Giorgio Venturini; Directed and Written by Ugo Liberatore; Photography, Leonida Barboni; Assistant Directors, Luigi Perelli, Robert Azderbal; Costumes, Nadia Vitali; A Filmes Cinematografica Production in Techniscope and Technicolor; December release. CAST: Bernard De Vries (Marco), Rosemarie Dexter (Nancy), Doris Kunstmann (Nora), Laura Troschel (Carla), Giovanni Petrucci (Luca), Efisio Cabras (Sergio), Brizio Montinaro (Pietro), Silvana Bacci (Karel), Hans Jurgen Neuman (Sailor).

DAY OF ANGER (National General) Producers, Alfonso Sansone, Enrico Chroscicky; Director, Tonino Valerii; Music, Riz Ortolani; Photography, Enzo Serafin; Story and Screenplay, Ernesto Gastaldi, Tonino Valerii, Renzo Genta; Based on novel by Ron Barker; In Techniscope and Technicolor; November release. CAST: Lee Van Cleef (Frank Talby), Giuliano Gemma (Mary Scott), Walter Rilla, Christa Linder, Ennio Balbo, Lukas Ammann, Andrea Bosic, Pepe Calvo, Giorgio Gargiullo, Anna Orso, Hans Otto Alberty, Nino Nini, Virgilio Gazzolo, Eleonora Morana, Benito Stefanelli.

JULIETTE DE SADE (Haven International) Producer, Ninki Maslansky; Co-Producers, James and Robert Brandt; Director, William Kiefer; In Eastmancolor; December release. CAST, Maria Pia Conte (Juliettè), Lea Nanni (Toni), Christine Delit (Clarissa), Angela DeLeo (Angela).

"In The Year Of The Pig"

Lee Van Cleef, Giuliano Gemma in "Day Of Anger"

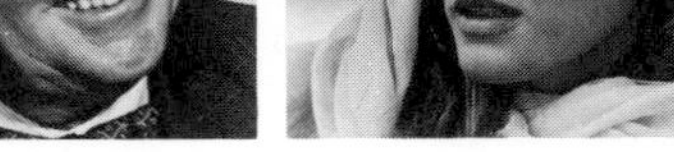

Alan Alda | Judith Anderson | Edward Andrews | Ursula Andress | Richard Attenborough

BIOGRAPHICAL DATA

(Name, real name, place and date of birth, and school attended)

ABBOTT, JOHN: London, June 5, 1905.

ADAMS, EDIE: (Elizabeth Edith Enke) Kingston, Pa., Apr. 16, 1931. Juilliard School of Music, Columbia.

ADAMS, JULIE: (Betty May) Waterloo, Iowa, Oct. 17, 1928. Little Rock Jr. College.

ADDAMS, DAWN: Felixstowe, Suffolk, Eng., Sept. 21, 1930. Royal Academy.

ADRIAN, IRIS: (Iris Adrian Hostetter) Los Angeles, May 29, 1913.

AGAR, JOHN: Chicago, Jan. 31, 1921.

AHERNE, BRIAN: Worcestershire, Eng., May 2, 1902. Malvern College, U. of London.

AHN, PHILIP: Los Angeles. Mar. 29, 1911. U. of Calif.

ALBERGHETTI, ANNA MARIA: Pesaro, Italy, May 15, 1936.

ALBERT, EDDIE: (Eddie Albert Heimberger) Rock Island, Ill., Apr. 22, 1908. U. of Minn.

ALBRIGHT, LOLA: Akron, Ohio, July 20, 1925.

ALDA, ALAN: NYC, Jan. 28, 1936, Fordham.

ALDA, ROBERT: (Alphonso D'Abruzzo) New York City, Feb. 26, 1914. NYU.

ALEJANDRO, MIGUEL: NYC, 1958.

ALLBRITTON, LOUISE: Oklahoma City, July 3, 1920. U. of Okla.

ALLEN, STEVE: New York City, Dec. 26, 1921.

ALLEN, WOODY: Brooklyn, Dec. 1, 1935.

ALLYSON, JUNE: (Ella Geisman) Westchester, N.Y., Oct. 7, 1923.

AMECHE, DON: (Dominic Amichi) Kenosha, Wisc., May 31, 1908.

AMES, ED: Boston, July 9, 1929.

AMES, LEON: (Leon Wycoff) Portland, Ind., Jan. 20, 1903.

ANDERSON, JUDITH: Adelaide, Australia, Feb. 10, 1898.

ANDERSON, MICHAEL, JR.: London, Eng., 1943.

ANDES, KEITH: Ocean City, N.J., July 12, 1920. Temple U., Oxford.

ANDRESS, URSULA: 1936.

ANDREWS, DANA: Collins, Miss., Jan. 1, 1912. Sam Houston College.

ANDREWS, EDWARD: Griffin, Ga., Oct. 9, 1914. U. Va.

ANDREWS, HARRY: Tonbridge, Kent, Eng., Nov. 10, 1911.

ANDREWS, JULIE: (Julia Elizabeth Wells) Oct. 1, 1935.

ANGEL, HEATHER: Oxford, Eng., Feb. 9, 1909. Wycombe Abbey School.

ANGELI, PIER: (Anna Maria Pierangeli) Sardinia, June 19, 1932.

ANN-MARGRET: Valsjobyn, Sweden, Apr. 28, 1941. Northwestern U.

ANSARA, MICHAEL: Lowell, Mass., Apr. 15, 1922. Pasadena Playhouse.

ANTHONY, TONY: Clarksburg, W. Va., Oct. 16, 1937. Carnegie Tech.

ARCHER, JOHN: (Ralph Bowman) Osceola, Neb., May 8, 1915. U. of S. Calif.

ARDEN, EVE: (Eunice Quedens) Mill Valley, Calif., Apr. 30, 1912.

ARKIN, ALAN: NYC, Mar. 26, 1934. LACC.

ARLEN, RICHARD: Charlottesville, Va., Sept. 1, 1900. St. Thomas College.

ARMSTRONG, LOUIS: New Orleans, July 4, 1900.

ARNAZ, DESI: Santiago, Cuba, Mar. 2, 1917. Colegio de Dolores.

ARNESS, JAMES: (Aurness) Minneapolis, Minn., May 26, 1923. Beloit College.

ARTHUR, JEAN: NYC, Oct. 17, 1908.

ARTHUR, ROBERT: (Robert Arthaud) Aberdeen, Wash., June 18. U. of Wash.

ASTAIRE, FRED: (Fred Austerlitz) Omaha, Neb., May 10, 1899.

ASTOR, MARY: (Lucile V. Langhanke) Quincy, Ill., May 3, 1906. Kenwood-Loring School.

ATTENBOROUGH, RICHARD: Cambridge, Eng., Aug. 29, 1923. RADA.

AULIN, EWA: Stockholm, Sweden, Feb. 14, 1950.

AUMONT, JEAN PIERRE: Paris, Jan. 5, 1913. French Nat'l School of Drama.

AUTRY, GENE: Tioga, Texas, Sept. 29, 1907.

AVALON, FRANKIE: (Francis Thomas Avallone) Philadelphia, Sept. 18, 1940.

AYLMER, FELIX: Corsham, Eng., Feb. 21, 1889. Oxford.

AYRES, LEW: Minneapolis, Minn., Dec. 28, 1908.

BACALL, LAUREN: (Betty Perske) NYC, Sept. 16, 1924. AADA.

BACKUS, JIM: Cleveland, Ohio, Feb. 25, 1913. AADA.

BADDELEY, HERMIONE: Shropshire, Eng., Nov. 13, 1908. Margaret Morris School.

BAILEY, PEARL: Newport News, Va., March 29, 1918.

BAIN, BARBARA: Chicago, Sept. 13, 1934. U. Ill.

BAKER, CARROLL: Johnstown, Pa., May 28, 1931. St. Petersburg Jr. College.

BAKER, DIANE: Hollywood, Feb. 25, USC.

BAKER, STANLEY: Glamorgan, Wales, Feb. 28, 1928.

BALIN, INA: Brooklyn, Nov. 12, 1937. NYU.

BALL, LUCILLE: Jamestown, N.Y., Aug. 6, 1911. Chatauqua Musical Inst.

BALSAM, MARTIN: NYC, Nov. 4, 1919. Actors Studio.

BANCROFT, ANNE: (Anna Maria Italiano) Bronx, N. Y., Sept. 17, 1931. AADA.

BANNEN, IAN: Airdrie, Scot., June 29, 1928.

BARDOT, BRIGITTE: Paris, 1934.

BARKER, LEX: (Alexander Crichlow Barker) Rye, N.Y., May 8, 1919.

BARRIE, WENDY: London, May 8, 1919.

BARRY, DONALD: (Donald Barry de Acosta) Houston, Tex. Texas School of Mines.

BARRY, GENE: (Eugene Klass) NYC, June 14, 1921.

BARRYMORE, JOHN BLYTH: Beverly Hills, Calif., June 4, 1932. St. John's Military Academy.

BARTHOLOMEW, FREDDIE: London, Mar. 28, 1924.

BASEHART, RICHARD: Zanesville, Ohio, Aug. 31, 1914.

BATES, ALAN: Allestree, Derbyshire, Eng., Feb. 17, 1934. RADA.

BAXTER, ALAN: East Cleveland, Ohio, Nov. 19, 1911. Williams U.

BAXTER, ANNE: Michigan City, Ind., May 7, 1923. Ervine School of Drama.

Brigitte Bardot

Jim Backus

Candice Bergen

Jim Brown

Coral Browne

BEAL, JOHN: (J. Alexander Bliedung) Joplin, Mo., Aug. 13, 1909. Pa. U.

BEATTY, ROBERT: Hamilton, Ont., Can., Oct. 19, 1909. U. of Toronto.

BEATTY, WARREN: Richmond, Virginia, March 30, 1937.

BEAUMONT, HUGH: Lawrence, Kan., Feb. 16, 1909. U. of Chattanooga, USC.

BEERY, NOAH, JR.: NYC, Aug. 10, 1916. Harvard Military Academy.

BEGLEY, ED: Hartford, Conn., Mar. 25, 1901. Conn. School for Boys.

BELAFONTE, HARRY: NYC, Mar. 1, 1927.

BELASCO, LEON: Odessa, Russia, Oct. 11, 1902.

BEL GEDDES, BARBARA: NYC, Oct. 31, 1922.

BELLAMY, RALPH: Chicago, June 17, 1905.

BELMONDO, JEAN PAUL: Paris, 1933.

BENNETT, BRUCE: (Herman Brix) Tacoma, Wash., U. of Wash.

BENNETT, JOAN: Palisades, N.J., Feb. 27, 1910. St. Margaret's School.

BENNY, JACK: (Jack Kubelsky) Waukegan, Ill. Feb. 14, 1894.

BERGEN, CANDICE: Los Angeles, 1946.

BERGEN, EDGAR: Chicago, Feb. 16, 1903. Northwestern U.

BERGEN, POLLY: Knoxville, Tenn., July 14, 1930. Compton Jr. College.

BERGERAC, JACQUES: Biarritz, France, May 26, 1927. Paris U. of Law.

BERGMAN, INGRID: Stockholm, Sweden, Aug. 29, 1917. Royal Dramatic Theatre School.

BERLE, MILTON: (Milton Berlinger) NYC, July 12, 1908. Professional Children's School.

BERLINGER, WARREN: Brooklyn, Aug. 31, 1937. Columbia University.

BEST, JAMES: Corydon, Ind., July 26, 1926.

BETTGER, LYLE: Philadelphia, Feb. 13, 1915. AADA.

BETZ, CARL: Pittsburgh, Mar. 9. Duquesne, Carnegie Tech.

BEYMER, RICHARD: Avoca, Iowa, Feb. 21, 1939.

BIKEL, THEODORE: Vienna, May 2, 1924. RADA.

BISHOP, JOEY: (Joseph Abraham Gottlieb) Bronx, NY, Feb. 3, 1918.

BISHOP, JULIE: (formerly Jacqueline Wells) Denver, Colo., Aug. 30, 1917. Westlake School.

BISSET, JACQUELINE: Waybridge, Eng., Sept. 13, 1944.

BIXBY, BILL: San Francisco, Jan. 22, 1934. U. Cal.

BLACKMER, SIDNEY: Salisbury, N.C., July 13, 1898. U. of N.C.

BLAINE, VIVIAN: (Vivian Stapleton) Newark, N.J., Nov. 21, 1924.

BLAIR, BETSY: (Betsy Boger) NYC, Dec. 11.

BLAIR, JANET: (Martha Jane Lafferty) Blair, Pa., Apr. 23, 1921.

BLAKE, AMANDA: (Beverly Louise Neill) Buffalo, N.Y., Feb. 20.

BLAKE, ROBERT: Nutley, N.J., 1933.

BLONDELL, JOAN: NYC, Aug. 30, 1909.

BLOOM, CLAIRE: London, Feb. 15, 1931. Badminton School.

BLUE, BEN: Montreal, Can., Sept. 12, 1901.

BLUE, MONTE: Indianapolis, Jan. 11, 1890.

BLYTH, ANN: Mt. Kisco, N.Y., Aug. 16, 1928. New Wayburn Dramatic School.

BOGARDE, DIRK: London, Mar. 28, 1921. Glasgow & Univ. College.

BOLGER, RAY: Dorchester, Mass., Jan. 10, 1906.

BOND, DEREK: Glasgow, Scot., Jan. 26, 1920. Askes School.

BONDI, BEULAH: Chicago, May 3, 1892.

BOONE, PAT: Jacksonville, Fla., June 1, 1934. Columbia U.

BOONE, RICHARD: Los Angeles. Stanford U.

BOOTH, SHIRLEY: NYC, Aug. 30, 1907.

BORGNINE, ERNEST: Hamden, Conn., Jan. 24, 1918. Randall School of Dramatic Art.

BOWMAN, LEE: Cincinnati, Dec. 28, 1914. AADA.

BOYD, STEPHEN: (William Millar) Belfast, Ire., 1928.

BOYER, CHARLES: Figeac, France, Aug. 28, 1899. Sorbonne U.

BRACKEN, EDDIE: NYC, Feb. 7, 1920. Professional Children's School.

BRADY, SCOTT: (Jerry Tierney) Brooklyn, Sept. 13, 1924. Bliss-Hayden Dramatic School.

BRAND, NEVILLE: Kewanee, Ill., Aug. 13, 1921.

BRANDO, JOCELYN: San Francisco, Nov. 18, 1919. Lake Forest College. AADA.

BRANDO, MARLON: Omaha, Neb., Apr. 3, 1924. New School of Social Research.

BRASSELLE, KEEFE: Elyria, Ohio, Feb. 7.

BRAZZI, ROSSANO: Bologna, Italy, 1916. U. of Florence.

BRENT, GEORGE: Dublin, Ire., Mar. 15, 1904. Dublin U.

BRENT, ROMNEY: (Romulo Larralde) Saltillo, Mex., Jan. 26, 1902.

BRIALY, JEAN-CLAUDE: Aumale, Algeria, 1933. Strasbourg Dramatic Cons.

BRIAN, DAVID: NYC, Aug. 5, 1914. CCNY.

BRIDGES, BEAU: Los Angeles, Dec. 9, 1941. UCLA.

BRIDGES, LLOYD: San Leandro, Calif., Jan. 15, 1913.

BRITT, MAY: (Maybritt Wilkins) Sweden, March 22, 1936.

BRODIE, STEVE: (Johnny Stevens) Eldorado, Kan., Nov. 25, 1919.

BROMFIELD, JOHN: (Farron Bromfield) South Bend, Ind., June 11, 1922. St. Mary's College.

BROOKS, GERALDINE: (Geraldine Stroock) NYC, Oct. 29, 1925. AADA.

BROWN, JAMES: Desdemona, Tex., Mar. 22, 1920. Baylor U.

BROWN, JIM: Manhasset, L.I., NY, Feb. 17, 1936. Syracuse U.

BROWN, JOE E.: Helgate, Ohio, July 28, 1892.

BROWN, TOM: NYC, Jan. 6, 1913. Professional Children's School.

BROWNE, CORAL: Melbourne, Aust., July 23, 1913.

BRUCE, VIRGINIA: Minneapolis, Sept. 29, 1910.

BRYNNER, YUL: Sakhalin Island, Japan, June 15, 1915.

BUCHHOLZ, HORST: Berlin, Ger., Dec. 4, 1933. Ludwig Dramatic School.

BUETEL, JACK: Dallas, Tex., Sept. 5, 1917.

BURKE, BILLIE: Washington, D.C., Aug. 7, 1885.

BURKE, PAUL: New Orleans, July 21, 1926. Pasadena Playhouse.

BURNETT, CAROL: San Antonio, Tex., Apr. 26, 1933. UCLA.

BURNS, GEORGE: (Nathan Birnbaum) NYC Jan. 20, 1896.

BURR, RAYMOND: New Westminster, B.C., Can., May 21, 1917. Stanford, U. of Cal., Columbia.

BURTON, RICHARD: (Richard Jenkins) Pontrhydyfen, S. Wales, Nov. 10, 1925. Oxford.

BUTTONS, RED: (Aaron Chwatt) NYC, Feb. 5, 1919.

BUZZI, RUTH: Wequetequock, R.I., July 24, 1936. Pasadena Playhouse.

Peggy Cass

Glen Campbell

Carol Channing

John Cassavetes

Adrienne Corri

BYGRAVES, MAX: London, Oct. 16, 1922. St. Joseph's School.

BYRNES, EDD: NYC, July 30, 1933. Haaren High.

CABOT, BRUCE: (Jacques de Bujac) Carlsbad, N.Mex. U. South.

CABOT, SUSAN: Boston, July 9, 1927.

CAESAR, SID: Yonkers, N.Y., Sept. 8, 1922.

CAGNEY, JAMES: NYC, July 1, 1904. Columbia.

CAGNEY, JEANNE: NYC, Mar. 25, 1919. Hunter College.

CAINE, MICHAEL: (Maurice Mickelwhite) London, Mar. 14, 1933.

CALHOUN, RORY: (Francis Timothy Durgin) Los Angeles, Aug. 8, 1923.

CALLAN, MICHAEL: (Martin Calininff) Philadelphia, Nov. 22, 1935.

CALVERT, PHYLLIS: London, Feb. 18, 1917. Margaret Morris School.

CALVET, CORINNE: (Corinne Dibos) Paris, Apr. 30. U. of Paris.

CAMERON, ROD: (Rod Cox) Calgary, Alberta, Can., Dec. 7, 1912.

CAMPBELL, GLEN: Apr. 22, 1935.

CANALE, GIANNA MARIA: Reggio Calabria, Italy, Sept. 12.

CANOVA, JUDY: Jacksonville, Fla., Nov. 20, 1916.

CAPUCINE: (Germaine Lefebvre) Toulon, France, Jan. 6, 1935.

CARDINALE, CLAUDIA: Italy, 1939.

CAREY, HARRY, JR.: Saugus, Calif., May 16. Black Fox Military Academy.

CAREY, MACDONALD: Sioux City, Iowa, Mar. 15, 1913. U of Wisc., U. of Iowa.

CAREY, PHILIP: Hackensack, N.J., July 15, 1925. U. of Miami.

CARMICHAEL, HOAGY: Bloomington, Ind., Nov. 22, 1899. Ind. U.

CARMICHAEL, IAN: Hull, Eng., June 18, 1920. Scarborough College.

CARNE, JUDY: (Joyce Botterill) Northampton, Eng., 1939. Bush-Davis Theatre School.

CARNEY, ART: Mt. Vernon, N. Y., Nov. 4, 1918.

CARON, LESLIE: Paris, July 1, 1931. Nat'l Conservatory, Paris.

CARRADINE, DAVID: Hollywood, Dec. 8, 1940. San Francisco State.

CARRADINE, JOHN: NYC, Feb. 5, 1906.

CARROLL, DIAHANN: (Johnson) NYC, July 17, 1935. NYU.

CARROLL, JOHN: (Julian LaFaye) New Orleans.

CARROLL, MADELEINE: West Bromwich, Eng., Feb. 26, 1906. Birmingham U.

CARROLL, PAT: Shreveport, La., May 5, 1927. Catholic U.

CARSON, JOHNNY: Corning, Iowa, Oct. 23, 1925. U. of Neb.

CASS, PEGGY: (Mary Margaret) Boston, May 21, 1925.

CASSAVETES, JOHN: NYC Dec. 9, 1929. Colgate College, Academy of Dramatic Arts.

CASTLE, PEGGIE: Appalachia, Va., Dec. 22, 1927. Mills College.

CAULFIELD, JOAN: Orange, N.J., June 1. Columbia U.

CERVI, GINO: Bologna, Italy, May 3, 1901.

CHAKIRIS, GEORGE: Norwood, O., Sept. 16, 1933.

CHAMBERLAIN, RICHARD: Beverly Hills, Cal., March 31, 1935. Pomona.

CHAMPION, GOWER: Geneva, Ill., June 22, 1921.

CHAMPION, MARGE: Los Angeles, Sept. 2, 1926.

CHANDLER, LANE: (Lane Oakes) Culbertson, Mont., June 4, 1899. Ill. U.

CHANEY, LON, JR.: (Creighton Chaney) Oklahoma City, 1915.

CHANNING, CAROL: Seattle, Jan. 31, 1921. Bennington.

CHAPLIN, CHARLES: London, Apr. 16, 1889.

CHAPLIN, GERALDINE: July 31, 1944.

CHAPLIN, SYDNEY: Los Angeles, Mar. 31, 1926. Lawrenceville.

CHARISSE, CYD: (Tula Ellice Finklea) Amarillo, Tex., Mar. 8, 1923. Hollywood Professional School.

CHASE, ILKA: NYC, Apr. 8, 1905.

CHEVALIER, MAURICE: Paris, Sept. 12, 1888.

CHIARI, WALTER: Veronea, Italy, 1930.

CHRISTIAN, LINDA: (Blanca Rosa Welter) Tampico, Mex., Nov. 13, 1923.

CHRISTIE, JULIE: Chukua, Assam, India, Apr. 14, 1941.

CHRISTOPHER, JORDAN: Youngstown, O., Oct. 23, 1940. Kent State U.

CHURCHILL, SARAH: London, Oct. 7, 1916.

CILENTO, DIANE: Queensland, Australia, Oct. 5, 1933. AADA.

CLARK, DANE: NYC, Feb. 18, 1915. Cornell and Johns Hopkins U.

CLARK, DICK: Mt. Vernon, N. Y., Nov. 30, 1929. Syracuse University.

CLARK, PETULA: England, 1932.

CLARKE, MAE: Philadelphia, Aug. 16, 1910.

CLEMENTS, STANLEY: Long Island, N.Y., July 16, 1926.

CLOONEY, ROSEMARY: Maysville, Ky., May 23, 1928.

COBB, LEE J.: NYC, Dec. 8, 1911. CCNY.

COBURN, JAMES: Laurel, Neb., Aug. 31, 1928. LACC.

COCA, IMOGENE: Philadelphia, Nov. 18, 1908.

COLBERT, CLAUDETTE: (Claudette Chauchoin) Paris, Sept. 13, 1907. Art Students League.

COLE, GEORGE: London, Apr. 22, 1925.

COLLINS, JOAN: London, May 23, 1933. Francis Holland School.

COMER, ANJANETTE: Dawson, Tex., Aug. 7, 1942. Baylor, Tex. U.

CONNERY, SEAN: Edinburgh, Scot., Aug. 25, 1930.

CONNORS, CHUCK: (Kevin Joseph Connors) Brooklyn, Apr. 10, 1924. Seton Hall College.

CONTE, RICHARD: (Nicholas Conte) NYC, Mar. 24, 1914. Neighborhood Playhouse.

COOGAN, JACKIE: Los Angeles, Oct. 26, 1914. Villanova College.

COOK, ELISHA, JR.: San Francisco, Dec. 26, 1907. St. Albans.

COOPER, BEN: Hartford, Conn., Sept. 30. Columbia U.

COOPER, GLADYS: Lewisham, Eng., Dec. 18, 1891.

COOPER, JACKIE: Los Angeles, Sept. 15, 1921.

COOPER, MELVILLE: Birmingham, Eng., Oct. 15, 1896. King Edward's School.

COOTE, ROBERT: London, Feb. 4, 1909. Hurstpierpont College.

CORCORAN, DONNA: Quincy, Mass., Sept. 29.

CORD, ALEX: (Viespi) Floral Park, L.I., Aug. 3, 1931. NYU, Actors Studio.

CORDAY, MARA: (Marilyn Watts) Santa Monica, Calif., Jan. 3, 1932.

COREY, JEFF: NYC, Aug. 10, 1914. Fagin School.

CORRI, ADRIENNE: Glasgow, Scot., Nov. 13, 1933. RADA.

CORTESA, VALENTINA: Milan, Italy, Jan. 1, 1925.

Ossie Davis

Kim Darby

Assaf Dayan

Angie Dickinson

Alain Delon

COSBY, BILL: Philadelphia, 1937. Temple U.

COTTEN, JOSEPH: Petersburg, Va., May 15, 1905.

COURTENAY, TOM: Hull, Eng., 1937. RADA.

COURTLAND, JEROME: Knoxville, Tenn., Dec. 27, 1926.

COWARD, NOEL: Teddington-on-the-Thames, Eng., Dec. 16, 1899.

COX, WALLY: Detroit, Dec. 6, 1924. CCNY.

CRABBE, BUSTER (LARRY): (Clarence Linden) Oakland, Calif., U. of S. Cal.

CRAIG, JAMES: (James H. Meador) Nashville, Tenn., Feb. 4, 1912. Rice Inst.

CRAIG, MICHAEL: India in 1929.

CRAIN, JEANNE: Barstow, Cal., May 25, 1925.

CRAWFORD, BRODERICK: Philadelphia, Dec. 9, 1911.

CRAWFORD, JOAN: (Billie Cassin) San Antonio, Tex., Mar. 23, 1908.

CRENNA, RICHARD: Los Angeles, 1927. USC.

CRISTAL, LINDA: (Victoria Moya) Buenos Aires, 1935.

CROSBY, BING: (Harry Lillith Crosby) Tacoma, Wash., May 2, 1904. Gonzaga College.

CROWLEY, PAT: Olyphant, Pa., Sept. 17, 1933.

CULP, ROBERT: Berkeley, Calif., Aug. 16, 1930. U. of Wash.

CUMMINGS, CONSTANCE: Seattle, Wash., May 15, 1910.

CUMMINGS, ROBERT: Joplin, Mo., June 9, 1910. Carnegie Tech.

CUMMINS, PEGGY: Prestatyn, N. Wales, Dec. 18, 1926. Alexandra School.

CURTIS, TONY: (Bernard Schwartz) NYC, June 3, 1925.

CUSHING, PETER: Kenley, Surrey, Eng., May 26, 1913.

CUTTS, PATRICIA: London, July 20, 1927. RADA.

DAHL, ARLENE: Minneapolis, Aug. 11, 1927. U. Minn.

DAMONE, VIC: (Vito Farinola) Brooklyn, June 12, 1928.

DANIELS, WILLIAM: Bklyn, Mar. 31, 1927. Northwestern.

DANTINE, HELMUT: Vienna, Oct. 7, 1918. U. Calif.

DANTON, RAY: NYC, Sept. 19, 1931. Carnegie Tech.

DARBY, KIM: (Deborah Zerby) North Hollywood, Cal., July 8, 1948.

DARCEL, DENISE: (Denise Billecard) Paris, Sept. 8, 1925. U. Dijon.

DARIN, BOBBY: (Robert Walden Cassotto) NYC, May 14, 1936. Hunter College.

DARREN, JAMES: Philadelphia, June 8, 1936. Stella Adler School.

DARRIEUX, DANIELLE: Bordeaux, France, May 1, 1917. Lycée LaTour.

DARVI, BELLA: (Bella Wegier) Sosnoviec, Poland, Oct. 23, 1928.

DA SILVA, HOWARD: Cleveland, Ohio, May 4, 1909. Carnegie Tech.

DAUPHIN, CLAUDE: Corbeil, France, Aug. 19, 1903. Beaux Arts School.

DAVIDSON, JOHN: Pittsburgh, Dec. 13, 1941. Denison U.

DAVIS, BETTE: Lowell, Mass., Apr. 5, 1908. John Murray Anderson Dramatic School.

DAVIS, OSSIE: Cogdell, Ga., Dec. 18, 1917. Howard U.

DAVIS, SAMMY, JR.: NYC, Dec. 8, 1925.

DAY, DENNIS: (Eugene Dennis McNulty) NYC, May 21, 1917. Manhattan College.

DAY, DORIS: (Doris Kappelhoff) Cincinnati, Apr. 3, 1924.

DAY, LARAINE: (Johnson) Roosevelt, Utah, Oct. 13, 1920.

DAYAN, ASSEF: Israel, 1945. U. Jerusalem.

DEAN, JIMMY: Plainview, Tex., Aug. 10, 1928.

DE CARLO, YVONNE: Vancouver, B.C., Can., Sept. 1, 1924. Vancouver School of Drama.

DE CORDOVA, ARTURO: Merida, Yucatan, May 8, 1908. Cavin Inst.

DEE, FRANCES: Los Angeles, Nov. 26, 1907. Chicago U.

DEE, JOEY: (Joseph Di Nicola) Passaic, N.J., June 11, 1940. Patterson State College.

DEE, SANDRA: (Alexandra Zuck) Bayonne, N. J., Apr. 23, 1942.

DE FORE, DON: Cedar Rapids, Iowa, Aug. 25, 1917. U. Iowa.

DE HAVEN, GLORIA: Los Angeles, July 23, 1925.

DE HAVILLAND, OLIVIA: Tokyo, Japan, July 1, 1916. Notre Dame Convent School.

DEL RIO, DOLORES: (Dolores Ansunsolo) Durango, Mex., Aug. 3, 1905. St. Joseph's Convent.

DENISON, MICHAEL: Doncaster, York, Eng., Nov. 1, 1915. Oxford.

DENNIS, SANDY: Hastings, Neb., Apr. 27, 1937. Actors Studio.

DEREK, JOHN: Hollywood, Aug. 12, 1926.

DE SICA, VITTORIO: Sora, Caserta, Italy, July 7, 1902.

DEVINE, ANDY: Flagstaff, Ariz., Oct. 7, 1905. Ariz. State College.

DE WILDE, BRANDON: Brooklyn, Apr. 9, 1942.

DE WOLFE, BILLY: (William Andrew Jones) Wollaston, Mass., Feb. 18.

DEXTER, ANTHONY: (Walter Reinhold Alfred Fleischmann) Talmadge, Neb., Jan. 19, 1919. U. Iowa.

DICKINSON, ANGIE: Kulm, N. Dak., Sept. 30, 1932. Glendale College.

DIETRICH, MARLENE: (Maria Magdalene von Losch) Berlin, Ger., Dec. 27, 1904. Berlin Music Academy.

DILLER, PHYLLIS: Lima, O., July 17, 1917. Bluffton College.

DILLMAN, BRADFORD: San Francisco, Apr. 14, 1930. Yale.

DOMERGUE, FAITH: New Orleans, June 16, 1925.

DONAHUE, TROY: (Merle Johnson) NYC, Jan. 27, 1937. Columbia U.

DONNELL, JEFF: (Jean Donnell) South Windham, Me., July 10, 1921. Yale Drama School.

DONNELLY, RUTH: Trenton, N.J., May 17, 1896.

DORS, DIANA: Swindon, Wilshire, Eng., Oct. 23, 1931. London Academy of Music.

DOUGLAS, KIRK: Amsterdam, N.Y., Dec. 9, 1916. St. Lawrence U.

DOUGLAS, MELVYN: (Melvyn Hesselberg) Macon, Ga., Apr. 5, 1901.

DOUGLAS, MICHAEL KIRK: Hollywood, 1945. UCal.

DRAKE, BETSY: Paris, Sept. 11, 1923.

DRAKE, CHARLES: (Charles Ruppert) NYC, Oct. 2, 1914. Nichols College.

DREW, ELLEN: (formerly Terry Ray) Kansas City, Mo., Nov. 23, 1915.

DRISCOLL, BOBBY: Cedar Rapids, Iowa, Mar. 3, 1937.

DRIVAS, ROBERT: Chicago, Nov. 21, 1938. U. Chi.

DRU, JOANNE: (Joanne LaCock) Logan, W. Va., Jan. 31, 1923. John Robert Powers School.

DUFF, HOWARD: Bremerton, Wash., Nov. 24, 1917.

DUKE, PATTY: NYC, Dec. 14, 1946.

Clint Eastwood

Samantha Eggar

Robert Forster

Barbara Ferris

Al Freeman, Jr.

DULLEA, KEIR: Cleveland, N.J., May 30, 1936. Neighborhood Playhouse, SF State Col.

DUNAWAY, FAYE: Tallahassee, Fla., Jan. 14, 1941. Fla. U.

DUNN, MICHAEL: Shattuck, Okla., Oct. 20, 1934. U. Mich.

DUNNE, IRENE: Louisville, Ky., Dec. 20, 1904. Chicago College of Music.

DUNNOCK, MILDRED: Baltimore, Jan. 25, 1906. Johns Hopkins and Columbia U.

DURANTE, JIMMY: NYC, Feb. 10, 1893.

DVORAK, ANN: (Ann McKim) NYC, Aug. 2, 1912.

EASTON, ROBERT: Milwaukee, Nov. 23, 1930. U. of Texas.

EASTWOOD, CLINT: San Francisco, May 31, 1931. LACC.

EATON, SHIRLEY: London, 1937. Aida Foster School.

EDEN, BARBARA: (Moorhead) Tucson, Ariz., 1934.

EDWARDS, VINCE: NYC, July 9, 1928. AADA.

EGAN, RICHARD: San Francisco, July 29, 1923. Stanford U.

EGGAR, SAMANTHA: London, 1940.

EKBERG, ANITA: Malmo, Sweden, Sept. 29, 1931.

ELLIOTT, DENHOLM: London, May 31, 1922. Malvern College.

ELSOM, ISOBEL: Cambridge, Eng., Mar. 16, 1894.

ELY, RON: (Ronald Pierce) Hereford, Tex. June 21, 1938.

EMERSON, FAYE: Elizabeth, La., July 8, 1917. San Diego State College.

ERDMAN, RICHARD: Enid, Okla., June 1, 1925.

ERICKSON, LEIF: Alameda, Calif., Oct. 27, 1914. U. of Calif.

ERICSON, JOHN: Dusseldorf, Ger., Sept. 25, 1926. AADA.

ESMOND, CARL: Vienna, June 14, 1906. U. of Vienna.

EVANS, DALE: (Frances Smith) Uvalde, Texas, Oct. 31, 1912.

EVANS, EDITH: London, Feb. 8, 1888.

EVANS, GENE: Holbrook, Ariz., July 11, 1922.

EVANS, MAURICE: Dorchester, Eng., June 3, 1901.

EWELL, TOM: (Yewell Tompkins) Owensboro, Ky., Apr. 29, 1909. U. of Wisc.

FABIAN: (Fabian Forte) Philadelphia, Feb. 6, 1940.

FABRAY, NANETTE: (Ruby Nanette Fabares) San Diego, Oct. 27, 1920.

FAIRBANKS, DOUGLAS, JR.: NYC, Dec. 9, 1909. Collegiate School.

FALK, PETER: NYC, Sept. 16, 1927. New School.

FARR, FELICIA: Westchester, N.Y., Oct. 4, 1932. Penn State College.

FARRELL, CHARLES: Onset Bay, Mass., Aug. 9, 1901. Boston U.

FARRELL, GLENDA: Enid, Okla., June 30, 1904.

FARROW, MIA: Los Angeles, 1945.

FAYE, ALICE: (Ann Lepert) NYC, May 5, 1915.

FELLOWS, EDITH: Boston, May 20, 1923.

FERNANDEL: (Fernand Joseph Desire Constandin) Marseilles, France, 1903.

FERRER, JOSE: Santurce, P.R., Jan. 8, 1912. Princeton U.

FERRER, MEL: Elberon, N.J., Aug. 25, 1917. Princeton U.

FERRIS, BARBARA: London 1943.

FIELD, BETTY: Boston, Feb. 8, 1913, AADA.

FIELD, SALLY: Pasadena, Cal., Nov. 6, 1946.

FIGUEROA, RUBEN: NYC 1958.

FINCH, PETER: London, Sept. 28, 1916.

FINNEY, ALBERT: Salford, Lancashire, Eng., May 9, 1936. RADA.

FISHER, EDDIE: Philadelphia, Aug. 10, 1928.

FITZGERALD, GERALDINE: Dublin, Ire., Nov. 24, 1914. Dublin Art School.

FLEMING, RHONDA: (Marilyn Louis) Los Angeles, Aug. 10, 1922.

FLEMYNG, ROBERT: Liverpool, Eng., Jan. 3, 1912. Haileybury College.

FOCH, NINA: Leyden, Holland, Apr. 20, 1924.

FONDA, HENRY: Grand Island, Neb., May 16, 1905. Minn. U.

FONDA, JANE: NYC, Dec. 21, 1937. Vassar.

FONDA, PETER: NYC, Feb. 23, 1939. U. of Omaha.

FONTAINE, JOAN: Tokyo, Japan, Oct. 22, 1917.

FORD, GLENN: (Gwylln Ford) Quebec, Can., May 1, 1917.

FORD, PAUL: Baltimore, Nov. 2, 1901. Dartmouth.

FOREST, MARK: (Lou Degni) Brooklyn, Jan. 1933.

FORREST, STEVE: Huntsville, Tex., Sept. 29. UCLA.

FORSTER, ROBERT: (Foster, Jr.) Rochester, N.Y., July 13, 1941. Rochester U.

FORSYTHE, JOHN: Penn's Grove, N.J., Jan. 29, 1918.

FOSTER, PRESTON: Ocean City, N.J., Aug. 24, 1904.

FOX, JAMES: London, 1939.

FRANCES, CONNIE: (Constance Franconero) Newark, N.J., Dec. 12, 1938.

FRANCIOSA, ANTHONY: NYC, Oct. 25, 1928.

FRANCIS, ANNE: Ossining, N. Y., Sept. 16.

FRANCIS, ARLENE: (Arlene Kazanjian) Boston, Oct. 20, 1908. Finch School.

FRANCKS, DON: Vancouver, Can., Feb. 28, 1932.

FRANZ, ARTHUR: Perth Amboy, N.J., Feb. 29, 1920. Blue Ridge College.

FRANZ, EDUARD: Milwaukee, Wisc., Oct. 31, 1902.

FREEMAN, AL, JR.: San Antonio, Texas, 1934. CCLA.

FREEMAN, MONA: Baltimore, June 9, 1926.

FURNEAUX, YVONNE: Lille, France, 1928. Oxford U.

GABEL, MARTIN: Philadelphia, June 19, 1912. AADA.

GABIN, JEAN: Villette, France, May 17, 1904.

GABOR, EVA: Budapest, Hungary, Feb. 11, 1925.

GABOR, ZSA ZSA: (Sari Gabor) Budapest, Hungary, Feb. 6, 1923.

GAM, RITA: Pittsburgh, Apr. 2, 1928.

GARBO, GRETA: (Greta Gustafson) Stockholm, Sweden, Sept. 18, 1906.

GARDINER, REGINALD: Wimbledon, Eng., Feb. 1903. RADA.

GARDNER, AVA: (Lucy Johnson) Smithfield, N.C., Dec. 24, 1922. Atlantic Christian College.

GARNER, JAMES: (James Baumgarner) Norman, Okla., Apr. 7, 1928. Berghof School.

GARNER, PEGGY ANN: Canton, Ohio, Feb. 3, 1932.

GARRETT, BETTY: St. Joseph, Mo., May 23, 1919. Annie Wright Seminary.

GARRISON, SEAN: NYC, Oct. 19, 1937.

GARSON, GREER: Ireland, Sept. 29, 1908.

GASSMAN, VITTORIO: Genoa, Italy, Sept. 1, 1922. Rome Academy of Dramatic Art.

GAVIN, JOHN: Los Angeles, Apr. 8. Stanford U.

GAYNOR, JANET: Philadelphia, Oct. 6, 1906.

GAYNOR, MITZI: (Francesca Mitzi Von Gerber) Chicago, Sept. 4, 1930.

GAZZARA, BEN: NYC, Aug. 28, 1930.

GENN, LEO: London, Aug. 9, 1905. Cambridge.

Greer Garson

Robert Goulet

Barbara Harris

Richard Harris

Susan Hayward

GIELGUD, JOHN: London, Apr. 14, 1904. RADA.

GILLMORE, MARGOLO: London, May 31, 1897. AADA.

GILMORE, VIRGINIA: (Sherman Poole) Del Monte, Calif., July 26, 1919. U. of Calif.

GINGOLD, HERMIONE: London, Dec. 9, 1897.

GISH, LILLIAN: Springfield, Ohio, Oct. 14, 1896.

GLEASON, JACKIE: Brooklyn, Feb. 26, 1916.

GODDARD, PAULETTE: (Levy) Great Neck, N.Y., June 3, 1911.

GOMEZ, THOMAS: NYC, July 10, 1905.

GORDON, RUTH: Wollaston, Mass., Oct. 30, 1896. AADA.

GOULD, ELLIOTT: (Goldstein): Bklyn, Aug. 29, 1938. Columbia U.

GOULET, ROBERT: Lawrence, Mass., Nov. 26, 1933. Edmonton School.

GRABLE, BETTY: St. Louis, Mo., Dec. 18, 1916. Hollywood Professional School.

GRAHAME, GLORIA: (Gloria Grahame Hallward) Los Angeles, Nov. 28, 1929.

GRANGER, FARLEY: San Jose, Calif., July 1, 1925.

GRANGER, STEWART: (James Stewart) London, May 6, 1913. Webber-Douglas School of Acting.

GRANT, CARY: (Archibald Alexander Leach) Bristol, Eng., Jan. 18, 1904.

GRANT, KATHRYN: (Olive Grandstaff) Houston, Tex., Nov. 25, 1933. UCLA.

GRAVES, PETER: (Aurness) Minneapolis, Mar. 18. U. of Minn.

GRAY, COLEEN: (Doris Jensen) Staplehurst, Neb., Oct. 23, 1922. Hamline U.

GRAYSON, KATHRYN: (Zelma Hedrick) Winston-Salem, N.C., Feb. 9, 1923.

GREENE, RICHARD: Plymouth, Eng., Aug. 25, 1918. Cardinal Vaughn School.

GREENWOOD, JOAN: London, 1919. RADA.

GREER, JANE: Washington, D.C., Sept. 9, 1924.

GREY, VIRGINIA: Los Angeles, Mar. 22, 1923.

GRIFFITH, ANDY: Mt. Airy, N.C., June 1, 1926. U. N.C.

GRIFFITH, HUGH: Marian Glas, Anglesey, N. Wales, May 30, 1912.

GRIZZARD, GEORGE: Roanoke Rapids, N.C., Apr. 1, 1928. U. N.C.

GUARDINO, HARRY: Brooklyn, Dec. 23, 1925.

GUINNESS, ALEC: London, Apr. 2, 1914. Pembroke Lodge School.

HACKETT, BUDDY: (Leonard Hacker) Brooklyn, Aug. 31, 1924.

HACKMAN, GENE: Danville, Ill., Jan. 30, 1931.

HALE, BARBARA: DeKalb, Ill., Apr. 18, 1922. Chicago Academy of Fine Arts.

HAMILTON, GEORGE: Memphis, Tenn., Aug. 12, 1939. Hackley School.

HAMILTON, MARGARET: Cleveland, Ohio, Dec. 9, 1902. Hathaway-Brown School.

HAMILTON, NEIL: Lynn, Mass., Sept. 9, 1899.

HARDING, ANN: (Dorothy Walton Gatley) Fort Sam Houston, Texas, Aug. 17, 1904.

HARRIS, BARBARA: (Sandra Markowitz) Evanston, Ill., 1937.

HARRIS, JULIE: Grosse Pointe, Mich., Dec. 2, 1925. Yale Drama School.

HARRIS, RICHARD: Limerick, Ire., Oct. 1, 1930.

HARRIS, ROSEMARY: Ashby, Eng., Sept. 19, 1930. RADA.

HARRISON, NOEL: London, Jan. 29, 1936.

HARRISON, REX: Huyton, Cheshire, Eng., Mar. 5, 1908.

HARTMAN, ELIZABETH: Youngstown, O., Dec. 23, 1941. Carnegie Tech.

HARVEY, LAURENCE: (Laruska Skikne) Yonishkis, Lithuania, Oct. 1, 1928. Meyerton College.

HATTON, RAYMOND: Red Oak, Iowa, July 7, 1892.

HAVER, JUNE: Rock Island, Ill., June 10, 1926.

HAVOC, JUNE: (June Hovick) Seattle, Wash., Nov. 8, 1916.

HAWKINS, JACK: London, Sept. 14, 1910. Trinity School.

HAYDEN, STERLING: (John Hamilton) Montclair, N. J., March 26, 1916.

HAYES, HELEN: (Helen Brown) Washington, D.C., Oct. 10, 1900. Sacred Heart Convent.

HAYES, MARGARET: (Maggie) Baltimore, Dec. 5, 1925.

HAYWARD, SUSAN: (Edythe Marrener) Brooklyn, June 30, 1919.

HAYWORTH, RITA: (Margarita Cansino) NYC, Oct. 17, 1919.

HECKART, EILEEN: Columbus, Ohio, Mar. 29, 1919. Ohio State U.

HEDISON, DAVID: Providence, R.I., May 20, 1929. Brown U.

HEFLIN, VAN: Walters, Okla., Dec. 13, 1910.

HEMMINGS, DAVID: Eng., 1938.

HENDERSON, MARCIA: Andover, Mass., July 22, 1932. AADA.

HENDRIX, WANDA: Jacksonville, Fla., Nov. 3, 1928.

HENREID, PAUL: Trieste, Jan. 10, 1908.

HEPBURN, AUDREY: Brussels, Belgium, May 4, 1929.

HEPBURN, KATHARINE: Hartford, Conn., Nov. 8, 1909. Bryn Mawr.

HESTON, CHARLTON: Evanston, Ill., Oct. 4, 1924. Northwestern U.

HEYWOOD, ANNE: (Violet Pretty) Birmingham, Eng., Dec. 11, 1933.

HICKMAN, DARRYL: Hollywood, Calif., July 28, 1933. Loyola U.

HICKMAN, DWAYNE: Los Angeles, May 18, 1934. Loyola.

HILL, STEVEN: Seattle, Wash., Feb. 24, 1922. U. Wash.

HILLER, WENDY: Bramhall, Cheshire, Eng., Aug. 15, 1912. Winceby House School.

HOFFMAN, DUSTIN: Los Angeles, Aug. 8, 1937. Pasadena Playhouse.

HOLBROOK, HAL: (Harold) Cleveland, O., Feb. 17, 1925.

HOLDEN, WILLIAM: O'Fallon, Ill., Apr. 17, 1918. Pasadena Jr. Coll.

HOLLIMAN, EARL: Tennasas Swamp, Delhi, La., Sept. 11. UCLA.

HOLLOWAY, STANLEY: London, Oct. 1, 1890.

HOLM, CELESTE: NYC, Apr. 29, 1919.

HOMEIER, SKIP: (George Vincent Homeier) Chicago, Oct. 5, 1930. UCLA.

HOMOLKA, OSCAR: Vienna, Aug. 12, 1898. Vienna Dramatic Academy.

HOOKS, ROBERT: Washington, D.C. Apr. 18, 1937. Temple.

HOPE, BOB: London, May 26, 1904.

HOPKINS, MIRIAM: Bainbridge, Ga., Oct. 18, 1902. Syracuse U.

HOPPER, DENNIS: Dodge City, Kan., May 17, 1936.

HORNE, LENA: Brooklyn, June 30, 1917.

HORTON, EDWARD EVERETT: Brooklyn, Mar. 18, 1888. Columbia U.

HORTON, ROBERT: Los Angeles, July 29, 1924. UCLA.

HOUGHTON, KATHARINE: Hartford, Conn., Mar. 10, 1945. Sarah Lawrence.

HOWARD, RONALD: Norwood, Eng., Apr. 7, 1918. Jesus College.

David Janssen

Shirley Jones

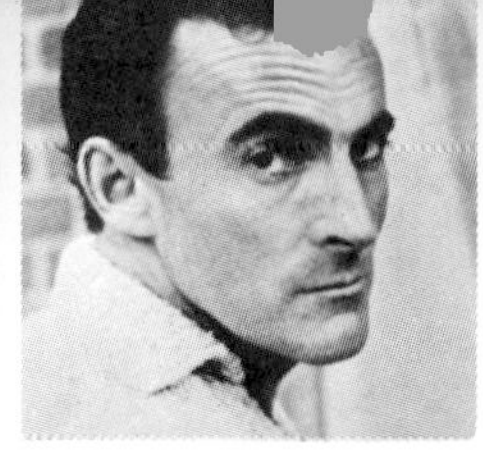
Page Johnson

Nancy Kwan

Aron Kincaid

HOWARD, TREVOR: Kent Eng., Sept. 29, 1916. RADA.

HOWES, SALLY ANN: London, July 20, 1934.

HUDSON, ROCK: (Roy Fitzgerald) Winnetka, Ill., Nov. 17, 1925.

HUNNICUTT, ARTHUR: Gravelly, Ark., Feb. 17, 1911. Ark. State.

HUNT, MARSHA: Chicago, Oct. 17, 1917.

HUNTER, IAN: Cape Town, S.A., June 13, 1900. St. Andrew's College.

HUNTER, KIM: (Janet Cole) Detroit, Nov. 12, 1922.

HUNTER, TAB: (Arthur Kelm) NYC, July 11, 1931.

HUSSEY, RUTH: Providence, R.I., Oct. 30, 1917. U. of Mich.

HUSTON, JOHN: Nevada, Mo., Aug. 5, 1906.

HUTTON, BETTY: (Betty Thornberg) Battle Creek, Mich., Feb. 26, 1921.

HUTTON, LAUREN (Mary): Charleston, SC., Nov. 17, 1943. Newcomb Col.

HUTTON, ROBERT: (Robert Winne) Kingston, N.Y., June 11, 1920. Blair Academy.

HYDE-WHITE, WILFRID: Gloucestershire, Eng., May 12, 1903. RADA.

HYER, MARTHA: Fort Worth, Tex., Aug. 10, 1930. Northwestern U.

IRELAND, JOHN: Vancouver, B.C., Can., Jan. 30, 1915.

IVES, BURL: Hunt Township, Ill., June 14, 1909. Charleston Ill. Teachers College.

JACKSON, ANNE: Alleghany, Pa. Sept. 3, 1926. Neighborhood Playhouse.

JAECKEL, RICHARD: Long Beach, N.Y., Oct. 10, 1926.

JAFFE, SAM: NYC, Mar. 8, 1898.

JAGGER, DEAN: Lima, Ohio, Nov. 7, 1903. Wabash College.

JANSSEN, DAVID: (David Meyer) Naponee, Neb., Mar. 27, 1930.

JARMAN, CLAUDE, JR.: Nashville, Tenn., Sept. 27, 1934.

JASON, RICK: NYC, May 21, 1926. AADA.

JEAN, GLORIA: (Gloria Jean Schoonover) Buffalo, N.Y., Apr. 14, 1928.

JEFFREYS, ANNE: Goldsboro, N.C., Jan. 26, 1923. Anderson College.

JERGENS, ADELE: Brooklyn, Nov. 26, 1922.

JESSEL, GEORGE: NYC, Apr. 3, 1898.

JOHNS, GLYNIS: Durban, S. Africa, Oct. 5, 1923.

JOHNSON, CELIA: Richmond, Surrey, Eng., Dec. 18, 1908. RADA.

JOHNSON, PAGE: Welch, W. Va., Aug. 25, 1930. Ithaca.

JOHNSON, RAFER: Hillsboro, Tex., Aug. 18, 1935. UCLA.

JOHNSON, RICHARD: Essex, Eng., 1927. RADA.

JOHNSON, VAN: Newport, R.I., Aug. 28, 1916.

JONES, CAROLYN: Amarillo, Tex., Apr. 28, 1933.

JONES, DEAN: Morgan County, Ala., Jan. 25, 1936. Asbury College.

JONES, JAMES EARL: Arkabutla, Miss., Jan. 17, 1931. U. Mich.

JONES, JENNIFER: (Phyllis Isley) Tulsa, Okla., Mar. 2, 1919. AADA.

JONES, SHIRLEY: Smithton, Pa., March 31, 1934.

JONES, TOM: (Thomas Jones Woodward) Pontypridd, Wales, June 7, 1940.

JOURDAN, LOUIS: Marseilles, France, June 18, 1921.

JURADO, KATY: (Maria Christina Jurado Garcia) Guadalajara, Mex., 1927.

KASZNAR, KURT: Vienna, Aug. 12, 1913. Gymnasium, Vienna.

KAUFMANN, CHRISTINE: Lansdorf, Graz, Austria, Jan. 11, 1945.

KAYE, DANNY: (David Daniel Kominski) Brooklyn, Jan. 18, 1913.

KAYE, STUBBY: NYC, Nov. 11, 1918.

KEDROVA, LILA: Greece, 1918.

KEEL, HOWARD: (Harold Keel) Gillespie, Ill., Apr. 13, 1919.

KEITH, BRIAN: Bayonne, N.J., Nov. 14, 1921.

KEITH, IAN: Boston, Feb. 27, 1899. AADA.

KEITH, ROBERT: Fowler, Ind., Feb. 10, 1898.

KELLY, GENE: Pittsburgh, Aug. 23, 1912. U. of Pittsburgh.

KELLY, GRACE: Philadelphia, Nov. 12, 1929. AADA.

KELLY, JACK: Astoria, N.Y., Sept. 16, 1927. UCLA.

KELLY, NANCY: Lowell, Mass., Mar. 25, 1921. Bentley School.

KENNEDY, ARTHUR: Worcester, Mass., Feb. 17, 1914. Carnegie Tech.

KENNEDY, GEORGE: NYC, Feb. 18, 1925.

KERR, DEBORAH: Helensburgh, Scot., Sept. 30, 1921. Smale Ballet School.

KERR, JOHN: NYC, Nov. 15, 1931. Harvard and Columbia.

KILEY, RICHARD: Chicago, Mar. 31, 1922. Loyola.

KINCAID, ARON: (Norman Neale Williams III) Los Angeles, June 15, 1943. UCLA.

KITT, EARTHA: North, S.C., Jan. 26, 1928.

KNIGHT, ESMOND: East Sheen, Eng., May 4, 1906.

KNIGHT, SHIRLEY: Goessel, Kan., July 5. Wichita U.

KNOWLES, PATRIC: (Reginald Lawrence Knowles) Horsforth, Eng., Nov. 11, 1911.

KNOX, ALEXANDER: Strathroy, Ont., Can., Jan. 16, 1907. Western Ontario U.

KNOX, ELYSE: Hartford, Conn., Dec. 14, 1917. Traphagen School.

KOHNER, SUSAN: Los Angeles, Nov. 11, 1936. U. of Calif.

KORVIN, CHARLES: (Geza Korvin Karpathi) Czechoslovakia, Nov. 21. Sorbonne.

KOSLECK, MARTIN: Barkotzen, Ger., Mar. 24, 1914. Max Reinhardt School.

KREUGER, KURT: St. Moritz, Switz., July 23, 1917. U. of London.

KRUGER, HARDY: Berlin, Ger., Apr. 12, 1928.

KRUGER, OTTO: Toledo, Ohio, Sept. 6, 1885. Michigan and Columbia U.

KWAN, NANCY: Hong Kong, May 19, 1939. Royal Ballet.

LAKE, VERONICA: (Constance Keane) Lake Placid, N.Y., Nov. 14, 1919. McGill U.

LAMARR, HEDY: (Hedwig Kiesler) Vienna, Sept. 11, 1915.

LAMAS, FERNANDO: Buenos Aires, Jan. 9, 1920.

LAMB, GIL: Minneapolis, June 14, 1906. U. of Minn.

LAMOUR, DOROTHY: Dec. 10, 1914. Spence's School.

LANCASTER, BURT: NYC, Nov. 2, 1913. NYU.

LANCHESTER, ELSA: (Elsa Sullivan) London, Oct. 28, 1902.

LANDIS, JESSIE ROYCE: Chicago, Nov. 25, 1904. Chicago Conservatory.

LANE, ABBE: Brooklyn, Dec. 14, 1935.

LANGAN, GLENN: Denver, Colo., July 8, 1917.

LANGE, HOPE: Redding Ridge, Conn., Nov. 28, 1933. Reed College.

LANGTON, PAUL: Salt Lake City, Apr. 17, 1913. Travers School of Theatre.

LANSBURY, ANGELA: London, Oct. 16, 1925. London Academy of Music.

LAURIE, PIPER: (Rosetta Jacobs) Detroit, Jan. 22, 1932.

Janet Leigh

Rick Lenz

Sophia Loren

Marcello Mastroianni

Shirley MacLaine

LAW, JOHN PHILLIP: Hollywood, Sept. 7, 1937. Neighborhood Playhouse.

LAWFORD, PETER: London, Sept. 7, 1923.

LAWRENCE, BARBARA: Carnegie, Okla., Feb. 24, 1930. UCLA.

LAWRENCE, CAROL: (Laraia) Melrose Park, Ill., Sept. 5, 1935.

LEDERER, FRANCIS: Karlin, Prague, Czechoslovakia, Nov. 6, 1906.

LEE, CHRISTOPHER: London, May 27, 1922. Wellington College.

LEE, GYPSY ROSE: (Rose Hovick) Seattle, Wash., Feb. 9, 1914.

LEE, MICHELE: (Dusiak) Los Angeles, June 24, 1942. LACC.

LEIGH, JANET: (Jeanette Helen Morrison) Merced, Calif., July 6, 1927. College of Pacific.

LEIGHTON, MARGARET: Barnt Green, Worcestershire, Eng., Feb. 26, 1922. Church of England College.

LEMBECK, HARVEY: Brooklyn, Apr. 15, 1923. U. of Ala.

LEMMON, JACK: Boston, Feb. 8, 1925. Harvard.

LENZ, RICK: Springfield, Ill., Nov. 21, 1939. U. Mich.

LESLIE, BETHEL: NYC, Aug. 3, 1929. Breaney School.

LESLIE, JOAN: (Joan Brodell) Detroit, Jan. 26, 1925. St. Benedict's.

LEVENE, SAM: NYC, 1907.

LEWIS, JERRY: Newark, N.J., Mar. 16, 1926.

LILLIE, BEATRICE: Toronto, Can., May 29, 1898.

LINCOLN, ABBEY: (Anna Marie Woolridge) Chicago.

LINDFORS, VIVECA: Uppsala, Sweden, Dec. 29, 1920. Stockholm Royal Dramatic School.

LISI, VIRNA: Rome, 1938.

LIVESEY, ROGER: Barry, Wales, June 25, 1906. Westminster School.

LLOYD, HAROLD: Burchard, Neb., July 28, 1893.

LOCKE, SONDRA: Shelbyville, Tenn., 1947.

LOCKHART, JUNE: NYC, June 25, 1925. Westlake School.

LOCKWOOD, MARGARET: Karachi, Pakistan, Sept. 15, 1916. RADA.

LOLLOBRIGIDA, GINA: Subiaco, Italy, 1928. Rome Academy of Fine Arts.

LOM, HERBERT: Prague, Czechoslovakia, 1917. Prague U.

LONDON, JULIE: (Julie Peck) Santa Rosa, Calif., Sept. 26, 1926.

LONG, RICHARD: Chicago, Dec. 17, 1927.

LOPEZ, PERRY: NYC, July 22, 1931. NYU.

LORD, JACK: (John Joseph Ryan) NYC, Dec. 30, 1930. NYU.

LOREN, SOPHIA: (Sofia Scicolone) Rome, Italy, Sept. 20, 1934.

LOUISE, ANITA: (Anita Louise Fremault) NYC, 1917. Professional Children's School.

LOUISE, TINA: (Blacker) Feb. 11, 1934.

LOY, MYRNA: (Myrna Williams) Helena, Mont., Aug. 2, 1905. Westlake School.

LUKAS, PAUL: Budapest, Hungary, May 26, 1895. Actors Academy of Hungary.

LUND, JOHN: Rochester, N.Y., Feb. 6, 1913.

LUNDIGAN, WILLIAM: Syracuse, N.Y., June 12, 1914. Syracuse U.

LUPINO, IDA: London, Feb. 4, 1918. RADA.

LYNDE, PAUL: Mt. Vernon, Ohio, June 13, 1926. Northwestern U.

LYNLEY, CAROL: NYC, Feb. 13, 1942.

LYNN, DIANA: (Dolly Loehr) Los Angeles, Oct. 7, 1926.

LYNN, JEFFREY: Auburn, Mass., 1910. Bates College.

LYON, SUE: Davonport, Iowa, July 10, 1946.

MacARTHUR, JAMES: Los Angeles, Dec. 8, 1937. Harvard.

MacGINNIS, NIALL: Dublin, Ire., Mar. 29, 1913. Dublin U.

MacLAINE, SHIRLEY: (Beatty) Richmond, Va., Apr. 24, 1934.

MacMAHON, ALINE: McKeesport, Pa., May 3, 1899. Barnard College.

MacMURRAY, FRED: Kankakee, Ill., Aug. 30, 1908. Carroll College.

MacRAE, GORDON: East Orange, N.J., Mar. 12, 1921.

MADISON, GUY: (Robert Moseley) Bakersfield, Calif., Jan. 19, 1922. Bakersfield Jr. College.

MAGNANI, ANNA: Alexandria, Egypt, Mar. 7, 1908. Rome Academy of Dramatic Art.

MAHARIS, GEORGE: Astoria, L.I., N.Y., Sept. 1, 1928. Actors Studio.

MAHONEY, JOCK: (Jacques O'Mahoney) Chicago, Feb. 7, 1919. U. of Iowa.

MALDEN, KARL: (Malden Sekulovich) Gary, Ind., Mar. 22, 1914.

MALONE, DOROTHY: Chicago, Jan. 30, 1925. S. Methodist U.

MARAIS, JEAN: Cherbourg, France, Dec. 11, 1913. St. Germain.

MARCH, FREDRIC: (Frederick McIntyre Bickel) Racine, Wisc., Aug. 31, 1897. U. of Wisc.

MARGO: (Maria Marguerita Guadalupe Boldao y Castilla) Mexico City, May 10, 1918.

MARGOLIN, JANET: NYC, July 25, 1943. Walden School.

MARLOWE, HUGH: (Hugh Hipple) Philadelphia, Jan. 30, 1914.

MARSHALL, BRENDA: (Ardis Anderson Gaines) Isle of Negros, P.I., Sept. 29, 1915. Texas State College.

MARSHALL, E. G.: Owatonna, Minn., June 18, 1910. U. of Minn.

MARTIN, DEAN: (Dino Crocetti) Steubenville, Ohio, June 17, 1917.

MARTIN, MARY: Wetherford, Tex., Dec. 1, 1914. Ward-Belmont School.

MARTIN, TONY: (Alfred Norris) Oakland, Cal., Dec. 25, 1913. St. Mary's College.

MARVIN, LEE: NYC, Feb. 19, 1924.

MARX, GROUCHO: (Julius Marx) NYC, Oct. 2, 1895.

MASON, JAMES: Huddersfield, Yorkshire, Eng., May 15, 1909. Cambridge.

MASON, PAMELA: (Pamela Kellino) Westgate, Eng., Mar. 10, 1918.

MASSEN, OSA: Copenhagen, Den., Jan. 13, 1916.

MASSEY, DANIEL: London, Oct. 10, 1933. Eaton and King's Colleges.

MASSEY, RAYMOND: Toronto, Can., Aug. 30, 1896. Oxford.

MASTROIANNI, MARCELLO: Italy, 1924.

MATTHAU, WALTER: (Matuschanskayasky) NYC, Oct. 1, 1923.

MATURE, VICTOR: Louisville, Ky., Jan. 29, 1916.

MAXWELL, MARILYN: Clarinda, Iowa, Aug. 3, 1922.

MAY, ELAINE: (Berlin) Philadelphia, Apr. 21, 1932.

MAYEHOFF, EDDIE: Baltimore, July 7. Yale.

McCALLUM, DAVID: Scotland, Sept. 19, 1933. Chapman Coll.

McCAMBRIDGE, MERCEDES: Joliet, Ill., March 17, 1918, Mundelein College.

McCARTHY, KEVIN: Seattle, Wash., Feb. 15, 1914. Minn. U.

McCLORY, SEAN: Dublin, Ire., March 8, 1924. U. of Galway.

McCLURE, DOUG: Glendale, Calif., May 11, 1938. UCLA.

McCREA, JOEL: Los Angeles, Nov. 5, 1905. Pomona College.

Barbara McNair

Roddy McDowall

Hayley Mills

Ricardo Montalban

Rita Moreno

McDERMOTT, HUGH: Edinburgh, Scot., Mar. 20, 1908.

McDOWALL, RODDY: London, Sept. 17, 1928. St. Joseph's.

McGAVIN, DARREN: Spokane, Wash., May 7, 1922. College of Pacific.

McGIVER, JOHN: NYC, Nov. 5, 1915. Fordham, Columbia U.

McGUIRE, DOROTHY: Omaha, Neb., June 14, 1919. Wellesley.

McKAY, GARDNER: NYC, June 10, 1932. Cornell.

McKENNA, VIRGINIA: London, June 7, 1931.

McNAIR, BARBARA: Chicago, March 4, 1939. UCLA.

McNALLY, STEPHEN: (Horace McNally) NYC, July 29, Fordham U.

McNAMARA, MAGGIE: NYC, June 18. St. Catherine.

McQUEEN, BUTTERFLY: Tampa, Fla., Jan. 8, 1911. UCLA.

McQUEEN, STEVE: Slater, Mo., Mar. 24, 1932.

MEADOWS, AUDREY: Wuchang, China, 1924. St. Margaret's.

MEADOWS, JAYNE: (formerly, Jayne Cotter) Wuchang, China, Sept. 27, 1923. St. Margaret's.

MEDFORD, KAY: (Maggie O'Regin) NYC, Sept. 14, 1920.

MEDWIN, MICHAEL: London, 1925. Instut Fischer.

MEEKER, RALPH: (Ralph Rathgeber) Minneapolis, Nov. 21, 1920. Northwestern U.

MELL, MARISA: Vienna, Austria, 1942.

MERCOURI, MELINA: Athens, Greece, Oct. 18, 1915.

MEREDITH, BURGESS: Cleveland, Ohio, Nov. 16, 1909. Amherst.

MEREDITH, LEE: (Judi Lee Sauls) Oct. 1947. AADA.

MERKEL, UNA: Covington, Ky., Dec. 10, 1903.

MERMAN, ETHEL: (Ethel Zimmerman) Astoria, N.Y., Jan. 16, 1909.

MERRILL, DINA: (Nedinia Hutton) NYC, Dec. 9, 1925. Geo. Wash. U.

MERRILL, GARY: Hartford, Conn., Aug. 2, 1915. Bowdoin, Trinity.

MIFUNE, TOSHIRO: Tsingtao, China, Apr. 1, 1920.

MILES, VERA: Boise City, Okla., Aug. 23, 1929.

MILLAND, RAY: (Reginald Truscott-Jones) Neath, Wales, Jan. 3, 1908. King's College.

MILLER, ANN: (Lucille Ann Collier) Chireno, Tex., Apr. 12, 1919. Lawler Professional School.

MILLER, MARVIN: St. Louis, July 18, 1913. Washington U.

MILLS, HAYLEY: London, Apr. 18, 1946. Elmhurst School.

MILLS, JOHN: Suffolk, Eng., Feb. 22, 1908.

MIMIEUX, YVETTE: Los Angeles, Jan. 8, 1941. Hollywood High.

MINEO, SAL: NYC, Jan. 10, 1939. Lodge School.

MINNELLI, LIZA: Los Angeles, Mar. 12, 1945.

MIRANDA, ISA: (Ines Sampietro) Milan, Italy, July 5, 1917.

MITCHELL, CAMERON: Dallastown, Pa., Nov. 1918. NY Theatre School.

MITCHELL, JAMES: Sacramento, Calif., Feb. 29, 1920. LACC.

MITCHUM, ROBERT: Bridgeport, Conn., Aug. 6, 1917.

MONTALBAN, RICARDO: Mexico City, Nov. 25, 1920.

MONTAND, YVES: (Yves Montand Livi) Mansummano, Tuscany, Oct. 13, 1921.

MONTGOMERY, ELIZABETH: Los Angeles, Apr. 15, 1933. AADA.

MONTGOMERY, GEORGE: (George Letz) Brady, Mont., Aug. 29, 1916. U. of Mont.

MONTGOMERY, ROBERT: (Henry, Jr.) Beacon, N.Y., May 21, 1904.

MOORE, CONSTANCE: Sioux City, Iowa, Jan. 18, 1922.

MOORE, DICK: Los Angeles, Sept. 12, 1925.

MOORE, KIERON: County Cork, Ire., 1925. St. Mary's College.

MOORE, MARY TYLER: Brooklyn, Dec. 29, 1937.

MOORE, ROGER: London, Oct. 14, 1927. RADA.

MOORE, TERRY: (Helen Koford) Los Angeles, Jan. 7, 1929.

MOOREHEAD, AGNES: Clinton, Mass., Dec. 6, 1906. AADA.

MORE, KENNETH: Gerrards Cross, Eng., Sept. 20, 1914. Victoria College.

MOREAU, JEANNE: France, 1928.

MORENO, RITA: (Rosita Alverio) Humacao, P.R., Dec. 11, 1931.

MORGAN, DENNIS: (Stanley Morner) Prentice, Wisc., Dec. 10, 1920. Carroll College.

MORGAN, HARRY (HENRY): (Harry Bratsburg) Detroit, Apr. 10, 1915. U. of Chicago.

MORGAN, MICHELE: (Simone Roussel) Paris, Feb. 29, 1920. Paris Dramatic School.

MORISON, PATRICIA: NYC, 1919.

MORLEY, ROBERT: Wiltshire, Eng., May 26, 1908. RADA.

MORRIS, CHESTER: NYC, Feb. 16, 1901. Art Students League.

MORRIS, GREG: Cleveland, O., 1934. Ohio State.

MORRIS, HOWARD: NYC, Sept. 4, 1919. NYU.

MORROW, VIC: Bronx, N.Y., Feb. 14, 1932. Fla. Southern College.

MORSE, ROBERT: Newton, Mass., May 18, 1931.

MOSTEL, ZERO: Brooklyn, Feb. 28, 1915. CCNY.

MURPHY, AUDIE: Kingston, Tex., June 20, 1924.

MURPHY, GEORGE: New Haven, Conn., July 4, 1904. Yale.

MURRAY, DON: Hollywood, July 31, 1929. AADA.

MURRAY, KEN: (Don Court) NYC, July 14, 1903.

NADER, GEORGE: Pasadena, Calif., Oct. 19, 1921. Occidental College.

NAGEL, CONRAD: Keokuk, Iowa, Mar. 16, 1897. Highland Park College.

NAPIER, ALAN: Birmingham, Eng., Jan. 7, 1903. Birmingham University.

NATWICK, MILDRED: Baltimore, June 19, 1908. Bryn Mawr.

NEAL, PATRICIA: Packard, Ky., Jan. 20, 1926. Northwestern U.

NEFF, HILDEGARDE: (Hildegard Knef) Ulm, Ger., Dec. 28, 1925. Berlin Art Academy.

NELSON, BARRY: (Robert Nielsen) Oakland, Cal., 1925.

NELSON, DAVID: NYC, Oct. 24, 1936. USC.

NELSON, GENE: (Gene Berg) Seattle, Wash., Mar. 24, 1920.

NELSON, HARRIET HILLIARD: (Peggy Lou Snyder) Des Moines, Iowa, July 18.

NELSON, LORI: (Dixie Kay Nelson) Sante Fe, N.M., Aug. 15, 1933.

NELSON, OZZIE: (Oswald) Jersey City, N.J., Mar. 20, 1907. Rutgers U.

NELSON, RICK: (Eric Hilliard Nelson) Teaneck, N.J., May 8, 1940.

NESBITT, CATHLEEN: Cheshire, Eng., Nov. 24, 1889. Victoria College.

NEWLEY, ANTHONY: Hackney, London, Sept. 21, 1931.

NEWMAN, PAUL: Cleveland, Ohio, Jan. 26, 1925. Yale.

NEWMAR, JULIE: (Newmeyer) Los Angeles, Aug. 16, 1935.

Hugh O'Brian

Patricia Neal

Anthony Perkins

Suzanne Pleshette

Michael J. Pollard

NICHOLS, MIKE: (Michael Igor Peschkowsky) Berlin, Nov. 1931. U. Chicago.

NICOL, ALEX: Ossining, N.Y., Jan. 20, 1919. Actors Studio.

NIELSEN, LESLIE: Regina, Saskatchewan, Can., Feb. 11, 1926. Neighborhood Playhouse.

NIVEN, DAVID: Kirriemuir, Scot., Mar. 1, 1910. Sandhurst College.

NOLAN, LLOYD: San Francisco, Aug. 11, 1902. Stanford U.

NORTH, SHEREE: (Dawn Bethel) Los Angeles, Jan. 17, 1933. Hollywood High.

NOVAK, KIM: (Marilyn Novak) Chicago, Feb. 18, 1933. LACC.

NUGENT, ELLIOTT: Dover, Ohio, Sept. 20, 1900. Ohio State U.

NUYEN, FRANCE: (Vannga) Marseilles, France, July 31, 1939. Beaux Arts School.

OBERON, MERLE: (Estelle Merle O'Brien Thompson) Tasmania, Feb. 19, 1911.

O'BRIAN, HUGH: (Hugh J. Krampe) Rochester, N.Y., Apr. 19, 1928. Cincinnati U.

O'BRIEN, EDMOND: NYC, Sept. 10, 1915. Fordham, Neighborhood Playhouse.

O'BRIEN, MARGARET: (Angela Maxine O'Brien) Los Angeles, Jan. 15, 1937.

O'BRIEN, PAT: Milwaukee, Nov. 11, 1899. Marquette U.

O'CONNELL, ARTHUR: NYC, Mar. 29, 1908. St. John's.

O'CONNOR, DONALD: Chicago, Aug. 28, 1925.

O'DONNELL, CATHY: (Ann Steely) Siluria, Ala., July 6, 1925. Oklahoma City U.

O'HARA, MAUREEN: (Maureen FitzSimons) Dublin, Ire., Aug. 17, 1921. Abbey School.

O'HERLIHY, DAN: Wexford, Ire., May 1, 1919. National U.

OLIVIER, LAURENCE: Dorking, Eng., May 22, 1907. St. Edward's, Oxford.

O'NEAL, PATRICK: Ocala, Fla., Sept. 26, 1927. U. of Fla.

O'SHEA, MICHAEL: NYC, Mar. 17, 1906.

O'SULLIVAN, MAUREEN: Byle, Ire., May 17, 1911. Sacred Heart Convent.

O'TOOLE, PETER: Connemara, Ireland, Aug. 2, 1932. RADA.

OWEN, REGINALD: Wheathampstead, Eng., Aug. 5, 1887. Tree's Academy.

PAGE, GERALDINE: Kirksville, Mo., Nov. 22, 1924. Goodman School.

PAGET, DEBRA: (Debralee Griffin) Denver, Aug. 19, 1933.

PAIGE, JANIS: (Donna Mae Jaden) Tacoma, Wash., Sept. 16, 1922.

PALANCE, JACK: Lattimer, Pa., Feb. 18, 1920. U. N.C.

PALMER, BETSY: East Chicago, Ind., Nov. 1, 1929. DePaul U.

PALMER, GREGG: (Palmer Lee) San Francisco, Jan. 25, 1927. U. Utah.

PALMER, LILLI: Posen, Austria, May 24, 1914. Ilka Gruning School.

PALMER, MARIA: Vienna, Sept. 5, 1924. College de Bouffement.

PAPAS, IRENE: Chiliomodion, Greece, 1929.

PARKER, CECIL: Hastings, Sussex, Eng., Sept. 3, 1897. St. Francis Xavier College.

PARKER, ELEANOR: Cedarville, Ohio, June 26, 1922. Pasadena Playhouse.

PARKER, FESS: Fort Worth, Tex., Aug. 16, 1927. USC.

PARKER, JEAN: (Mae Green) Deer Lodge, Mont., Aug. 11, 1918.

PARKER, SUZY: (Cecelia Parker) San Antonio, Tex., Oct. 28, 1933.

PARKER, WILLARD: (Worster Van Eps) NYC, Feb. 5, 1912.

PARKINS, BARBARA: Vancouver, Can., May 22, 1945.

PARSONS, ESTELLE: Lynn, Mass., Nov. 20, 1927. Boston U.

PARSONS, LOUELLA: Freeport, Ill., Aug. 6, 1893. Dixon College.

PATRICK, NIGEL: London, May 2, 1913.

PATTERSON, LEE: Vancouver, Can., 1929. Ontario College of Art.

PAVAN, MARISA: (Marisa Pierangeli) Cagliari, Sardinia, June 19, 1932. Torquado Tasso College.

PEACH, MARY: Durban, S. Africa, 1934.

PEARSON, BEATRICE: Denison, Tex., July 27, 1920.

PECK, GREGORY: La Jolla, Calif., Apr. 5, 1916. U. of Calif.

PEPPARD, GEORGE: Detroit, Oct. 1, 1933. Carnegie Tech.

PERKINS, ANTHONY: NYC, Apr. 14, 1932. Rollins College.

PERREAU, GIGI: (Ghislaine) Los Angeles, Feb. 6, 1941.

PETERS, JEAN: (Elizabeth) Canton, Ohio, Oct. 15, 1926. Ohio State U.

PICERNI, PAUL: NYC, Dec. 1, 1922. Loyola U.

PICKENS, SLIM: (Louis Bert Lindley, Jr.) Kingsberg, Calif., June 29, 1919.

PICKFORD, MARY: (Gladys Mary Smith) Toronto, Can., Apr. 8, 1893.

PIDGEON, WALTER: East St. John, N.B., Can., Sept. 23, 1898.

PINE, PHILLIP: Hanford, Calif., July 16, 1925. Actors' Lab.

PLEASENCE, DONALD: Workshop, Eng., Oct. 5, 1919. Sheffield School.

PLESHETTE, SUZANNE: NYC, Jan. 31, 1937. Syracuse U.

PLUMMER, CHRISTOPHER: Toronto, Can., Dec. 13, 1927.

PODESTA, ROSANA: Tripoli, June 20, 1934.

POITIER, SIDNEY: Miami, Fla., Feb. 20, 1924.

POLLARD, MICHAEL J.: Pacific, N.J., May 30, 1939.

POWELL, ELEANOR: Springfield, Mass. Nov. 21, 1913.

POWELL, JANE: (Suzanne Burce) Portland, Ore., Apr. 1, 1929.

POWELL, WILLIAM: Pittsburgh, July 29, 1892. AADA.

POWERS, MALA: (Mary Ellen) San Francisco, Dec. 29, 1921. UCLA.

PRENTISS, PAULA: (Paula Ragusa) San Antonio, Tex., Mar. 4, 1939. Northwestern U.

PRESLE, MICHELINE: (Micheline Chassagne) Paris, Aug. 22, 1922. Rouleau Drama School.

PRESLEY, ELVIS: Tupelo, Miss., Jan. 8, 1935.

PRESNELL, HARVE: Modesto, Calif., Sept. 14, 1933. USC.

PRESTON, ROBERT: (Robert Preston Meservey) Newton Highlands, Mass., June 8, 1918. Pasadena Playhouse.

PRICE, DENNIS: Twyford, Eng., 1915. Oxford.

PRICE, VINCENT: St. Louis, May 27, 1911. Yale.

PRINCE, WILLIAM: Nicholas, N.Y., Jan. 26, 1913. Cornell U.

PROVINE, DOROTHY: Deadwood, S.D., Jan. 20, 1937. U. of Wash.

PROWSE, JULIET: Bombay, India, Sept. 25, 1936.

PURCELL, NOEL: Dublin, Ire., Dec. 23, 1900. Irish Christian Brothers.

PURDOM, EDMUND: Welwyn Garden City, Eng., Dec. 19. St. Ignatius College.

QUAYLE, ANTHONY: Lancashire, Eng., 1913. Old Vic School.

QUINN, ANTHONY: Chihuahua, Mex., Apr. 21, 1915.

RAFFERTY, FRANCES: Sioux City, Iowa, June 26, 1922. UCLA.

Oliver Reed

Lee Remick

Cesar Romero

Romy Schneider

Michael Sarrazin

RAFT, GEORGE: NYC, 1903.

RAINES, ELLA: (Ella Wallace Rains Olds) Snoqualmie Falls, Wash., Aug. 6, 1921. U. of Washington.

RANDALL, TONY: Tulsa, Okla., Feb. 26, 1920. Northwestern U.

RANDELL, RON: Sydney, Australia, Oct. 8, 1920. St. Mary's College.

RAY, ALDO: (Aldo DaRe) Pen Argyl, Pa., Sept. 25, 1926. UCLA.

RAYE, MARTHA: (Margie Yvonne Reed) Butte, Mont., Aug. 27, 1916.

RAYMOND, GENE: (Raymond Guion) NYC, Aug. 13, 1908.

REAGAN, RONALD: Tampico, Ill., Feb. 6, 1911. Eureka College.

REASON, REX: Berlin, Ger., Nov. 30, 1928. Pasadena Playhouse.

REDFORD, ROBERT: Santa Monica, Calif., Aug. 18, 1937. AADA.

REDGRAVE, LYNN: London, Mar. 8, 1943.

REDGRAVE, MICHAEL: Bristol, Eng., Mar. 20, 1908. Cambridge.

REDGRAVE, VANESSA: London, Jan. 30, 1937.

REDMAN, JOYCE: County Mayo, Ire., 1919. RADA.

REED, DONNA: (Donna Mullenger) Denison, Iowa, Jan. 27, 1921. LACC.

REED, OLIVER: Wimbledon, Eng., 1938.

REEVES, STEVE: Glasgow, Mont., Jan. 21, 1926.

REID, ELLIOTT: NYC, Jan. 16, 1920.

REINER, CARL: NYC, Mar. 20, 1922. Georgetown.

REMICK, LEE: Quincy, Mass., Dec. 14, 1935. Barnard College.

RENNIE, MICHAEL: Bradford, Eng., Aug. 25, 1909. Cambridge.

RETTIG, TOMMY: Jackson Heights, N.Y., Dec. 10, 1941.

REYNOLDS, DEBBIE: (Mary Frances Reynolds) El Paso, Tex., Apr. 1, 1932.

REYNOLDS, MARJORIE: Buhl, Idaho, Aug. 12, 1921.

RHOADES, BARBARA: Poughkeepsie, N.Y., 1947.

RICH, IRENE: Buffalo, N.Y., Oct. 13, 1897. St. Margaret's School.

RICHARDS, JEFF: (Richard Mansfield Taylor) Portland, Ore., Nov. 1. USC.

RICHARDSON, RALPH: Cheltenham, Eng., Dec. 19, 1902.

RICKLES, DON: NYC, May 8, 1926. AADA.

RIGG, DIANA: Doncaster, Eng., July 20, 1938. RADA.

ROBARDS, JASON: Chicago, July 26, 1922. American Academy of Dramatic Art.

ROBERTSON, CLIFF: La Jolla, Calif., Sept. 9, 1925. Antioch College.

ROBINSON, EDWARD G.: (Emanuel Goldenberg) Bucharest, Rum., Dec. 12, 1893. Columbia U.

ROBSON, FLORA: South Shields, Eng., Mar. 28, 1902. RADA.

ROCHESTER: (Eddie Anderson) Oakland, Calif., Sept. 18, 1905.

ROGERS, CHARLES "BUDDY": Olathe, Kan., Aug. 13, 1904. U. of Kan.

ROGERS, GINGER: (Virginia Katherine McMath) Independence, Mo., July 16, 1911.

ROGERS, ROY: (Leonard Slye) Cincinnati, Nov. 5, 1912.

ROLAND, GILBERT: (Luis Antonio Damasco De Alonso) Juarez, Mex., Dec. 11, 1905.

ROMAN, RUTH: Boston, Dec. 23. Bishop Lee Dramatic School.

ROMERO, CESAR: NYC, Feb. 15, 1907. Collegiate School.

ROONEY, MICKEY: (Joe Yule, Jr.) Brooklyn, Sept. 23, 1920.

ROSS, KATHARINE: Hollywood, Jan. 29, 1943.

ROTH, LILLIAN: Boston, Dec. 13, 1910.

ROWLANDS, GENA: Cambria, Wisc., June 19, 1936.

RUGGLES, CHARLES: Los Angeles, Feb. 8, 1892.

RULE, JANICE: Cincinnati, Aug. 15, 1931.

RUSH, BARBARA: Denver, Colo., Jan. 4. U. of Calif.

RUSSELL, JANE: Bemidji, Minn., June 21, 1921. Max Reinhardt School.

RUSSELL, JOHN: Los Angeles, Jan. 3, 1921. U. of Calif.

RUSSELL, KURT: Springfield, Mass., March 17, 1951.

RUSSELL, ROSALIND: Waterbury, Conn., June 4, 1911. AADA.

RUTHERFORD, ANN: Toronto, Can., 1924.

RUTHERFORD, MARGARET: London, May 11, 1892. Wimbledon Hill School.

RYAN, ROBERT: Chicago, Nov. 11, 1913. Dartmouth.

SAINT, EVA MARIE: Newark, N.J., July 4, 1924. Bowling Green State U.

ST. JACQUES, RAYMOND: (James Arthur Johnson) Conn.

ST. JOHN, BETTA: Hawthorne, Calif., Nov. 26, 1929.

ST. JOHN, JILL: (Jill Oppenheim) Apr. 19.

SANDERS, GEORGE: St. Petersburg, Russia, July 3, 1906. Brighton College.

SANDS, TOMMY: Chicago, Aug. 27, 1937.

SAN JUAN, OLGA: NYC, Mar. 16, 1927.

SARGENT, RICHARD: (Richard Cox) Carmel, Cal., 1933. Stanford U.

SARRAZIN, MICHAEL: Quebec City, Can., May 22, 1940.

SAVALAS, TELLY: (Aristotle) Garden City, N.Y., 1924. Columbia.

SAXON, JOHN: (Carmen Orrico) Brooklyn, Aug. 5, 1935.

SCALA, GIA: Liverpool, Eng., Mar. 3, 1936. Stella Adler School.

SCHELL, MARIA: Vienna, Jan. 15, 1926.

SCHELL, MAXIMILIAN: Vienna, Dec. 8, 1930.

SCHNEIDER, ROMY: Vienna, Sept. 23, 1938.

SCOFIELD, PAUL: Hurstpierpont, Eng., Jan. 21, 1922. London Mask Theatre School.

SCOTT, GEORGE C., Wise, Va., Oct. 18, 1927. U. of Mo.

SCOTT, GORDON: (Gordon M. Werschkul) Portland, Ore., Aug. 3, 1927. Oregon U.

SCOTT, MARTHA: Jamesport, Mo., Sept. 22, 1914. U. of Mich.

SCOTT, RANDOLPH: Orange County, Va., Jan. 23, 1903. U. of N.C.

SEARS, HEATHER: London, 1935.

SEBERG, JEAN: Marshalltown, Iowa, Nov. 13, 1938. Iowa U.

SECOMBE, HARRY: Swansea, Wales, Sept. 8, 1921.

SELLERS, PETER: Southsea, Eng., Sept. 8, 1925. Aloysius College.

SELWART, TONIO: Wartenberg, Ger., June 9, 1906. Munich U.

SEYLER, ATHENE: (Athene Hannen) London, May 31, 1889.

SEYMOUR, ANNE: NYC, Sept. 11, 1909. American Laboratory Theatre.

SHARIF, OMAR: (Michel Shalboub) Alexandria, Egypt, Apr. 10, 1933.

SHATNER, WILLIAM: Montreal, Can., Mar. 22, 1931. McGill U.

SHAW, SEBASTIAN: Holt, Eng., May 29, 1905. Gresham School.

SHAWLEE, JOAN: Forest Hills, N.Y., Mar. 5, 1929.

Elke Sommer

Maximilian Schell

Inger Stevens

Jean-Louis Trintignant

Pamela Tiffin

SHAWN, DICK: (Richard Schulefand) Buffalo, N.Y., Dec. 1. U. of Miami.

SHEARER, MOIRA: Dunfermline, Scot., Jan 17, 1926. London Theatre School.

SHEARER, NORMA: Montreal, Can., Aug. 10, 1904.

SHEEN, MARTIN: (Ramon Estevez) Dayton, O., Aug. 3, 1940.

SHEFFIELD, JOHN: Pasadena, Calif., Apr. 11, 1931. UCLA.

SHORE, DINAH: (Frances Rose Shore) Winchester, Tenn., Mar. 1, 1917. Vanderbilt U.

SHOWALTER, MAX: (Formerly Casey Adams) Caldwell, Kan., June 2, 1917. Pasadena Playhouse.

SIDNEY, SYLVIA: NYC, Aug. 8, 1910. Theatre Guild School.

SIGNORET, SIMONE: (Simone Kaminker) Wiesbaden, Ger., Mar. 25, 1921. Solange Sicard School.

SILVERS, PHIL: (Philip Silversmith) Brooklyn, May 11, 1912.

SIM, ALASTAIR: Edinburgh, Scot., 1900.

SIMMONS, JEAN: London, Jan. 31, 1929. Aida Foster School.

SIMON, SIMONE: Marseilles, France, Apr. 23, 1914.

SINATRA, FRANK: Hoboken, N.J., Dec. 12, 1915.

SKELTON, RED: (Richard Skelton) Vincennes, Ind., July 18, 1913.

SLEZAK, WALTER: Vienna, Austria, May 3, 1902.

SMITH, ALEXIS: Penticton, Can., June 8, 1921. LACC.

SMITH, JOHN: (Robert E. Van Orden) Los Angeles, Mar. 6, 1931. UCLA.

SMITH, KATE: (Kathryn Elizabeth) Greenville, Va., May 1, 1909.

SMITH, KENT: NYC, Mar. 19, 1907. Harvard U.

SMITH, ROGER: South Gate, Calif., Dec. 18, 1932. U. of Ariz.

SOMMER, ELKE: Germany, 1941.

SORDI, ALBERTO: Rome, Italy, 1925.

SOTHERN, ANN: (Harriet Lake) Valley City, N.D., Jan. 22, 1909. Washington U.

STACK, ROBERT: Los Angeles, Jan. 13, 1919. USC.

STAMP, TERENCE: London, 1940.

STANG, ARNOLD: Chelsea, Mass., Sept. 28, 1925.

STANLEY, KIM: (Patricia Reid) Tularosa, N.M., Feb. 11, 1921. U. of Tex.

STANWYCK, BARBARA: (Ruby Stevens) Brooklyn, July 16, 1907.

STAPLETON, MAUREEN: Troy, N.Y., June 21, 1925.

STEEL, ANTHONY: London, May 21, 1920. Cambridge.

STEELE, TOMMY: London, Dec. 17, 1936.

STEIGER, ROD: Westhampton, N.Y., Apr. 14, 1925.

STERLING, JAN: (Jane Sterling Adriance) NYC, Apr. 3, 1923. Fay Compton School.

STERLING, ROBERT: (Robert Sterling Hart) Newcastle, Pa., Nov. 13, 1917. U. of Pittsburgh.

STEVENS, CONNIE: (Concetta Ann Ingolia) Brooklyn, Aug. 8, 1938. Hollywood Professional School.

STEVENS, INGER: (Inger Stensland) Stockholm, Sweden, Oct. 18, 1934. Columbia U.

STEVENS, MARK: (Richard) Cleveland, Ohio, Dec. 13, 1922.

STEVENS, STELLA: (Estelle Eggleston) Hot Coffee, Miss., 1936.

STEWART, ELAINE: Montclair, N.J., May 31, 1929.

STEWART, JAMES: Indiana, Pa., May 20, 1908. Princeton.

STEWART, MARTHA: (Martha Haworth) Bardwell, Ky., Oct. 7, 1922.

STOCKWELL, DEAN: Hollywood, March 5.

STORM, GALE: (Josephine Cottle) Bloominton, Tex., Apr. 5, 1922.

STRASBERG, SUSAN: NYC, May 22, 1938.

STRAUSS, ROBERT: NYC, Nov. 8, 1913.

STREISAND, BARBRA: Brooklyn, Apr. 24, 1942.

STRUDWICK, SHEPPERD: Hillsboro, N.C., Sept. 22, 1907. U. of N.C.

SULLIVAN, BARRY: (Patrick Barry) NYC, Aug. 29, 1912. NYU.

SULLY, FRANK: (Frank Sullivan) St. Louis, 1910. St. Teresa's College.

SWANSON, GLORIA: (Josephine Swenson) Chicago, Mar. 27, 1898. Chicago Art Inst.

SWINBURNE, NORA: Bath, Eng., July 24, 1902. RADA.

SYLVESTER, WILLIAM: Oakland, Calif., Jan. 31, 1922. RADA.

SYMS, SYLVIA: London, 1934. Convent School.

TALBOT, LYLE: (Lysle Hollywood) Pittsburgh, Feb. 8, 1904.

TALBOT, NITA: NYC, Aug. 8, 1930. Irvine Studio School.

TAMBLYN, RUSS: Los Angeles, Dec. 30.

TANDY, JESSICA: London, June 7, 1909. Dame Owens' School.

TAYLOR, DON: Freeport, Pa., Dec. 13, 1920. Penn State U.

TAYLOR, ELIZABETH: London, Feb. 27, 1932. Byron House School.

TAYLOR, KENT: (Louis Weiss) Nashua, Iowa, May 11, 1907.

TAYLOR, ROD: (Robert) Sydney, Aust., Jan. 11, 1930.

TEAL, RAY: Grand Rapids, Mich., Jan. 12, 1902. Pasadena Playhouse.

TEMPLE, SHIRLEY JANE: Santa Monica, Calif., Apr. 23, 1928.

TERRY-THOMAS: (Thomas Terry Hoar Stevens) Finchley, London, July 14, 1911. Ardingly College.

THATCHER, TORIN: Bombay, India, Jan. 15, 1905. RADA.

THAXTER, PHYLLIS: Portland, Me., Nov. 20, 1921. St. Genevieve School.

THOMAS, DANNY: (Amos Jacobs) Deerfield, Mich., Jan. 6, 1914.

THOMAS, MARLO: (Margaret) Detroit, Nov. 21, 1943.

THOMPSON, MARSHALL: Peoria, Ill., Nov. 27, 1925. Occidental College.

THORNDIKE, SYBIL: Gainsborough, Eng., Oct. 24, 1882. Guild Hall School of Music.

TIERNEY, GENE: Brooklyn, Nov. 20, 1920. Miss Farmer's School.

TIERNEY, LAWRENCE: Brooklyn, Mar. 15, 1919. Manhattan College.

TIFFIN, PAMELA: (Wonso) Oklahoma City, Oct. 13, 1942.

TODD, RICHARD: Dublin, Ire., June 11, 1919. Shrewsbury School.

TOPOL: (Chaim Topol) Tel-Aviv, Israel, 1936.

TORN, RIP: Temple, Tex., Feb. 6, 1931. U. Tex.

TOTTER, AUDREY: Joliet, Ill., Dec. 20.

TRAVERS, BILL: Newcastle-on-Tyne, Eng., Jan. 3, 1922.

TRAVIS, RICHARD: (William Justice) Carlsbad, N.M., Apr. 17, 1913.

TREMAYNE, LES: London, Apr. 16, 1913. Northwestern, Columbia, UCLA.

TRINTIGNANT, JEAN-LOUIS: Pont-St. Esprit, France, 1930. Dullin-Balachova Drama School.

TRUEX, ERNEST: Kansas City, Mo., Sept. 19, 1890.

Tom Tryon

Mae West

Nicol Williamson

Susannah York

Scott Wilson

TRYON, TOM: Hartford, Conn., Jan. 14, 1926. Yale.

TUCKER, FORREST: Plainfield, Ind., Feb. 12, 1919. George Washington U.

TURNER, LANA: (Julia Jean Mildred Frances Turner) Wallace, Idaho, Feb. 8, 1920.

TUSHINGHAM, RITA: Liverpool, Eng. 1942.

TYLER, BEVERLY: (Beverly Jean Saul) Scranton, Pa., July 5, 1928.

ULRIC, LENORE: New Ulm, Minn., July 21, 1894.

USTINOV, PETER: London, Apr. 16, 1921. Westminster School.

VACCARO, BRENDA: Brooklyn, Nov. 18, 1939. Neighborhood Playhouse.

VALLEE, RUDY: (Hubert) Island Pond, Vt., July 28, 1901. Yale.

VALLI, ALIDA: Pola, Italy, May 31, 1921. Rome Academy of Drama.

VAN DOREN, MAMIE: (Joan Lucile Olander) Rowena, S.D., Feb. 6, 1933.

VAN DYKE, DICK: West Plains, Mo., Dec. 13, 1925.

VAN FLEET, JO: Oakland, Cal., 1922.

VAN ROOTEN, LUIS: Mexico City, Nov. 29, 1906. U. of Pa.

VAUGHN, ROBERT: NYC, Nov. 22, 1932. USC.

VENUTA, BENAY: San Francisco, Jan. 27, 1911.

VERDON, GWEN: Culver City, Calif.; Jan. 13, 1925.

VITALE, MILLY: Rome, Italy, July 16, 1938. Lycée Chateaubriand.

VOIGHT, JON: Yonkers, N.Y., Dec. 29, 1938. Catholic U.

VYE, MURVYN: Quincy, Mass., July 15, 1913. Yale.

WAGNER, ROBERT: Detroit, Feb. 10, 1930.

WALKER, CLINT: Hartford, Ill., May 30, 1927. USC.

WALKER, NANCY: (Ann Myrtle Swoyer) Philadelphia, May 10, 1921.

WALLACH, ELI: Brooklyn, Dec. 7, 1915. CCNY, U. of Tex.

WALLIS, SHANI: London, Apr. 5, 1941.

WALSTON, RAY: New Orleans, Nov 22, 1918. Cleveland Playhouse.

WANAMAKER, SAM: Chicago, 1919. Drake.

WARD, BURT: (Gervis) Los Angeles, July 6, 1945.

WARDEN, JACK: Newark, N.J., Sept. 18, 1920.

WARREN, LESLEY ANN: NYC, Aug. 16, 1946.

WASHBOURNE, MONA: Birmingham, Eng., Nov. 27, 1903.

WATERS, ETHEL: Chester, Pa., Oct. 31, 1900.

WATLING, JACK: London, Jan. 13, 1923. Italia Conti School.

WAYNE, DAVID: (Wayne McKeehan) Travers City, Mich., Jan. 30, 1916. Western Michigan State U.

WAYNE, JOHN: (Marion Michael Morrison) Winterset, Iowa, May 26, 1907. USC.

WEAVER, DENNIS: Joplin, Mo., June 4, 1925. U. Okla.

WEAVER, MARJORIE: Crossville, Tenn., Mar. 2, 1913. Indiana U.

WEBB, ALAN: York, Eng., July 2, 1906. Dartmouth.

WEBB, JACK: Santa Monica, Calif., Apr. 2, 1920.

WELCH, RAQUEL: (Tejada) Chicago, Sept. 5, 1942.

WELD, TUESDAY: (Susan) NYC, Aug. 27, 1943. Hollywood Professional School.

WELDON, JOAN: San Francisco, Aug. 5, 1933. San Francisco Conservatory.

WELLES, ORSON: Kenosha, Wisc., May 6, 1915. Todd School.

WERNER, OSKAR: Vienna, Nov. 13, 1922.

WEST, MAE: Brooklyn, Aug. 17, 1892.

WHITE, CAROL: London, Apr. 1, 1944.

WHITE, JESSE: Buffalo, N.Y., Jan. 3, 1919.

WHITE, WILFRID HYDE: Gloucestershire, Eng., May 12, 1903. RADA.

WHITMAN, STUART: San Francisco, Feb. 1, 1929. CCLA.

WIDMARK, RICHARD: Sunrise, Minn., Dec. 26, 1914. Lake Forest U.

WILCOXON, HENRY: British West Indies, Sept. 8, 1905.

WILDE, CORNEL: NYC, Oct. 13, 1915. CCNY, Columbia.

WILDING, MICHAEL: Westcliff, Eng., July 23, 1912. Christ's Hospital.

WILLIAMS, EMLYN: Mostyn, Wales, Nov. 26, 1905. Oxford.

WILLIAMS, ESTHER: Los Angeles, Aug. 8, 1923.

WILLIAMS, GRANT: NYC, Aug. 18, 1930. Queens College.

WILLIAMS, JOHN: Chalfont, Eng., Apr. 15, 1903. Lancing College.

WILSON, FLIP: (Clerow Wilson) Jersey City, N. J., Dec. 8, 1935.

WILSON, MARIE: Anaheim, Calif., Dec. 30, 1917. Cumnock School.

WILSON, SCOTT: Atlanta, Ga., 1942.

WINDSOR, MARIE: (Emily Marie Bertelson) Marysvale, Utah, Dec. 11, 1924. Brigham Young University.

WINTERS, JONATHAN: Dayton, Ohio, Nov. 11, 1925. Kenyon College.

WINTERS, ROLAND: Boston, Nov. 22, 1904.

WINTERS, SHELLEY: (Shirley Schrift) St. Louis, Aug. 18, 1922. Wayne U.

WINWOOD, ESTELLE: Kent, Eng., Jan. 24, 1883. Lyric Stage Academy.

WITHERS, GOOGIE: Karachi, India, Mar. 12, 1917. Italia Conti School.

WOOD, NATALIE: (Natasha Gurdin) San Francisco, July 20, 1938.

WOOD, PEGGY: Brooklyn, Feb. 9, 1894.

WOODWARD, JOANNE: Thomasville, Ga., Feb. 27, 1931. Neighborhood Playhouse.

WOOLAND, NORMAN: Dusseldorf, Ger., Mar. 16, 1910. Edward VI School.

WRAY, FAY: Alberta, Can., Sept. 10, 1907.

WRIGHT, TERESA: NYC, Oct. 27, 1918.

WYATT, JANE: Campgaw, N.J., Aug. 10, 1912. Barnard College.

WYMAN, JANE: (Sarah Jane Fulks) St. Joseph, Mo., Jan. 4, 1914.

WYMORE, PATRICE: Miltonvale, Kan., Dec. 17, 1927.

WYNN, KEENAN: NYC, July 27, 1916. St. John's.

WYNN, MAY: (Donna Lee Hickey) NYC, Jan. 8, 1930.

YORK, DICK: (Richard Allen York) Fort Wayne, Ind., Sept. 4, 1928. DePaul U.

YORK, SUSANNAH: London, 1942.

YOUNG, ALAN: (Angus) North Shield, Eng., Nov. 19, 1919.

YOUNG, GIG: (Byron Barr) St. Cloud, Minn., Nov. 4, 1913. Pasadena Playhouse.

YOUNG, LORETTA: (Gretchen) Salt Lake City, Jan. 6, 1913. Immaculate Heart College.

YOUNG, ROBERT: Chicago, Feb. 22, 1907.

ZETTERLING, MAI: Sweden, May 27, 1925. Ordtuery Theatre School.

ZIMBALIST, EFREM, JR.: NYC, Nov. 30, 1923. Yale.

OBITUARIES

AHEARNE, TOM, 63, character actor of stage, tv, and screen, died in NYC of influenza on Jan. 5, 1969. Began career in silent films at 16. He appeared in many major tv series, and his last films were "No Way To Treat A Lady," "What's So Bad About Feeling Good?," and "Three In The Attic." His wife survives.

ALEXANDER, BEN, 58, screen, radio, tv, and stage actor, was found dead of natural causes in his Hollywood home on July 5, 1969. He had been dead for several days. Probably best known as Jack Webb's partner on the "Dragnet" tv series, and his own "Felony Squad." Began career at 3 in DeMille's "Each Pearl A Tear," and later appeared in "Self-Made Failure," "All Quiet On The Western Front," "A Wise Child," "Are These Our Children?," "Mystery Ship," "Stage Mother," "This Day and Age," and "It's A Wise Child."

ANDREWS, STANLEY, 77, veteran screen, radio and tv actor, died in Los Angeles on June 23, 1969. He played the Old Ranger on both the radio and tv "Death Valley Days" serial. Among his many movies are "Escape From Devil's Island," "Devil's Playground," "Meet John Doe, "Coast Guard," "Kit Carson," "Time Out For Rhythm," "North To The Klondike," "Michigan Kid," "Northwest Stampede," and "Southwest Passage."

AUERBACH, JOSEF, 85, producer, died in NYC on March 29, 1969. He produced Hedy Lamarr's "Ecstacy" in 1933. Fled Czechoslovakia in 1941 and came to the U.S. to form Film Classics. Later won an "Oscar" for his 1963 film "Chagall." Surviving are his widow, 2 daughters and a son.

BACCALONI, SALVATORE, 69, opera star and film actor, died in NYC Dec. 31, 1969. His film career began in 1957 in "Full of Life," followed by "Fanny," "The Pigeon That Took Rome," "Merry Andrew," "Rock-a-bye Baby." His widow survives.

BARZELL, WOLFE, 72, film and stage actor, died of a heart attack while fishing at Acapulco, Mex., on Feb. 14, 1969. Born in Poland, toured Europe in Yiddish theatre before making Bdwy debut. Among his many films were "The Blue Angel," and "The King of Kings." His widow survives.

BATES, BARBARA, 43, film actress, died Mar. 18, 1969 in her native Denver, Colo. Among her film credits are "Salome Where She Danced," "Cheaper By The Dozen," "All About Eve," "Quicksand," "I'd Climb the Highest Mountain," "Belles On Their Toes," "Outcasts of Poker Flat," "The Caddy," "Rhapsody," "Campbell's Kingdom," and "Inspector General." For 2 years she appeared in the tv series "It's a Great Life." She retired in 1962. She was the widow of Cecil Coan. Her mother and 2 sisters survive.

BEAL, ROYAL, 69, retired actor, died of cancer in Keene, N.H., on May 20, 1969. His career of more than 40 years spanned stage, radio, tv, and films. Screen credits include "Lost Boundaries," "Death of A Salesman," "Anatomy of A Murder." His wife and 2 daughters survive.

BELGADO, MARIA, 63, veteran character actress, died in Hollywood after a short illness on June 24, 1969. She had appeared in films for 37 years. Surviving is her actress daughter, Rosita Delva.

BENDER, RUSSELL, 59, film and tv actor, died in Hollywood on Aug. 16, 1969. The last of his many films was "Born Wild." His wife and 2 sons survive.

BENNETT, ENID, 71, silent film star, died of a heart attack in her Malibu, Calif. home on May 14, 1969. Her films include "The Red Lily," "Robin Hood," "Waterloo Bridge," and "The Seahawk." She retired in 1931 but appeared later in a few films, including "Intermezzo." She was the wife of producer Sidney Franklin.

Barbara Bates

Enid Bennett (1916)

John Boles (1937)

Mildred Davis

Mitzi Green (1937)

Sonja Henie

BOLES, JOHN, 73, actor-singer, died of a heart attack in his San Angelo, Tex., home on Feb. 27, 1969. He had lived there since 1955. Gloria Swanson brought him to films in 1927 for "Loves of Sunya." Other movie credits include "Only Yesterday," "The Desert Song," "Rio Rita," "Resurrection," "Message to Garcia," "Stella Dallas," "Imitation of Life," "Music In The Air," "Craig's Wife," "The Littlest Rebel," "Curly Top," and his last in 1954 "Babes in Bagdad." Surviving are his wife and 2 daughters.

BONANOVA, FORTUNIO, 73, former operatic baritone and character actor, died of a cerebral hemorrhage on Apr. 2, 1969 in Woodland Hills, Calif., where he was recovering from a stroke. Made film debut in 1924 in "Don Juan" in Spain, and his U.S. debut in 1941 in "Citizen Kane." He also appeared in "Five Graves to Cairo," "September Affair," "An Affair To Remember," "Going My Way," "The Moon is Blue," "Jaguar," "Brazil," "That Night in Rio," and his last, "Hector the Stowaway Dog." He had appeared in over 1000 films. His widow and daughter survive.

BRACKETT, CHARLES, 77, writer and producer, died in his Bel-Air home on Mar. 9, 1969, after a long illness. With Billy Wilder, he won "Oscars" for "Sunset Boulevard," and "The Lost Weekend," and on his own won for "Titanic." His wife and daughter survive.

CIANNELLI, EDUARDO, 80, Italian-born film and stage character actor, died of cancer in Rome on Oct. 8, 1969. He had appeared in such films as "Winterset," "The Front Page," "For Whom The Bells Toll," "Gunga Din," "Strange Cargo," "Foreign Correspondent," "The Brotherhood," "Secret of Santa Vittoria," and his last "Boot Hill." Two sons survive.

COLLYER, BUD, 61, radio and tv host, died of a circulatory ailment on Sept. 8, 1969 in Greenwich, Conn. He hosted such shows as "Break The Bank," "To Tell The Truth," "Beat The Clock," and "Feather Your Nest." Surviving are his wife, a son, and 2 daughters.

CORRIGAN, LLOYD, 69, actor, writer, and director, died Nov. 5, 1969 at the Motion Picture Country Home in Woodland Hills, Calif. Arthritis had confined him for several years. Made film debut in 1925 in DeMille's "The Splendid Crime," followed by many others, including "Ghost Breakers," "A Girl, A Guy, and A Gob," "The Great Man's Lady," "Lady Luck," "The Chase," "The Bride Goes Wild," "Dancing In The Dark," "My Friend Irma Goes West," "Son of Paleface," and "It's A Mad, Mad, Mad, Mad World." He also wrote many screenplays, including "It," "Red Hair," "Saturday Night Kid," and son of the Fu Manchu series. No survivors.

D'ARCY, ROY, 75, vaudeville, stage and screen actor, died Nov. 15, 1969 in Redlands, Calif. Usually portraying a villain, he appeared in such films as "The Merry Widow," "The Masked Bride," "The Temptress," "Bardelys the Magnificent," "Valencia," "La Boheme," "The Road to Romance," and "The Black Watch."

DAVIS, MILDRED, 68, film ingenue who retired after her marriage in 1923 to Harold Lloyd, died of a coronary in Santa Monica, Calif., Aug. 18, 1969. Before her marriage she appeared with Mr. Lloyd in a number of two-reelers, and then as his leading lady in "A Sailor Made Man," "Grandma's Boy," "Dr. Jack," and "Safety Last." Surviving besides her husband are a son and two daughters.

DeAUBRY, DIANE, 79, vaudeville, musical comedy, and silent film star, died of a heart attack May 23, 1969 in Santa Monica, Calif. She was billed as "The Girl with the Million Dollar Eyes," and starred in Biograph and World Co. films. She retired in 1930. Surviving are a son and daughter.

DEUTSCH, ERNST, 78, German-born film and stage actor, died of a heart attack in his Berlin home on March 22, 1969. He was Max Reinhardt's leading man before fleeing Nazi Germany in 1933. Among his last films was "The Third Man." His widow survives.

JUDY GARLAND
1922-1969

Martita Hunt (1949)

Jeffrey Hunter (1962)

Rex Ingram (1966)

DIXON, HARLAND, 83, top vaudeville dancer, Broadway star, and former dance director for Warner Bros., died June 27, 1969 in Jackson Heights, N.Y. His widow survives.

DOWLING, CONSTANCE, 49, former stage and screen actress, died of a cardiac arrest in Los Angeles on Oct. 28, 1969. After appearing on Broadway, went to Hollywood in 1943 and appeared in such films as "Up In Arms," "Gog," "Black Angel," "The Well Groomed Bride," "The Flame," "Mad About Opera," "A Voice in Your Heart," "Miss Italy," "Knickerbocker Holiday," and "Blind Spot." She retired in 1954 after her marriage to producer Ivan Tors, who survives, as do three sons, and her sister actress Doris Dowling.

EVANS, REX, 66, British-born character actor, died April 3, 1969 following surgery in Glendale, Calif. After appearing on Broadway, he was seen in such films as "Camille," "It Should Happen to You," "The Prince and The Pauper," and "The Matchmaker." A brother survives.

FLEMING, IAN, 80, stage and film actor, died in London, Jan. 1, 1969. Perhaps his best known film character was Dr. Watson in a series of Sherlock Holmes films. He also appeared in "The Forsyte Saga."

FORSTER, RUDOLF, 84, Austrian-born stage and film actor, died Oct. 25, 1969 in Vienna where he was still active. Among his many films were "Threepenny Opera," "Ariadne," "Dreaming Lips," "Hamlet," and "Morgenrot." His widow survives.

FOSTER, DONALD, 80, veteran actor for more than 50 years on stage, film, and tv, died in Hollywood on Dec. 23, 1969 after a long illness. His more recent film credits include "The Al Capone Story," "Horse Soldiers," "Please Don't Eat The Daisies," and "All In A Night's Work." On tv he had roles in "Dragnet," "Bewitched," "Perry Mason," "Profiles in Courage," and "Run For Your Life." His widow, a son and daughter survive.

FREUND, KARL, 79, cameraman for six decades, died May 3, 1969 in Santa Monica, Calif. He was the innovative technician behind many early film classics. He won an Academy Award in 1937 for "The Good Earth." He had been chief cinematographer for Desilu Productions.

GARLAND, JUDY, 47, vaudeville, stage and screen star, was found dead June 22, 1969 in her London home from an accidental over-dose of sleeping pills. After beginning her career in vaudeville at 30 months, she became a star of films at 15, and appeared in over 35, including "Broadway Melody of 1938," "Love Finds Andy Hardy," "Every Sunday," "Babes in Arms," "Little Nellie Kelly," "For Me and My Gal," 'The Harvey Girls," "Meet Me In St. Louis," "Ziegfeld Follies," "The Pirate," "Easter Parade," "A Star Is Born," "Summer Stock," "The Clock," "Judgement at Nuremberg," and "A Child Is Waiting." She became synonymous with the song "Over the Rainbow" from "The Wizard of Oz," for which performance she received a special Academy Award in 1939. Surviving are her fifth husband of 3 months, Mickey Deans, and 3 children, Lorna and Joseph Luft, and singer-actress Liza Minnelli.

GOETZ, WILLIAM, 66, who rose from assistant director to head of Universal studios, died of cancer Aug. 15, 1969 in his home in Holmby Hills, Calif. His widow and 2 daughters survive.

GORCEY, LEO, 52, stage and film actor, died June 2, 1969 after a long illness in Oakland, Calif. For nearly 20 years he was the "Dead End Kid," and then one of "The Bowery Boys" until he retired in 1956. Other films include "East Side Kids," "Crime School," "Hell's Kitchen," "Angels with Dirty Faces," "Battle of City Hall," and "Destroyer." Surviving are his fifth wife and a son and daughter.

GRAFF, WILTON, 64, stage and film actor, died Jan. 13, 1969 in Pacific Palisades, Calif. Among his many films were "Take Me Out To The Ball Game," "The West Point Story," "Springfield Rifle," "Lili," "The Benny Goodman Story," "Lust for Life," and "Compulsion." His widow and daughter survive.

GREEN, KENNETH, 61, one of the fat boys in the "Our Gang" series, died of a heart attack Feb. 24, 1969 while working in Warner Bros. transportation department. Surviving are his widow and daughter.

GREEN, MITZI, 48, screen and stage actress, died May 24, 1969 of cancer in Huntington Beach, Calif. Began her career at 3 and became a child star as "Little Mitzi." Among her films were "Tom Sawyer," "Huckleberry Finn," "Skippy," "Little Orphan Annie," "Girl Crazy," and "TransAtlantic Merry-Go-Round." She is survived by her husband, director Joseph Pevney, and four children.

GURIE, SIGRID, 58, former film actress, died Aug. 14, 1969 in Mexico City. Born in Brooklyn and reared in Norway, before making Hollywood debut in 1934. She appeared in such films as "Algiers," "Rio," "The Dark Streets of Cairo," "The Forgotten Woman," "Three Faces West," "Sword of the Avenger," "Sofia," and "The Green Hornet Strikes Again." Her second husband survives.

HAYES, GEORGE "GABBY," 83, veteran character actor, died Feb. 9, 1969 of a heart ailment in Burbank, Calif. Before he retired in 1960, he had appeared in over 200 films, mostly westerns. Was probably best known as Hopalong Cassidy's sidekick. He also had his own tv show. His wife died in 1957. A brother and sister survive.

HECHT, TED, 61, stage and film character actor, died June 24, 1969 in Hollywood. He had appeared in the tv series "China Smith," and in such films as the Abbott and Costello series, "The Cyclone Lover," "Badmen of Tombstone," "Blue Grass of Kentucky," and "So Proudly We Hail." A daughter survives.

HENIE, SONJA, 57, Oslo-born international ice-skating and film star, died Oct. 12, 1969 of leukemia while en route on an ambulance plane to her home in Oslo. Three-time Olympic figure-skating champion made her Hollywood film debut in 1936 in "One in a Million," followed by such films as "Sun Valley Serenade," "Wintertime," "It Happened on Ice," "Thin Ice," "My Lucky Star," "Everything Happens at Night," "It's A Pleasure," and "Countess of Monte Cristo." Her Hollywood Ice Revues were major attractions throughout the U. S. for many years. Her third husband, Nils Onstad, a Norwegian shipowner, survives.

HENNECKE, CLARENCE R., 74, veteran film character actor, died Aug. 28, 1969 in his Santa Monica, Calif. home. He was an original Keystone Kop, and later turned to scriptwriting and character parts in films and tv. A sister survives.

HOLLIDAY, MARJORIE, 49, film actress, died June 16, 1969 of a brain hemorrhage. She appeared in almost every Betty Grable film, as well as many others. She retired from acting after her marriage to actor Michael St. Angel. Her husband and a son survive.

HUNT, MARTITA, 69, screen and stage actress, died June 13, 1969 in her London home. She had suffered for years from bronchial asthma. Her first film was "I Was A Spy" followed by many others including "Bunny Lake Is Missing," "The Unsinkable Molly Brown," "Admirable Crichton," "Great Expectations," "The Fan," "Becket," and "Anastasia."

HUNTER, JEFFREY, 42, actor, died May 27, 1969 after brain surgery in Van Nuys, Calif. Made film debut in 1951 in "14 Hours," and subsequently appeared in "Call Me Mister," "The Frogmen," "Belles on Their Toes," "3 Young Texans," "The Searchers," "7 Angry Men," "Hell to Eternity," "Sgt. Rutledge," "The True Story of Jesse James," "The Last Hurrah," "King of Kings," and "Brainstorm." His third wife and 3 sons survive.

INGRAM, JACK, 66, character actor, died Feb. 20, 1969 of a heart attack in Canoga Park, Calif. Entered films in 1929 and played mostly heavies in many westerns and serials, and also appeared in "Rebellion," and "Dick Tracy Returns." His widow survives.

Boris Karloff

Rod LaRocque

Frank Lawton (1934)

Barton MacLane (1967)

Eric Portman (1962)

Georges Renevant (1920)

INGRAM, REX, 73, stage and film actor for more than 50 years, died Sept. 19, 1969 of a heart attack in Hollywood. Made film debut in 1920 in the Tarzan series, subsequently appearing in "The Green Pastures," "Lord Jim," "Beau Geste," "The Sign of the Cross," "Huckleberry Finn," "Thief of Baghdad," "Talk of the Town," "Sahara," "Cabin in the Sky," "King Solomon's Mines," "The Ten Commandments," "Anna Lucasta," "Elmer Gantry," "Your Cheating Heart," and "Desire in the Dust." He was also seen in several tv series. His second wife and a daughter survive.

KARLOFF, BORIS, 81, master of horror roles on stage and film, died Feb. 2, 1969 in Midhurst, Sussex, Eng., of a respiratory disease. His role in the 1931 film "Frankenstein" made him a star, and he subsequently appeared in several sequels based on the same character, the last being "Frankenstein 1970." He was the Chinese detective James Lee Wong, and also Dr. Fu Manchu, and was also in "The Body Snatchers," "Tower of London," "The Walking Dead," "The Man They Could Not Hang," "The Mummy," "Bedlam," "Young Donovan's Kid," "You'll Find Out," and his last "Targets." His second wife and a daughter survive.

KOHLMAR, FRED, 64, motion picture producer, died Oct. 13, 1969 of lung cancer in Hollywood. His films include "Picnic," "Pal Joey," "Les Miserables," "Bye Bye Birdie," "Call Me Madam," "Dear Brigitte," and his last "The Only Game in Town." Surviving is his widow, actress Maxine Marshall.

LANPHIER, JAMES F., 48, actor, died of a stroke in Los Angeles Feb. 11, 1969. His films include "Operation Mad Ball," "Pink Panther," "Lost Balloon," "The Party," and "Darling Lili." He had also appeared in several tv series. His parents and a brother survive.

LaROCQUE, ROD, 70, silent screen star who was also successful in talkies, died Oct. 15, 1969 in his Beverly Hills home. Among his many films from 1919 were "The Ten Commandments," "Gigolo," "Resurrection," "Hold 'Em, Yale," "Captain Swagger," "The Love Pirate," "Our Dancing Daughters," "Our Modern Maidens," "One Romantic Night," "S.O.S. Iceberg," "Mystery Woman," "Feet of Clay," "Forbidden Paradise," "A Society Scandal," "Triumph," "The Coming of Amos," "The Fighting Eagle," "Let Us Be Gay," "The Locked Door," "The Hunchback of Notre Dame," "Preview Murder Mystery," "Till We Meet Again," and "Meet John Doe." Once called "second only to Valentino" as a screen lover, he married screen siren Vilma Banky in one of Hollywood's most lavish weddings. His widow survives.

LAWTON, FRANK, 64, British stage and film actor, died in his London home on June 10, 1969. Among his many films were "Young Woodley," "David Copperfield," "Cavalcade," and "A Night to Remember." He is survived by his widow, musical comedy star, Evelyn Laye.

LOCHER, FELIX, 87, character actor, died March 13, 1969 in Hollywood. Began his career at 73 and appeared in more than 50 films, and on tv. Surviving are two daughters, and a son, actor Jon Hall.

LOESSER, FRANK, 59, composer and lyricist, died of lung cancer July 28, 1969 in NYC. In addition to many songs, he wrote "Guys and Dolls," "Where's Charley?," "Most Happy Fella," and "How To Succeed in Business . . ." His song "Baby, It's Cold Outside" for the film "Neptune's Daughter" won the 1948 Academy Award. He is survived by his second wife, actress-singer Jo Sullivan, 3 daughters and a son.

LOGAN, ELLA, 56, Scottish-born singer-actress, died of cancer on May 1, 1969 in Burlingame, Calif. Her film appearances include "Top of the Town," "Flying Hostess," and "Woman Chases Man." A daughter survives.

MacLANE, BARTON, 66, stage, tv, and film actor, died of pneumonia in Santa Monica on Jan. 1, 1969. Often portraying the villain, he appeared in more than 150 films, including "The Treasure of Sierra Madre," "The Maltese Falcon," "San Quentin," "Half Breed," "Glenn Miller Story," "All Through the Night," "Western Union," "Men Without Souls," "You Only Live Once," "Prison Break," "Bullets or Ballots," "Best of the Bad Men," "Dr. Jekyll and Mr. Hyde," and "Town Tamer." He was in the tv "Outlaws" series. Surviving are his widow, former actress Charlotte Wynters, a son and daughter.

McCAREY, LEO, 71, "Oscar"-winning writer, director, and producer, died July 5, 1969 of emphysema in Santa Monica, Calif. He received two Academy Awards for his screenplay and direction of "Going My Way" which he also produced, and an "Oscar" in 1937 for his direction of "The Awful Truth," instead of for "Make Way for Tomorrow" which he considered his best film. His other films include "The Bells of St. Mary's," "Belle of the Nineties," "Ruggles of Red Gap," "The Milky Way," "Love Affair," "The Cowboy and The Lady," and "An Affair to Remember." His widow and daughter survive.

McHUGH, JIMMY, 75, prolific composer of numerous popular songs, and of scores for 55 films, died of a heart attack on May 23, 1969 in his Beverly Hills home. After 1930, he wrote almost exclusively for films. Some of his best known songs are "I Can't Give You Anything But Love, Baby," "The Sunny Side of the Street," "Comin' In on A Wing and a Prayer," "I'm In The Mood For Love," "I Feel A Song Comin' On," and "It's A Most Unusual Day." A son survives.

McNEAR, HOWARD, 64, radio, film, and tv character actor, died after a long illness on Jan. 3, 1969 in Hollywood. He had appeared in numerous films and tv serials. His last running role was on the "Andy Griffith Show."

MILLARD, HARRY WILLIAMS, 41, actor and producer, died of cancer in NYC on Sept. 2, 1969. He had appeared in "The Last Mile," and "American Roulette," and in "The Defenders" and "The F.B.I." television series. Was president of his own GHM Film Co. His parents and 2 brothers survive.

MINNER, KATHRYN, 77, actress, died May 26, 1969 of a heart attack in Van Nuys, Calif. Over a long film career, she did small parts in numerous pictures. Her most recent film credits include "The Love Bug," "Miracle in My Pocket," "Blackbeard's Ghost," and on tv appeared in "Gunsmoke," and "Petticoat Junction." A daughter survives.

MOWBRAY, ALAN, 72, London-born actor, died of a heart attack in Hollywood on March 25, 1969. He had appeared in more than 400 movies, and on Broadway. He became a citizen in 1933 and was a founder of Screen Actors Guild. His many film credits include "Alexander Hamilton," "Hotel Continental," "The World and The Flesh," "Sherlock Holmes," "Charlie Chan in London," "My Man Godfrey," "Topper," "That Hamilton Woman," "A Yank at Eton," "Holy Matrimony," "Captain from Castile," "You're My Everything," "The Jackpot," "I Wake Up Screaming," "The King and I," "Androcles and the Lion," "Ma and Pa Kettle at Home," and "The Man Who Knew Too Much." He starred in the "Colonel Flack" tv series. His wife, former actress Lorayne Carpenter, and a daughter survive.

NEWBERG, FRANK, 83, veteran film actor, died Nov. 11, 1969 at the Motion Picture Country Home in Woodland Hills, Calif., where he had resided for the past 7 years. Appeared in vaudeville before moving to California where he had roles in over 100 films, including "The Jazz Singer." A daughter survives.

PORTMAN, ERIC, 66, stage and screen actor, died from heart trouble in his home in Cornwall, Eng., on Dec. 7, 1969. His film credits from 1939 include "The Invaders," "One of Our Aircraft Is Missing," "Uncensored," "Squadron Leader X," "Escape to Danger," "We Dive at Dawn," "Great Day," "Men of Two Worlds," "Deep Blue Sea," "The Naked Edge," "Freud," "West 11," "The Belford Incident." He retired only a few months prior to his death.

Thelma Ritter (1955)

Gladys Swarthout (1935)

Sharon Tate

Peter Van Eyck (1965)

Ruth White

Charles Winninger

RENEVANT, GEORGES, 75, Paris-born retired stage and film actor, died after a long illness on Jan. 2, 1969 in Guadalajara, Mex., where he had lived for several years. His film credits include "Rio Rita," "Our Hearts Were Young and Gay," "Captain Eddie," and "The Catman of Paris." Surviving is his widow, former actress Selena Royle.

RITTER, THELMA, 63, stage and film actress, died of a heart attack in NY on Feb. 5, 1969. Began film career in 1946 in "Miracle on 34th Street," and subsequently appeared in over 20 pictures, among which were "Letter to 3 Wives," "Father Was A Fullback," "All About Eve," "I'll Get By," "Mating Season," "With A Song in My Heart," "The Farmer Takes A Wife," "Pickup on South Street," "Titanic," "Rear Window," "Pillow Talk," "The Misfits," "Birdman of Alcatraz," "Move Over, Darling," "Boeing-Boeing," and "The Incident." Surviving are her husband, Joseph Moran, a son and actress daughter Monica Moran.

RYAN, DICK, 72, veteran actor of vaudeville, radio, films, and tv, died Aug. 12, 1969 in Burbank after a long illness. His widow survives.

SCHENCK, NICHOLAS M., 87, Russian immigrant who became head of MGM, died March 3, 1969, of a stroke in Miami Beach. As head of a huge corporation embracing MGM and Loew's Theatres, his judgments affected the investment of millions of dollars, the careers of many screen stars, and the power of the studio's west coast production chiefs. Surviving are his second wife, and 3 daughters.

SEFF, MANUEL, 74, writer for stage, screen, and tv, died of a heart ailment Sept. 22, 1969 in NYC. original movie scripts, including "College Coach," He had produced more than 45 screenplays and "Footlight Parade," and "Married Bachelor." His widow and 2 daughters survive.

SELIGMAN, SELIG, 51, independent motion picture producer, author, and former vice president of ABC, died of a heart attack on June 20, 1969 in his Hollywood home. His most recent picture was "Charly" for which Cliff Robertson received an Academy Award. His widow and 5 children survive.

SHERMAN, FRED E., 64, character actor, died May 20, 1969 following a stroke in Woodland Hills, Calif. His most recent films include "Behind Green Lights," "Lady in the Lake," and "Some Like It Hot." On tv he had appeared in such series as "Perry Mason," "I Love Lucy," "Life with Father," "Dick Van Dyke Show," "Bonanza," and "Andy Griffith Show." Surviving is his widow, actress Claire Carleton.

SINGLETON, CATHERINE, 65, silent film star, and Miss Universe of 1926, died Sept. 9, 1969 at her home in Fort Worth, Tex. She appeared in over a dozen silent films, and in the Ziegfeld Follies. A daughter survives.

STEPPAT, ILSE, 52, German screen and stage actress, died Dec. 22, 1969 in West Berlin. Her last film was "On Her Majesty's Secret Service," preceded by such films as "Marriage in the Shadow," "The Man Who Wanted To Live Twice," "Capt. Wrongski," "The Bridge," and "The Confessions of Felix Krull." She was married to film director Max Nosseck.

SWARTHOUT, GLADYS, 64, former opera and film star, died July 8, 1969 of rheumatic fever in her villa outside Florence, Italy. On the screen she appeared in "Rose of the Rancho," "Give Us This Night," "Champagne Waltz," "Romance In The Dark," and "Ambush." She retired in 1957 and with her second husband, Frank M. Chapman, moved to Italy. He died in 1966. A sister survives.

TALMADGE, NATALIE, 70, silent screen star, and sister of Constance and the late Norma Talmadge, died in a Santa Monica Hospital on June 19, 1969. Never particularly interested in a film career, she nevertheless appeared in several pictures as Buster Keaton's leading lady, and in several others, including "A Tale of Two Cities," and "The New Moon." Divorced from the late Buster Keaton, two sons survive.

TATE, SHARON, 26, promising film actress, was found murdered in her Belair home on Aug. 9, 1969. From 1963, she had appeared in "The Americanization of Emily," "The Sandpiper," "Fearless Vampire Killers," "The Wrecking Crew," "The Wheeler-Dealers," "Don't Make Waves," "Valley of the Dolls," and her last "12 Places." Surviving is her husband, director Roman Polanski.

TAYLOR, ROBERT, 57, film star for more than 30 years, died June 8, 1969 of lung cancer in Santa Monica, Calif. One of Hollywood's most glamorous leading men appeared in over 70 pictures, including "Camille," "There's Always Tomorrow," "Society Doctor," "West Point of the Air," "Broadway Melody of 1936," "Magnificent Obsession," "Billy the Kid," "Waterloo Bridge," "The Crowd Roars," "Johnny Eager," "Her Cardboard Lover," "Ivanhoe," "Bataan," "Song of Russia," "The High Wall," "The Bribe," "Ambush," "His Brother's Wife," "This Is My Affair," "Quo Vadis," "Rogue Cop," "A Yank at Oxford," "Where Angels Go," "Johnny Tiger," and "The Night Walker." In 1961 he starred in his own tv series "The Detectives." Surviving are his second wife, former actress Ursula Thiess, a son and a daughter.

Robert Taylor (1964)

TERRANOVA, DINO, 65, stage and film actor, died April 27, 1969 in his Miami home. His most recent films were "Flipper" and "The Brotherhood." His widow survives.

TONG, KAM, 62, film and tv actor, died Nov. 8, 1969 in his Costa Mesa, Calif. home. Among his many film credits are "Flower Drum Song," and "Love Is A Many Splendored Thing." Surviving are his widow, a son and daughter.

VAN EYCK, PETER, 56, German-born actor, died near Zurich, Switzerland on July 15, 1969 after a long illness. Often portraying a Nazi, he had appeared in such films as "And So To Bed," "Station 6 Sahara," "The World in My Pocket," "The Rest Is Silence," "Rosemary," "The Glass Tower," "Flesh and Desire," "Address Unknown," "The Imposter," "The Hitler Gang," "Five Graves to Cairo," "The Moon Is Down," "Rommel," "The Spy Who Came in From the Cold," and "Shalako." His widow and daughter survive.

VON STERNBERG, JOSEF, 75, Vienna-born director, died of a heart ailment in Hollywood on Dec. 22, 1969. Probably achieved his greatest fame directing Marlene Dietrich, whom he discovered, in "The Blue Angel," "Morocco," "Dishonored," "Shanghai Express," "Blonde Venus," "The Scarlet Empress," and "The Devil Is A Woman." Other films were "The Exquisite Sinner," "Underworld," "Docks of New York," "The Last Command," "The Case of Lena Smith," "The Shanghai Gesture," and his last two in 1953 "Jet Pilot," and "Macao." His widow, a son and daughter survive.

WALBURN, RAYMOND, 81, veteran stage and film actor whose career spanned 59 years, died in NYC on July 26, 1969 after a long illness. He had appeared in more than 80 movies, among which were "Broadway Bill," "Count of Monte Cristo," "Thanks A Million," "The Great Ziegfeld," "Mr. Deeds Goes To Town," "Born to Dance," "And The Angels Sing," "Hail The Conquering Hero." His second wife survives.

WHITE, RUTH, 55, stage, film, and tv actress, died of cancer in Perth Amboy, N. J. on Dec. 3, 1969. She won an "Emmy" for her tv performance in "Little Moon of Alban," and appeared in such movies as "Edge of The City," "Up the Down Staircase," "To Kill A Mockingbird," "The Nun's Story," "Midnight Cowboy," "The Reivers," and her last, "The Pursuit of Happiness." A sister and two brothers survive.

WHITNEY, CLAIRE, 79, one of silent films first leading ladies, died in Los Angeles on Aug. 27, 1969. Among her credits are such films as "Life's Shop Window," "The Nigger," "Fine Feathers," "A Free Soul," "Room 909," and "Enlighten Thy Daughter." Surviving is her husband, actor Robert Emmett Keane.

WILLIAMS, HUGH, 65, British film, and stage actor, and playwright, died Dec. 7, 1969 after surgery in a London hospital. As a film actor, he appeared in "One of Our Aircraft Is Missing," "Wuthering Heights," "Charley's Aunt," "The Holly and The Ivy," "Outcast Lady," "An Ideal Husband," "Take My Life," and many others. He is survived by his wife and co-author, actress Margaret Vyner, 2 sons and a daughter.

WILLIAMS, RHYS, 71, veteran character actor of stage, films, and tv, died in a Santa Monica hospital on May 28, 1969. Among his many films are "The Corn Is Green," "You Came Along," "Blood on The Sun," "The Spiral Staircase," "The Bells of St. Mary's," "If Winter Comes," "Moss Rose," "Tenth Avenue Angel," "Bad Boy," "Kiss Tomorrow Goodbye," "Son of Dr. Jekyll," "Never Trust A Gambler," "Mutiny," "Les Miserables," "Meet Me At The Fair," "Julius Caesar," "The Kentuckian," "Nightmare," "Brigadoon," "How Green Was My Valley," "Johnny Guitar," "Chicken Every Sunday," "Gentleman Jim," and "The Trouble With Women." His widow and two sons survive.

WINNINGER, CHARLES, 84, veteran character actor of stage, films, radio and tv, died at his Palm Springs home on Jan. 19, 1969 after a long illness. Probably most famous for the role of Cap'n Andy that he created in "Show Boat," his career had spanned 70 years, from vaudeville to tv. Among his film credits are "The Canadian," "Night Nurse," "Cafe Metropole," "3 Smart Girls," "3 Girls Grow Up," "The Go Getter," "Babes in Arms," "Ziegfeld Girl," "Nothing Sacred," "Little Nellie Kelly," "Belle of the Yukon," "Sunday Dinner for a Soldier," "State Fair," "Destry Rides Again," "The Sun Shines Bright," "The Perilous Journey," "A Lady Takes A Chance," "Fifth Avenue Girl," "Flesh and Fantasy," "Coney Island," "Give My Regards to Broadway," "Father Is A Bachelor," and "Las Vegas Shakedown." Surviving is his second wife, former actress Gertrude Walker.

INDEX